Praise for *Assassins of the Turquoise Palace:*

"*Assassins of the Turquoise Palace* throws light on the rivalries and fears within Iran's cast exile community. . . . Carefully researched and vividly written . . . In addition to being a lively account of an extraordinary trial, [it] can be read as an unsettling reminder of the dangers of excessive zeal." —*The New York Times Book Review*

"Insightful and detailed . . . A rumination on the Islamic Republic's culture of terror, and as such it delves into the personal lives of the victims [and] their broken families . . . [A] captivating narrative."
—*Frontline,* PBS.org

"[A] riveting account . . . [Hakakian] deploys all of her talents as a former producer at *60 Minutes* and a poet in her native Farsi to tell the human and political story behind the news. . . . A nonfiction political thriller of a very high order." —*Kirkus Reviews*, (starred review)

"[A] groundbreaking book" —*Jerusalem Post*

"Even as they continue to breach every known international law, all the while protesting at interventions in their 'internal affairs,' the theocrats in Tehran stand convicted of mounting murderous interventions in the affairs of others. Roya Hakakian's beautiful book mercilessly exposes just one of these crimes, and stands as tribute to the courageous dissidents and lawyers who managed one of that rarest of human achievements; an authentic victory for truth and justice. May its publication speed the day when the mullahs stand in the dock, and when the civilized people of Persia gain control of their own destiny." —Christopher Hitchens

"Roya Hakakian brilliantly documents . . . Tehran's 1992 attack on the Mykonos restaurant in Berlin." —Wall Street Journal.com

"A thoroughly researched, dramatically told account . . . Readers will find everything they could ask for . . . and more. . . . [A] fine book."
—*Washington Independent Book Review*

"This is a brilliant, riveting book, with all the elements of a great thriller—a horrific crime, sociopathic villains, international intrigue, personal betrayals, a noble prosecutor, and an honorable judge. And it is all too real: with remarkably comprehensive reporting and brisk, smart writing, Roya Hakakian has told a great story but, more important, she has made plain the lethal immorality at the heart of Iran's regime."

—Joe Klein, political columnist, *Time*

"Admirable . . . [Hakakian] does a worthy job of presenting the facts through the eyes of the men who survived the shooting and the German authorities who prosecuted the case." —*Publishers Weekly*

"Roya Hakakian is something rare: a poet turned investigative reporter. The outcome of this unusual fusion is a work of journalistic revelation, written so fluidly and gorgeously, it is a masterpiece."

—Lesley Stahl, correspondent, *60 Minutes*

"Masterfully documented." —*National Post*

"Hakakian's meticulously documented account of the Mykonos incident is a powerful rejoinder, as well as a lesson in ruthlessness and conscience . . . Hakakian's narrative shines." —*Jewish Ideas Daily*

"Hakakian is also a poet, and her style has an intensity of purpose. The details she marshals and the overlapping points of view she records invite the reader to bear witness to the events described . . . more tangled than a fictional thriller perhaps, but no less gripping."

—*World Affairs Journal*

"As the world contemplates the pressing predicament of Iran, Roya Hakakian offers one possible solution through a riveting tale that is most timely and profoundly urgent. This superb true story is much more than an international *In Cold Blood*—it is a stunning parable of the central struggle of our times between totalitarianism and the rule of law."

—R. James Woolsey, Director of Central Intelligence, 1993–1995

Assassins *of the* Turquoise Palace

Also by Roya Hakakian

Journey from the Land of No

Assassins *of the* Turquoise Palace

Roya Hakakian

Grove Press
New York

Published simultaneously in Canada
Printed in the United States of America

ISBN-13: 978-0-8021-4597-0

Grove Press
an imprint of Grove/Atlantic, Inc.
841 Broadway
New York, NY 10003

Distributed by Publishers Group West

www.groveatlantic.com

12 13 14 10 9 8 7 6 5 4 3 2 1

For my two suns
E & K

To the Reader

This is a work of nonfiction. The characters and events depicted in this book are real. The material has been drawn from video archives, television and radio interviews, personal Web sites, and the notes and diaries of the individuals involved. There was also a wealth of trial reports, notes, memorandums, police documents, and newspaper and magazine articles to which I gained access. Moreover, I conducted my own interviews with many individuals whose lives had been touched by the case. Dialogue has been reconstructed based on the recollections of interviewees or been taken from the actual reports or transcripts. For a more comprehensive catalog of all the material used, a quick character reference or a glossary of unfamiliar terms, please see "Sources" at the end of the book.

Assassins *of the* Turquoise Palace

Anytime I open my mouth to say something about the sad turn of events in my country, people worry that their funny man has become too political. I don't know what it means to be political. All I am is a resister against a band of thugs. I want for my homeland all the good things that forced us into exile in the West. I want freedom. If that loses me fans by making me political, if it makes me a target of the thugs, if it endangers my life and the life of my family, so be it!

—Hadi Khorsandi, exiled Iranian satirist against whom Ayatollah Khomeini issued a fatwa in 1980

1

Berlin, Germany, September 17, 1992. After nearly an hour prowling Prager Street, surveying the restaurant in its cul-de-sac, two hulking, bearded figures rolled their collars up to their eyes and burst inside. A third man stood guard at the entrance. It was 10:47 p.m.

They darted through the main dining hall, past a lonely customer nursing a last drink. Through an archway, they entered the back room, where a party of eight sat at a corner table. The taller of the two intruders stationed himself behind one of the diners, facing the eldest among them—a bald, bespectacled man in a gray suit who was addressing everyone. No one was yet aware of their arrival. The speaker, suddenly meeting the intruder's dark gaze, froze in midspeech. Another guest asked what was wrong with him. The answer came from the intruder.

"You sons of whores!"

He thrust his gloved hand into the sports bag that hung on his shoulder. Then, a click.

A shout came from the table. "Friends, it's an assassi—"

The trail of his call faded in the roaring sound that followed. In the dimly lit air, sparks of fire flashed at the intruder's hip. Bullets pierced the side of the bag, riddled the guests.

After two rounds—twenty-six bullets—the barrage ceased. The air was thick with the smell of gunpowder. Of the eight guests, everyone had stooped or fallen, except one. The eldest guest was still in his chair, head slumped, blood tinting his white shirt, blending with the busy pattern of his tie. Another victim was doubled over, breathing noisily, gasping for air. His face was smashed into a mug of beer. The golden liquid was slowly darkening.

The second shooter walked up to the table, tucked his bare hand under his belt, and drew out a gun. No one stirred. He aimed at the eldest man and fired three bullets into his head. Then he turned to one of the bodies on the floor, a young, slender man dressed in what, until moments before, had been a crisp white shirt. Pointing his gun at the back of the man's head, he fired a single shot. Then he turned to the next body and aimed once more. But before he pulled the trigger, his accomplice motioned him to leave.

They bolted out of the restaurant. The guard joined them at the door. They ran toward a sky-blue BMW that was idling at the intersection across the cul-de-sac. The lead shooter reached it first. He grabbed the handles and swung both front and back passenger doors open. As he jammed himself beside the driver, he threw the bag behind him. The other two shoved themselves in the backseat. The driver stomped on the accelerator, nearly running over a pedestrian as he took off. Across the intersection, the engine of a black Mercedes roared, and it, too, took off and swerved onto a side street.

In their wake, everything was once again as it had been on so many nights before. The breeze blew gently. A light drizzle fell softly. But lights had come on in the few windows overlooking the restaurant. A handful of neighbors had awakened. On the fourth floor balcony of the building next to the restaurant, a young woman clutched the railing, leaning downward. Her auburn hair flowed over her white uniform, her skin still warm from the bike ride home. She peered intently at the sidewalk below, looking for the source of the blast that had shaken the floor of her living room. She was a curious bystander then, soon a witness to detail her account of the tremor beneath her feet, the tremor that would ripple through the continent in the months to come.

2

Terrorists nowadays! It's not enough that they kill you; they must also insult you as they do it.

Hadi Khorsandi, exiled Iranian satirist

On a Sunday morning in June 1989, six-year-old Sara Dehkordi received the news she had been praying for.

The phone rang at six o'clock and Sara's mother, who answered it, was surprised to hear the voice of the neighbor's girl at the other end. She asked the girl the reason for calling so early. But the seven-year-old had assumed her most adult tone and insisted that the matter could only be discussed with Sara, and that "No, Mrs. Dehkordi! It absolutely *can't* wait."

Shohreh handed the receiver to her daughter and within moments squeals of glee filled the drowsy air of their apartment.

Sara climbed into her bunk bed, designed and built by her father, and reaching for a stash of crayons beneath the mattress she withdrew one and scrawled the word "hooray" on the ceiling.

Her parents appeared at the door, mystified. "What's going on, *moosh mooshak*?" her mother asked—"little mouse" in Persian.

Sara stuck her head between the wooden railings of the bed and cried out, "He's dead!"

Of all the images Shohreh and Noori Dehkordi kept in their minds, the child's head framed by the railings—dark curls filling the spaces her petite face left empty—was among the most endearing. Sara was their only child, the sole heir to all the youthful idealism they still held to as they approached their middle years. Cultivate boldness in her now, they thought, and she would learn to tackle ideas in adulthood. During their traditional Sunday family strolls through Berlin's Tiergarten Park, if Sara climbed a tree, their first reminder to her was not "Be careful!" It was, "Is this the highest you can go?"

Sara was at home in the outdoors and expressed her feelings, immensely joyous on that particular morning, more physically than verbally.

"Dead-o, dead!" she shouted a last time. Then she jumped onto her trampoline, her dark locks flying, took a bow, and announced, "Hooray, hooray, Khomeini is dead!"

It was June 4, 1989, and Ayatollah Ruholla Khomeini, the supreme leader, the ultimate authority for Shiite Muslims around the world, had died of old age a day earlier at his residence in Tehran. Sara's stunned parents turned and stared at each other, until Shohreh finally asked, "How do you know?"

"Turn on the radio! The neighbors just heard it on the radio!"

Noori switched on his shortwave radio and tuned in to the Persian-language BBC. The correspondent was excitedly narrating scenes of mourning on the streets. The couple stood facing each other in silence. A few moments passed, and once again it was Shohreh who spoke, in a daze. "Could it be?"

Noori was wholly focused on the broadcast, deaf to his wife.

"The bastard goes to sleep one night and doesn't wake up!" Shohreh went on talking to herself. "Can't be, after all that! Shouldn't be!"

All that was the couple's shorthand for everything they had lost since the Ayatollah's rise to power in 1979. Their home and homeland, parents, relatives, and friends—Shohreh and newborn Sara had fled from Iran in 1983, and Noori followed a year later—those were their most tangible losses. There were also the intangibles. They missed the melody of Persian in their ears, the scent of herbs wafting from their neighbors' kitchens. They missed the Thursday night gatherings at Naderi Café, even the bad poetry their friends recited feverishly. They missed the heat of the steaming beets peddlers wrapped in paper cones and dropped in their palms on cold autumn days. How could a year become new amid the winter's freeze? They missed their own sensible New Year, Nowrouz, ringing in the spring every March.

But they were no strangers to Germany. Shohreh and Noori met in Berlin in 1972, while they were studying abroad. She spotted him in the common hall of her dormitory a few days after she arrived. Her eyes had drifted indifferently over the many faces in the room till he came into view.

How fitting, she thought upon hearing others call his name, that this man, with eyes so deeply dark and radiant, should be called Noori, *luminous*.

She did her best to seem unaffected despite her flushed cheeks, trying to veil her excitement in the haze of smoke from her cigarette, until he stepped before her and asked her name.

"Shoh-reh!" She drew out the syllables, breathing the *h*'s deeply for sensuous effect and boasted, "As in *famous*, your luminous!"

"As you clearly deserve to be!" he had said with admiration. Then matching her impishness with his own confidence, he added, "And will be, if you stick with me!"

In Berlin, they fell in love with each other, and with the single conviction that defined their youth. The phrase that crossed their lips as often as *I love you* in those days was *Down with the Shah!* They had each declared a major for the university records, but what consumed them most was the overthrow of Iran's last monarch, Shah Mohammad Reza Pahlavi. If they were not in class attending a perfunctory lecture or making love, they were with friends plotting the next anti-Shah demonstration, drafting another anti-Shah flyer. It was in West Berlin, the seat of the free Europe, where politicians aired criticisms of their rivals, writers openly taunted their leaders, and comedians freely ridiculed all things venerable, that they realized they wanted the same things for their country. And in 1978, when a revolution swept through Iran, they left Berlin jubilantly. They joined thousands of chanting Iranians on the streets of Tehran on the January day the Shah flew out, when grown men and women celebrated by dancing in the streets, as passing traffic honked and turned on wipers. The Ayatollah returned from exile two weeks after that and, days later, on a sunny mid-February morning, the Royal Army caved in and 2,500 years of monarchy ended.

They had no reason to fear the Ayatollah. In his many speeches and interviews from exile in the suburbs of Paris, he insisted that he wanted nothing other than to see the Shah go and to return to the holy city of Qom, where he could resume his religious studies at a seminary. Why fear a man whose ways reminded them of Mahatma Gandhi, who pitted himself against the extravagance of the rulers by wearing a modest robe, sleeping on a cot, and eating a simple dinner of bread and yogurt?

Barely a year later, after he had strengthened his grip on power, the Ayatollah abandoned the moderate Iranians he had once tried to court. He broke all the promises that had helped win them over. Instead of Qom, he took up residence in Tehran. He banned all newspapers and political parties, shut down universities to "cleanse" them through a "cultural revolution," and began hounding the opposition, among them secular students of the previous era, the likes of Noori and Shohreh—executing, arresting, and imprisoning thousands, and forcing thousands more to flee, which caused an exodus unlike any other throughout the nation's ancient history.

"What will happen now?" Shohreh wondered.

The shock on Noori's face slowly lifted. At forty-six, he still felt young enough to hope. He cheerfully prophesied, "It'll be the end of them, little lady. You'll see."

There was a party at the Dehkordi home that Sunday. Friends, fellow Iranian exiles, came to visit, bearing sweets and flowers. For Sara, that Sunday marked a moment of personal triumph. All her life, she had believed that the Ayatollah and the men her parents described to her as his soldiers were the only threat to her family. For months, she had secretly prayed in the direction of Tehran, from the windows of her Berlin bedroom. With the Ayatollah's death, the fears that had always beset her life perished. At last, childhood, with its blithe abandon, was hers.

But only briefly. On September 17, 1992, a Thursday afternoon, Shohreh, who had a cold, picked Sara up from school and brought her home earlier than usual so they could all have dinner together before Noori left for a meeting. The mother rarely cooked but she had prepared her famous beans and potatoes. Eating as a family was a tradition they upheld with more fervor in those days. After many years of marriage, the couple were dreaming of another child, which was why Noori had built a bunk bed for Sara. The idea of a newborn had infused their home with unspoken mirth. Having only two children was a compromise for Noori who wanted several more.

After dinner, Noori and Sara went about the bedtime routine, though it was too early to turn the lights out. He helped her into her pajamas and fluffed her pillow, knowing full well that Sara's head never remained on it for long. Instead of reading to her, he improvised a lullaby, something she preferred to her tired books. Sara loved her father's creations. (God, she would not dispute, had made the world outside. But the lovely world within, bunk bed and all, was her father's invention.) Noori, the penniless bohemian, knew how to suffuse a child's senses with immeasurable wealth.

"For the sake of honey," he softly sang in the girl's ear, then paused.

Sara burst into song, "We must forgive the sting."

He nodded and hummed another line, borrowing from the poems of Rumi and Hafez, the poets he had known as a child and wanted his daughter to know, "For the sake of the rose—"

Sara chirped again, "We must forgive the thorn."

"For the sake of the moth—"

Sara, who always grew more alert with every verse, quickly added, "We must forgive the flame."

Noori kissed her forehead once again. "For the sake of your *baba,* who must leave this very minute to not keep his friends waiting, my *moosh mooshak,* we must forgive goodbyes. Be especially nice to your sick mom till I get back!"

With Sara settled in her room, Noori went into the kitchen and threw his arms around his wife, who was standing at the sink. He squeezed her, without turning her face to his, and whispered in her ear, "Don't bother with the dishes now. I'll get to them later."

Then kissing the side of her neck, he bid her farewell with the same unsuspecting words as always, "See you shortly, little lady!"

3

> During an interrogation, a political activist in Iran was asked why he had the picture of Jesus on his dorm wall but not that of the Supreme Leader. The activist said, "If they drive nails through the Leader and post him alongside the road just like Jesus, I'll have his picture on the wall too."
>
> *Hadi Khorsandi, exiled Iranian satirist*

Noori Dehkordi left his apartment that evening dressed in a pair of black pants and the silk sapphire shirt Shohreh had given him on his forty-sixth birthday, carrying a black leather satchel, and walked to the subway. It was nearly six o'clock. Noori did not drive. Why so dexterous a man felt uneasy behind the wheel was a question Noori, who could not afford a car, put to rest by declaring himself against all "lazyfying contraptions." To most places, he walked or biked.

Their building on the southwest intersection of Alt-Moabit and Rathenauer was the kind of plain cement and steel construction that had mushroomed throughout the country in the late 1940s to quickly house those made homeless by war. In a neighborhood of mostly well-established Arab and Turkish immigrants, the less well-off Dehkordis never expected their rental application for #120 to be accepted. Even after it was, they celebrated warily, worried that the landlord might reverse his decision. Sidewalks cluttered with peddlers and small shops, a bookstore specializing in legal texts, a Turkish eatery with a revolving skewer dripping with grease at the entrance, and boutiques with permanent "Final Sale of the Season" signs on display—all of this was enough reminiscent of Tehran to dull their pangs of homesickness. Sara's day care and favorite playground were within walking distance. So was the Tiergarten, where the family's favorite bike path stretched along its canal. Only the courthouse, the sprawling majestic edifice enclosed in wrought-iron gates, seemed to be out of place. Through their living room windows, the Dehkordis had a view of the courthouse's unsightly temporary prison webbed in razor wire, an eyesore for which their dislike would soon turn into hatred.

Noori had looked forward to this evening for days. His old friend Sadegh Sharafkandi, nicknamed "the Doctor," was in town and Noori was on his way to a small dinner in the visitor's honor. The nickname had originated in the early 1970s, after Sharafkandi received his PhD in analytical chemistry from a French university. But like most degrees that the students of his generation earned, it became useless at home, no more than a glorified line in his biography. After returning from France, he began to teach chemistry in a school in Iran's Kurdistan, only to find that his pupils, stricken with poverty and prejudice, could not contemplate atoms and molecules. They did not need a teacher. They needed an advocate. And so he shed the chemist and fashioned himself into an activist. For him, and most educated youth of his era, activism was not an ambition, a career, or even a choice. It was an inevitable detour along the way to a future good enough to afford the likes of chemists.

Twenty years since his days in France, the young scientist was now the chairman of Iran's Democratic Party of Kurdistan, founded at the end of World War II to attain equal rights for the Kurds. The party, beloved by the Kurds though banned in Iran, was recognized in Europe, and the Doctor had been invited to address the annual International Congress of the Social Democratic Party. The event was a rare occasion for the Doctor. It brought him to Europe from his clandestine underworld in the mountains of Kurdistan.

For most Iranians, Kurdistan was a forsaken place where the news was often grim, a reminder of some of their history's inglorious moments. But Noori was not afraid to stare the ugly past in the face. He likened Kurds to Native Americans. The comparison was hardly exact, he knew, but he drew it nonetheless to provoke those of his compatriots who readily castigated America for its sins against its own people. After all, both people were perennially haunted by a historic tragedy that had come to them through loss of territory. Both were more indigenous to the regions they inhabited than those who ruled them. Though the word "tribal" was no longer used to describe them, each community had steadfastly maintained, against all assaults, its unique culture, language, tradition, and way of life. The mountains had once been the Kurds' only home, their source of life and livelihood, the landscape they eternally celebrated in folk tunes as their "best friend." They still wore traditional costumes—men in loose-fitting shirts and pants, with shawls wrapped around the waist; women in iridescent, ankle-length dresses and headgear. And they still suffered. The Kurds were Sunni—a minority of nearly four million among Iran's fifty million Shiite. Their ancient territory, last intact in 520 AD, once stretched from southern Turkey and northern Iraq to western Iran and eastern Syria. Military attacks over the centuries tore it apart, leaving the Kurds to perpetually fight to reconquer the lost land, or at least win enough autonomy to live according to their own traditions.

For Noori, the avid reader of history, 520 AD was hardly a distant past. He often quoted the famous line "Iran is where the Kurd is," to say that the Kurds were the very essence of the Iranian tradition, and being at peace as a nation had to begin with peace for the Kurds. Besides, Noori had a debt to the Kurds. In the early 1980s, when the new regime had begun to persecute secular intellectuals, Kurdistan became a safe haven for many on the run. Shohreh and Sara had already left for Germany, but Noori, forced into hiding, fled to Kurdistan. The Kurds safely smuggled him on horseback across the border. For having reunited him with his family, he never forgot his debt, not even in Berlin.

A balmy early autumn day was ending in a tender drizzle. He had almost reached Prager Street. His destination was the northernmost end of the block, in a narrow cul-de-sac cars usually avoided. Shaded by tall elms and plane trees, the restaurant at number 2A nestled just where the curve of the blind alley began. On one side stood an elegant six-story building with balconies overlooking the street. On the other was the backyard of a nursery school where the colored eggs of Easter still dangled from the branches of autumnal trees, giving the surroundings an air of innocence.

When the telephone rang, Parviz Dastmalchi did not answer it. He had looked forward to spending a few quiet hours stretched on his living-room couch, reading through his manuscript. The prospect of publishing a first book had eclipsed all the misfortunes that could have otherwise spurred a midlife crisis: divorce, separation from his only child, Salomeh, and a lonely life in exile. Writing, though he had started late, kept his spirit in place while he made the necessary adjustments.

But the phone kept on ringing and, at last, he answered it.

"Excellency, how goes it?" came the sound of his best friend Noori, whose voice was tinged with distress. Parviz immediately asked what was wrong.

"No one's here," Noori answered.

"Where's *here*?"

"The restaurant. Where else?"

Puzzled, Parviz asked why Noori was there at all. For a few moments, each answered the other with questions of his own, until Noori relented. "Stop with the Q and A, Excellency! I'm here with the Kurds. With the Doctor and his two deputies. And *you*? Why on earth are you home? I told you about this days ago."

The charge of not being on time or missing a date was not one Parviz, who preached punctuality, took lightly. In his calendar, as he read aloud from it to Noori, the dinner was marked for the following night.

The distress in Noori's voice gave way to resignation. "Aziz told you it was on Friday, didn't he? The buffoon has been calling people, telling them to come Friday night. How he got that into his head is beyond me."

The Doctor, Noori explained, had long been booked on an early morning flight to Paris on Friday and various receptions at the conference had claimed every other evening on his schedule except Thursday.

Learning of the blunder, Parviz said, "Aha! This is what I call a disaster of the quintessentially Iranian kind! We're never on time. We can't coordinate a simple meeting and we wonder why the mullahs are running our country. Bah!"

But Noori, in no mood to self-reflect, said, "Spare me the punditry for now! There's just the four of us and Aziz. The place is dead, Excellency! You've got to come! You've got to come and make me look good."

Parviz knew he had to go. Yet he could not help resisting. His work day was to start unusually early the next day and sleep was not something he did without anymore.

"Come now!" Noori replied with loving banter. "Stop sounding like an old man. We won't start dinner without you. Praise the Almighty!"

• • •

Praise the Almighty, the famous sign-off by the devout atheist. It was loyalty to their twenty-year-old friendship that moved Parviz from his couch that night—loyalty and also hope.

The year 1992 seemed full of promise. The eight-year war between Iran and Iraq had long ended. The Ayatollah was mostly a memory. Extremism had lost its allure for Iranians. The nation had distanced itself from its radical rulers. Many among the exiles believed 1992 was about to deliver what 1979 had only promised and that it was time for the opposition to prepare itself. The new president, Rafsanjani, had lifted the ban on many publications the Ayatollah had outlawed. He spoke of moderation, tolerance, and national reconciliation. He had issued a call inviting all exiles to return home: "The motherland needs its children to set aside the old divisions and return home to rebuild what years of war destroyed."

Only a few thought the call to be a ploy to lure the opposition back to the country to annihilate them once and for all. The rest welcomed it as the sign of a new, milder political season. Since the revolution, nothing had divided the diaspora the way Rafsanjani's conciliatory gesture had. The opposition that had mostly spoken with one voice against the regime was torn asunder by the sudden friendliness of the old enemy.

Noori was among the hopeful. And it was hope that had moved him to arrange the gathering that night. He had invited several of the most notable local exiles to meet the Doctor over dinner, thinking the encounter might draw them

—members of Iran's disarrayed opposition—into unity. He believed they were on the cusp of change and that repatriation was only a matter of time, though the fancy word meant nothing to him other than simply going home. He had written many articles citing the latest political developments as proof that the tide was turning in favor of reform in Iran. Yet no amount of polemical smoke could cloud his true motive, at least not to those closest to him. He regretted the uncompromising attitude, the radicalism, of his university days, though he still kept the guise of a wiry rebel: earth-tone Che Guevara attire, large spectacles, and a bushy mustache that curled under his fleshy upper lip. Over twenty years of activism, first against the Shah and then against the Ayatollah, had only led to what he, on good days, referred to as "a historic failure of infinite proportions," and on bad, by whatever single-syllable vulgarism that came to his restless mind. He rarely said so, and when he did it was only after a few drinks, but all radicalism had got him was from bad, a king, to worse, a cleric. The thought of forever remaining a dissident and growing old in exile dispirited him. Idealism had led him to a profession he had hoped would satisfy his desire to make a difference in the world. He and Parviz were both working at the Red Cross supervising the resettlement of refugees in Berlin, each raising a family on a social worker's salary but while Parviz was content, Noori felt expendable. Age had brought him the opposite of what he had expected. Instead of forgoing the loss of small things, he longed for them. He did not want new and better things, but the old imperfect ones he had known as a child. He dreamed of his family home, especially the third floor library he had built—sawing, sanding, and staining each shelf to last a lifetime—*his* lifetime.

In a few minutes Parviz was dressed and the lateness of the hour did not keep him from composing his trademark boyish yet professorial look—the first owing to his ready, mischievous smile and full head of chestnut hair, which refused graying, and the second to the immaculate dress shirt and sharply pressed trousers on his small frame. He grabbed his parka and the article, "The Kurds of Iran Today," to read on the road.

By the time Parviz arrived, the boxed menus and the wrought-iron fixtures at either side of the restaurant's entrance were already lit. The nights were growing chilly, and the sidewalk tables had been carted to storage. Only a stack of white rubber chairs remained, beside a row of potted junipers. Even after a year of being in Iranian hands, the restaurant had kept its Greek appearance. On the front window the image of four doves circling a windmill remained, along with the words Taverna Restaurant scripted in antique lettering above the name—Mykonos.

For nearly a year, 2A Prager Street had been the haunt of the diaspora. But its popularity was no reflection on the owner. Aziz, a fellow exile, knew nothing about running a business, nor was he a connoisseur to be trusted with matters of taste or decor. The expatriates came because they saw pieces of themselves in the restaurant's awkward ambience. Nostalgia made the imperfections of the place endearing, as did its imperfect host, Aziz, *dear* in Persian, the language of their nostalgia. The dirty gray carpeting, the institutional white paint on the walls, the potted vines thickly layered with dust, the plastic flowers with missing petals, and the unframed, sun-faded posters of the Greek isles tacked here and there all reminded them of the flaws of their displaced selves. Mykonos was familiar. Mykonos was what they thought they deserved. And Aziz, despite his inadequacies, knew how to invoke their sympathies so that tolerating his poor cooking seemed like their duty, an exercise in patriotism.

Inside, Parviz found Maria, the blonde Ukrainian barmaid, leaning on the counter, listlessly listening to the lone customer in the main hall. Aziz had been turning away customers, except this loyal, mildly hunched German regular who, from his usual table by the bar, exchanged an occasional line with the barmaid. Making a crisscrossing motion with his hands, Aziz had apologized to everyone who walked in that night in his broken German, *Chef no here. He sick. Kitchen closed.*

Noori's voice could be heard in the main hall as he fumed in the back room of the restaurant. "Tell me this! Tell me only this! How could you say to people *Friday* night when I'd clearly told you *Thursday*?"

Of his original list of sixteen guests none had shown up. Aziz's voice echoed, stammering an answer, "Listen, Noori *mola*."

Mola, as in "mentor," had long been Aziz's term for Noori. "You said Friday night. I swear on my two children's lives, you said Friday night. 'Aziz,' you said, 'call 'em up,' you said, 'tell 'em we're meeting the Doctor at Mykonos on Friday night,' is what you said."

The answer flabbergasted Noori, who threw his hands up and refused to say more than, "Impossible!" But Aziz would not give in. "I don't hold a candle to you, *mola jaan,* but my memory is rock solid. Friday night is what you said."

They were seated around a long, wobbly table Aziz had arranged by joining three small tables together. At the head, the Doctor and Noori sat side by side, their backs against the wall, facing the open room and the Doctor's two deputies. Had there been no confusion about the timing, the meeting would have been a rare chance to hear from the Doctor, the beloved regional leader who had national potential. But by eight-thirty, Parviz was the only one to arrive.

They all rose to welcome Parviz. "I was in my pajamas when Noori called, thinking the meeting was for tomo—"

With a gentle pat on the back, the Doctor interrupted Parviz to stop the exhausted argument from starting once again. Aziz resumed his duties as host. He ran a scraper over the tablecloth to clear crumbs, lit the candles, and emptied the ashtrays into his palms before walking away. Noori cast a last look of dismay in Aziz's direction, then turned his attention to Parviz. He offered Parviz the other empty seat beside the Doctor, but seeing beer on the table Parviz chose to sit across from them, where he had an uncluttered path to the men's room. No sooner had they settled in their chairs than they rose to welcome two other unexpected arrivals. Two Iranian cabdrivers had stopped to pick up dinner but Aziz had urged them to stay, hoping to make up for the missing audience.

Within minutes, a last guest arrived.

"*Huzzah*! Look who's here!" Aziz rushed to the door. "Our own Mr. Mehdi, who'd otherwise never set foot in my joint."

Mehdi, who was a former wrestling champion, pressed a sinewy forearm to his chest, giving a gentle bow, and greeted everyone. Aziz, trying to lighten the mood, exclaimed, "This way, please! Let the champ get through! Mr. Mehdi! Mr. Mehdi! You're just as rare a sight around here as the absent Prophet Mahdi you were named after."

Mehdi was there for Noori's sake who had called earlier that evening urging him to come. A star athlete and an engineering graduate of Sharif, Iran's most prestigious university, Mehdi could have remained in Iran relishing his status as a celebrity. But the glories of fame fell short of life's daily indignations once he left the ring and crossed the threshold from wrestler to citizen. At least living as a cabdriver in Berlin afforded him consistency—he was the same invisible immigrant wherever he went.

"You're a gem to come," Noori, brimming with gratitude, whispered in Mehdi's ear, then offered him the empty chair on his right.

"With all due respect, Doctor, you ought to take better care of yourself. You need security. You need guards," one of the guests began, once everyone had settled around the table.

But the Doctor waved away the advice. Bodyguards were an expensive indulgence to the Doctor, who represented an impoverished people. Or perhaps it was the metaphysical streak in him, in every Iranian, that made him dismissive of death, as if his cause was too great to yield to mortal concerns. The Doctor's security had long preoccupied the thoughts of his supporters—something he always tried to ease by telling a favorite anecdote.

"'Life and death are the two sides of the same coin.' A Peshmerga fighter in the mountains of Kurdistan taught me this. With his walking stick, he drew a line in the dirt, stood to one side of it, looked into my eyes, and said, '*Kaak* Doctor, this is life.' Then leapt to the other side of the line, looked into my eyes again, and said, 'This is death, *Kaak* Doctor.' He taught me to see how closely death shadows us all. There's no point in fearing what's always with us. There's no telling when, but a few seconds is all that separates us from the next world."

How fatalistic, Parviz thought. What he believed the Kurds and all disenchanted Iranians needed was not a mystic but a pragmatic leader who refused to surrender, most of all to death. But before he had sounded his objection, the Doctor had moved on and was answering a question about Kurdistan and the state of its people. The Doctor was an attentive listener. He compensated for his lacking charisma with avuncular gentleness. His civility was endearing. He spooned condiments into everyone's dish and cordially got up when anyone rose from his seat. Even in his fiercest official pose—decked in combat uniform with a gun strapped to his back—the balding, full-cheeked Doctor looked no more menacing than a crossing guard at an intersection. Had he not been born among a persecuted people, he would have been a professor or a researcher in a laboratory. But all that was left of his years of learning was a pair of wire-rimmed glasses and the title *Doctor*.

Despite the Doctor's warmth, the exchange quickly lost its vigor. Of his two deputies, one was silent and the other, too eager to speak, incessantly interrupted everyone. Parviz was growing restless. He wanted to go home but knew he could not. Noori would not let him, at least not until dinner had been served.

At nine o'clock the telephone at 7 Senftenberger Ring in north Berlin rang once. Within seconds, it rang again. Then, no more. The four men inside the apartment did not pick up the receiver. For six days they had prepared for this moment—for the two rings that let them know their targets had arrived.

For six days, they had remained in a cramped dormitory studio, leaving only on essential errands. That morning, they had been busy wiping off doorknobs, kitchen counters, cabinet handles, and refrigerator shelves, all the surfaces where their fingertips might have left a trace. That afternoon, two of the men had gone to the local Woolworth's store to buy a sports bag. They had returned within the hour with a black and green bag marked Sportino, purchased for 24.95 DM in cash—a final investment in the stock of malice.

The day before, the pair had driven to a deserted spot, a *blind location* in their own vernacular, where they received a delivery without seeing the deliverer. A cache of weapons had been left in a fruit carton, which they retrieved and locked up in the trunk of their BMW. In the early morning hours of the next day, the sixth and last day, the team's leader left before anyone was awake and returned that afternoon with an envelope of photographs. He ordered one of the men to fetch the fruit carton from the BMW's trunk. Then behind locked doors and drawn shades he circulated the photos—mainly portraits—among his underlings. There were images of a bald, middle-aged man with round features, wearing a pair of wire-rimmed glasses. In others, the same face appeared next to two younger men, mustached and clean-shaven, their dark hair parted to one side, their expressions subdued.

The contents of the carton also passed hands—a machine gun, a handgun, several dozen bullets, and two silencers. They disassembled and reassembled the pieces, loading and unloading each, cocking them, taking aim, shooting blanks, until everyone felt at ease with them. Then they placed the pieces back in the carton and locked it in the car's trunk once again. The BMW was perfectly indistinct beside the other cars on the block, though not for long. Soon, its every detail—the softness of its shade of blue, its plate number, B-AR 5503, its purchase price of 3120 DM—would be repeated like a new popular tune on the lips of reporters and investigators.

At sunset, the men spread their mats, stood in the direction of Ka'aba, and began a final prayer before leaving on their mission, code named the "Great Alavi Shout." Alavi as in Shiite, the faith they claimed as their own.

After the two single rings, their leader announced, "It's time!"

Two of his underlings left the apartment and drove away in the BMW. He and the remaining man also headed out. They hailed a taxi, which they rode to a midway point. When they exited the taxi, they descended the stairs into a subway station, walked through an underground tunnel, and ascended the stairs at the other end. When they surfaced, they hailed another taxi.

By nine-thirty, all four men had reunited near the Mykonos. An hour later, a black Mercedes pulled to the curb at the intersection opposite the cul-de-sac. The team leader approached the car and exchanged a few words with its passengers. Returning, he walked along the small alley separating the playground of the nursery from the back lot of the restaurant. Through the window overlooking the small room, he peered inside, then walked over to the BMW and unlocked its trunk.

4

> Scotland Yard called to warn me that they'd received a tip about a terrorist plot against me. Their best advice was to never be on time for an appointment. "A half-hour delay is one Iranian tradition I always observe, I said." The Yard man shook his head. "Then God help you, because your killers are Iranian, too."
>
> —*Hadi Khorsandi, exiled Iranian satirist*

It was after ten when dinner was finally served. Aziz laid several trays of assorted kebabs and saffron rice on the table, along with perfunctory bowls of tomato wedges and iceberg lettuce. He kept shuttling to the table, being both chef and host, lingering only to fill empty glasses or replenish the trays. In the main hall, the German regular was still nursing his nightcap when two dark-haired men charged in and scurried past him.

As they were making their way through the restaurant, Aziz approached the guests once more. He pointed to the guest of honor, and asked, "Would the Doctor like any more beer?"

The Doctor did not turn toward the host, or answer him. His cheeks went bloodless, his eyes suddenly vacant. His gaze was fixed upon the archway where he had spotted the two strangers. A sense of foreboding filled the room, the feeling that something was dreadfully awry. Someone, seeing the change on the Doctor's face, suspecting a heart attack, shouted, "Noori, see what's wrong with the Doctor!"

And that was how death announced itself that night, unceremoniously, only as a blush vanishing, pink turning sallow. The swiftness, the simpleness of it had paralyzed them before a single bullet had been shot.

Parviz felt a presence beside him. From the corner of his eye, he quickly traced a set of steely legs beneath an impressive outline upward along a thick torso to a pair of dark eyes, connected eyebrows, and a widow's peak . . . *but the face?* It was only partly visible. The obscurity of the face alarmed him. His nerves mutinous, he threw himself back to take cover under the table behind him.

The predators, standing tall, had yet to fire. The prey were hunched in chairs or lay prostrate on the floor. The ones to survive would strain to remember what had passed in the hours before the shooting began or after it had ended, but these in-between moments, this purgatory, would vividly, indelibly, brand their memories. A menacing voice boomed, cursing in Persian. The shout was followed by steady explosions that flashed through the dim air like the embers of a dying fire. The shell casings rang on the floor—the men collapsing, their chairs falling, the wall behind them cracking with each bullet. Blood sprayed on what remained of a dinner of meat and rice, speckling the empty china like remnants of some crimson garnish, dotting the uneaten bread in the straw baskets, beading upon the petals of the plastic flowers in their stubby vases. One of the wounded men clutched the tablecloth as he fell, dragging it with him, spilling bottles. Beer and water streaked the cloth and dampened the neon-blue layer beneath. The print of his bleeding hand stained one end of the white fabric.

Danger summoned the wrestler in Mehdi. He shouted a warning, then dragged the elbows of his tablemates as he dove under the table. The person to his left followed the trajectory of his tug. The one to his right did not. Noori collapsed onto the table.

When the barrage ceased, a hush fell over the room, more petrifying than the disquiet it succeeded. Parviz stole a glance at his surroundings. Another shooter walked up and fired three more shots at the Doctor. His gun, like the machine gun, sounded muffled. *Silencers!* Parviz could see the shooter's elbow jerk backward with every blow, then turn to aim at the Doctor's deputy who lay next to him. A single muffled echo reverberated in the air. Expecting the elbow, clad in black leather, to pause over him next, Parviz shut his eyes and waited. But the next sounds were of rustling feet, heavy steps rushing past then fading away.

Fear had muted everything but the unconscious groans of the wounded. Nothing moved. Nothing gave a sound. Until at last, Mehdi called out.

"Noori?"

There was no answer. He called again, "Doctor?"

Only silence. "Mr. Abdoli?"

Still, no one gave a sound. "Mr. Ardalan? Aziz?"

At the other end of the room, someone stirred. Finally, a voice.

"Mehdi?"

"Yes! Aziz? Is that you?"

"No. It's Parviz."

The sound of Mehdi's voice restored Parviz. He got to his feet and walked to the main hall. He was going to dial the police from the phone at the bar, but the German diner had already done so. Instead, Parviz called a friend and relayed the news. "They came to Mykonos and shot us all. I don't know who's alive and who's dead. Tell everyone!"

The two cabdrivers among the guests, also unhurt, were standing in the main hall, dazed and too frightened to leave. Parviz retraced his steps to the back room. Under the archway, he froze, standing where the shooters had stood moments ago, gazing at what they had left behind. Arms to one side, neck drooped over a shoulder, the Doctor remained seated, as if to deny his enemies the pleasure of witnessing his fall. Under the table where Parviz had taken cover, one of the Doctor's two deputies lay on his side, blood streaming from the corner of his mouth. The other, facedown, had fallen within a few feet of his spot at the table, as if the force of the bullets had ejected him from his chair. Aziz was on his back, motionless.

Parviz scanned the table. The glass and china were intact. A few vases had tipped when someone had grabbed onto the tablecloth to break his fall. Suddenly he caught sight of Noori, whose face was propped up by his mug of beer, overflowing with blood. His glasses had slipped—a lens pressing against his forehead. A wet murky stain was widening across his sapphire shirt. With seven bullets lodged in his chest, he was unconscious, breathing strained breaths.

The image of the wounded Noori would seal two decades of Parviz's memories, spanning Berlin and Tehran—Sunday afternoons on the volleyball court, evenings in the kitchen serving as Noori's sidekick, late nights of drinking at the Bierkeller, the endless hours of debating, drafting statements, rewording the phrases of a flyer while inhaling the nicotine-riddled air that always hovered about Noori, weekends in the outdoors, watching Noori teach the malcontented children of newly arrived immigrants the secrets of survival in the woods—how to build a fire, climb a rock, weave a net, knot a rope. This bloody creature was that Noori, the chef, the writer, the debater, the debonair socialite, the friend Parviz had come to tonight to make look good.

He walked over to him. He wanted to lift Noori, hold him, soothe him. But he fought the urge, lest moving him worsened his condition. He stepped gingerly away, till he felt the wall against his back. Then his knees gave. He slithered to the floor and squatted shoulder to shoulder beside Mehdi. The two did not speak. They stared at the floor with damp eyes neither moved a hand to wipe.

Suddenly, Aziz stood up. He tried to walk but instead he let out a moan and collapsed, and kept on moaning. In the distance, the faint shrieking of sirens was growing louder. A man entered the restaurant. Parviz, startled by the sight, shouted, "Get away! Who the hell are you?"

Flashing a badge, the plainclothes officer shouted the same question at Parviz. Minutes later, Noori and Aziz were strapped onto stretchers and driven away in two ambulances. The bodies of the Doctor and his two deputies were left untouched. Only three square cardboard signs were placed next to each: 1, 2, and 3.

Yousef Amin wanted to be anywhere but in the backseat of that BMW. By his own calculation, he was not all that guilty. He had only been a watchman at the door of the restaurant. He had refused to kill, and did not want to be sitting in the same car with killers. The BMW jerked forward, speeding and braking without heeding road signs, barely keeping from crashing. To Yousef's relief, the driver finally headed for the highway, but soon took the first exit and steered the car back onto the city streets again, resuming the madness.

The team leader barked at Yousef from the front seat. "Put the gun in the bag! Now!"

In the frantic rush to escape, the second shooter had thrown his piece into the car, and it lay in plain sight on the passenger floor. Yousef picked it up with a ski mask and dropped it into the sports bag. The car neared a crowded square. At a traffic light, the two shooters slipped out. Yousef followed next. With everyone gone, the driver was alone behind the wheel of the incriminating vehicle, in possession of the incriminating bag. The operation had been flawlessly planned and executed until the moment of shooting, but not beyond. He drove aimlessly, looking for a desolate block to leave the car. Then he found himself on Cicero Street. He pulled over, shut the engine, grabbed the sports bag, and fled the car, unaware that he had blocked a driveway. The bag was all that was left to be rid of. He found a lot full of cars. He flung the bag under one of them. Unburdened at last, he ran into the night.

In a small room at Berlin's police headquarters, Parviz stared out the window, waiting for the interrogating officer who had left to take a phone call. When he returned, he told Parviz that Noori, the restaurant owner, had died in the hospital.

Parviz rushed to correct him.

"Sir, please! Watch what you say! The restaurant owner's name is Aziz. You're trying to say Aziz died. Aziz, not Noori. Two different men."

The officer checked his notes, then asked who Noori Dehkordi was, to which Parviz responded with confidence, "Not a restaurant owner. No! Anything but that."

"Well, he's the one who just died."

Parviz looked at the officer, his gaze blank as a blind man's. Tears streaked his face. He was not the crying kind, least of all in public. But at 3 a.m. on September 18, 1992, he was not the kind of man he used to be.

The officer brought him a glass of water and two pills, then softly urged Parviz to take them. He followed the order mindlessly. In the spartan room, there was no more than a desk, a file cabinet, a set of chairs, and the glare of fluorescent lights above. Parviz tried to think but fear and fury kept getting in his way. To Parviz Dastmalchi, the fatherless boy from Tehran's poor Sarsabil neighborhood, there was no problem that could not be solved, no adversity he could not overcome through thinking. He had always been pragmatic, able to reduce the most intangible matters to their elements. When his childhood allowance had been too small, he earned more by tutoring classmates in math. By fourteen he had worked at a tea factory wrapping tea boxes in cellophane, skinned and chopped onions for the corner grocer, getting paid by the kilo, and earned the reputation of a fledgling entrepreneur by supplying local peddlers with bags he made from the pages of his old notebooks—each pack of ten for one rial.

The fear he felt was not of death. Death had haunted him from the womb. (His mother, who had nicknamed him "the invincible" at birth, had tried to abort him, but Parviz, the fetus, had survived the intervention.) The fear he had was of another's control over the circumstances of his death and, by extension, of another's control over the circumstances of his life. He feared indignity. He had sacrificed much to live as a free man but the destiny he had tried to avoid had come looking for him. That night he had, but only narrowly, escaped becoming yet another number, sixty-five to be exact.

Five hundred Iranians had been on a list to be murdered; at least sixty of them (possibly more) had already been shot, stabbed, or beheaded in Paris, Maryland, Manila, Bombay, Karachi, Istanbul, Vienna, Wembley, Larnaca, Geneva, Stockholm, Sulaymaniyah, Tokyo, New Jersey, and, five weeks earlier, in the suburbs of Bonn. On this night a malicious hand had crossed out four more names: sixty-one, Noori Dehkordi; sixty-two, Dr. Sadegh Sharafkandi; sixty-three, Homayoun Ardalan; sixty-four, Fattah Abdoli.

The list had been drawn up by Ayatollah Khomeini in 1980, one year after his rise to power. The names belonged to those he had branded "enemies of Islam." Three years after his death, the orders were reinstated by his successor. These were the first death sentences the Ayatollah issued, before the word *fatwa* entered the Western lexicon or Salman Rushdie became a household name. The Ayatollah's footmen were on a worldwide hunt for everyone on the list—writers, artists, poets, intellectuals, and even satirists. Scores of dissidents living inside Iran had long been silenced, imprisoned, or executed. Those abroad were learning that even if they could flee the Ayatollah, they could not flee the fate he had dictated for them.

The list also included many in the political opposition, several Kurds among them. The Ayatollah's hatred for the Kurds was an old one. It ran so deep that he could not withhold it even before he was securely in power. After the 1979 revolution, when a new constitution was being drafted, he barred representatives of the mostly Sunni Kurds from the process. The constitution that was ultimately ratified favored the Shiite majority. After the fall of the Shah, a spirit of unity had swept over the nation and the Ayatollah, seizing upon the public euphoria, invited all minorities to forgo ethnic demands and instead become a single Muslim nation. But the Kurds refused. They held fast to their own dream of autonomy. Years before a second word, *jihad,* entered the Western lexicon, the Ayatollah invoked it to declare war against the Kurds.

Iran was already at war with Iraq on its western frontier. So this other war against five hundred infidels had to be waged covertly. "We will export our revolution," he promised. His shipments of aid were reaching far and wide, from the shores of Lebanon to the poor neighborhoods of Algiers. But for expatriates, his only export was terror. His scheme was run by henchmen who were recruited from around the globe. In Berlin, his funds poured into the city's main Shiite mosque where his agents identified promising congregants and gave them jobs in innocuous grocery stores or other small businesses, which served as fronts for their sinister operations. It would be several years until terror networks began to strike against Western targets. But the Ayatollah's fledgling cells, growing under Europe's oblivious skin, were already at work destroying the lives of expatriates, creating a blueprint for the next, more ambitious generation of killers.

Parviz sat disoriented before his interrogator. He knew with perfect clarity, even without proof, who had sent the assassins to the restaurant. So did a handful of Europe's most powerful politicians. After all, these culprits were not unknown. They were a recurring cadre of killers. A former pilot in Iran's Royal Army was assassinated in Geneva in

1989 by the same shooter who, a year later, attempted to assassinate the Saudi ambassador to Sweden. He evaded arrest or was quickly released both times, investigators would ultimately discover, and went on to become the chief shooter at Mykonos.

He was not the only one. Others like him had attacked exiles throughout Europe and escaped as law enforcement authorities looked on. A few were briefly detained but were quietly deported to Iran in the name of "national interest." In Austria and France, after two such assassinations took place in the 1980s, both countries cited "national interests" and escorted the killers onto planes bound for Iran. Each time an assassin returned home safely, Tehran rewarded Europe by arranging for the release of a European hostage held captive somewhere in the lawless corners of the world. Europe accepted Tehran's math: dozens of dead Iranian exiles equaled one free European citizen.

These deaths were merely an inconvenience to the politicians who were boosting their careers by negotiating with Tehran and facilitating trade. They were granting asylum to Iranian dissidents at their borders, giving them the illusion of having reached a safe haven. But they were also turning a blind eye to assassins crossing the same borders.

Parviz did not know the details of this dark history, but he intuited its essence, and it was what he told the interrogating officer when he asked who Parviz thought was behind the crime. The officer noted the statement in the file but appeared skeptical.

Dawn had broken by the time the questioning ended and Parviz was allowed to leave. He stepped into the hallway, looking for Mehdi or the others. Instead, he found Shohreh. The two rushed to each other and embraced.

He wailed, "They killed them, Shohreh. They killed them."

"How's Noori?" she whimpered.

Deaf to her words, he went on, "Our dear ones. . . . all gone. The Kurds. Dead as stone on the floor. Blood all over. Oh, Shohreh. Aziz, poor Aziz . . ."

They shook with weeping and talked without listening to the other. She asked again through sobs, "Noori, Parviz, Noori! What happened to Noori?"

But he only wept. She released herself from his embrace, looked into his eyes, and repeated her question. This time, he heard her. That Shohreh had not yet learned of her husband's death stunned him. In a daze, he simply echoed her, "Noori?" then resumed wailing.

Shohreh pressed. "Yes, Noori. Tell me, what happened to him? Will he be all right? What will I do if something happens to him?"

Parviz averted his gaze from hers. Standing before Shohreh, faced with her yearning, valor failed him. He mumbled, "He was breathing the last time I saw him."

Then, without pause, he turned on his heel and hurried down the hallway, looking for the exit.

5

Ever since that night at the Mykonos restaurant, Parviz Dastmalchi won't have dinner unless it's served under the table.

—*Hadi Khorsandi, exiled Iranian satirist*

Bruno Jost first heard of the murders at the Mykonos restaurant in the men's room of his office, the chief federal prosecutor's headquarters in Karlsruhe, some four hundred miles from Berlin. From behind the stall door, the prosecutor received a briefing from his superior.

"Quadruple homicides of top Iranian Kurds at a Greek place in Berlin, sometime around twenty-three hundred hours last night. Quite a scene, Mr. Jost. Could be linked to the other Kurdish case you've got on your plate." The superior relayed the crux of what he had learned in a phone call from the BND, Germany's intelligence agency.

The conversation continued against the backdrop of rushing water and the hissing of a hand dryer. They discussed the assassins' probable identities as they walked the long corridor to Jost's office. He was in the throes of a case involving the PKK, the armed separatist group of Turkish Kurds. He could not help suspecting there was a link between that case and the murders in Berlin. For a militant group, an assassination would be the swiftest solution to a dispute over leadership.

"The victims being high-profile political types, the killers being most likely foreign agents," Jost said, more in rumination than inquiry, "this ought to be our case, don't you agree?"

He was hoping to take on what seemed to be a new piece to the puzzle he was trying to solve.

His superior, the head of the terrorism division, shared Jost's intuition and asked him to make a few preliminary inquiries.

Bruno Jost made two calls—one to the Berlin police and one to the federal police—to assess the scope of the case, which, if it proved vast enough to be deemed a threat to the nation's security, his office would claim as its own.

At forty-two, Bruno Jost had reached his moment of professional reckoning. He wanted a case consequential enough to put his skills and mettle to the test. Such a case, he believed, seldom came a prosecutor's way, and, if it did, only once. His professional lot thus far had included a notable medley of drug and terrorism cases. But even the most demanding of them, one brought against the former East

German officials after reunification—grueling enough to keep him in Leipzig, far from home for six months—had not quenched or exhausted but only conditioned him for an Olympian run.

A prosecutor's ambition is usually the mark of his opportunism, his eagerness to stage a performance in the courtroom in the hopes that politicians might take notice and promotion might follow. But in Germany a prosecutor rises through the ranks only by merit—a series of rigorous tests and internal peer reviews. Courtroom drama hardly has a place in this universe, where the prosecutor is neither the adversary of the accused nor the victim's defender, but an objective agent on a mission to find the truth. He is the nonpartisan trustee who must follow all leads against, or in favor of, all sides. His success or failure hardly reflects his oratory or panache. It comes long before the curtain rises on the courtroom stage, during the many days, weeks, or even months of grueling investigation, culminating in the indictment. The ensuing trial is not a battle between two adversarial parties. It is a thorough examination of the merits of that indictment that is, in essence, the prosecutor's last word, his discovery, his verdict on the matter the judges set out to examine.

The prospect of such a monastic quest had preoccupied Jost from boyhood, as he read favorites by Charles Dickens (*Oliver Twist,* in particular), Karl May, Albert Schweitzer (for Jost, too, had a passion for distant lands), and Daniel Defoe's *Robinson Crusoe*—the latter having left him ever daydreaming about scenarios of his own solitary encounters with great odds. Jost's tanned face, small hands, salt and pepper hair (more pepper than salt in 1992), and disarming lilac eyes belied his fierceness. The decor of his office was equally misleading, seeming more like the tidy quarters of a lovelorn youth than the workplace of a middle-aged attorney. On his walls hung a poster of Gustav Klimt's *The Kiss* and a picture of snow-covered prairie. There were two overgrown plants in need of repotting on a shelf and a few unframed cartoons tacked above his desk next to the file cabinet on which pictures of his family were propped. These tokens of serenity camouflaged his inner intensity. Law was the most consuming passion of his life. He had afforded the luxuries of marriage and children only because his wife, Angela, who often found herself alone in the face of domestic trials, was unusually resourceful. His father had been a hospital attendant, his mother, a homemaker. Law had been the antidote to his inner adolescent tumult—the mark of his mutiny against his lowly filial destiny. It took no more than skimming a few vocational brochures at a high school job fair for Jost to discover his future. In his teenage state, becoming a prosecutor seemed a noble profession. When he finally entered one of Germany's most prestigious offices, Jost was an unfettered prodigy who owed no one for his ascent.

After the phone calls, Jost pondered what he had learned. Two facts loomed larger than any others. The first was that the killers had insulted their victims not in Kurdish but in Persian, which probably meant they were not Kurds. The second was that the crime in Berlin had a precursor in Vienna. Three years earlier, another Iranian Kurdish leader, the predecessor of the main target at Mykonos, had also been assassinated. Though the assassins were still at large, the three-year investigation by the Austrian investigators pointed to Iran's embassy in Vienna.

The telephone rang. Chief Federal Prosecutor Alexander von Stahl had heard the news in his car, en route to work. He had immediately called to tell his office to begin working on the case.

"We'll take it now and worry about proving why it's ours later," were the words of von Stahl, whose elegant, baritone voice had a tinny echo on the mobile telephone.

Von Stahl's next call would be to his press secretary, he assured Jost, to arrange a noon press conference. In the meantime, he instructed Jost to take charge of the investigation in Berlin.

On his way to the airport, Bruno Jost drafted the statement that would become the emblem of his career. It began with a description of the incident and then, in a paragraph, he summarized his earliest suspicions about the culprits.

The pattern of the execution—particularly the profile of the victims who were all members of the opposition—speaks to the political motivation behind this crime. Based on the current evidence, the following are the possible culprits:

1) *PKK as the rival of the Democratic Party of Kurdistan. The possible reasons may be: In the past the PKK has widely and routinely attacked competing movements. In these instances, it has not shied*

away from murder. Another clue may be that one of the perpetrators shot Sadegh Sharafkandi with a handgun, even though he had already been shot by a machine gun.

2) *An Iranian governmental agency may also be a suspect since the gathering was of a group of Iranian opposition members. That one of the perpetrators shouted an expletive in Persian speaks of a punitive or vengeful act on behalf of a governmental organization.*

To this he added several legal citations to justify the federal prosecutor's claim to the case. At the bottom, dispensing with titles and prefixes, he wrote only: *Jost*

Berlin beckoned, and the prosecutor had one regret. He would be missing his wife on the night of their twenty-second wedding anniversary, something he hoped to rectify with a loving phone call. He expected to be home in a few days. Neither he nor Angela could have known that they would remain apart for six weeks, or that September 18 would some day be not simply the reminder of their union, but also of the ordeal that put that union through its toughest trial.

Sara Dehkordi knew something was amiss when she woke up to find her parents gone and her aunt at her bedside. The morning grew stranger when she learned she would be skipping school. Instead, the two of them went out and wandered through the streets. And when her aunt bought all the frivolous things Sara pointed to in shop windows—the small indulgences her parents never permitted—her foreboding worsened. Never had getting her wish made her so miserable.

Sara was not the only little girl to skip school that day. At his apartment, the first call Parviz made was to his former wife. Hearing the cheerful voice of his daughter at the other end, he grumbled, "You're home, Salomeh. *Warum?*" He broke into German as they often did together, speaking a mix of tongues, one of the mixed blessings of their overlapping worlds.

Salomeh said that her mother had allowed her a day off, then handed the receiver to her for proof. Parviz's ex came on and he whispered, "Listen! I can't say much now, but keep Salomeh away from television today."

Calls! All he wanted to do was make calls. He paced the apartment—from his living room couch, past the television set where the news was on, to the balcony for air, to the telephone on his bedroom desk, to the stove in the kitchen where he was boiling water for tea—over and over again. His morning routine had vanished. The thought of eating or going to bed did not enter his mind. Only, *calls*! He dialed his secretary at Berlin's Red Cross where he was a supervising social worker managing the affairs of refugees. "I won't be in today," he told her and, when asked why, he broke into a sob.

"Were you robbed? Is your mother dead? Is your daughter missing?" came the secretary's frantic questions.

All he could say to her was, "Turn on the news!"

• • •

He took a shower. Under the rushing water, he stood with eyes wide open. If he closed them, the image of the extended arm in a black leather sleeve would plague his mind. It was not until the streaming water struck his body that he felt the aching in his right cheek and temple and remembered the blow to his right side upon falling off his chair at the restaurant.

The age of real-time news had not dawned, and reporters were not yet looking for him. On an ordinary morning, he would have reveled in the peace. But against the uproar within him, quiet was the antithesis of peace. *More calls!* He dialed another number. It was that of a friend, an editorial writer on the board of the progressive daily *Berliner Zeitung*.

"Hello there. This is Parviz."

"Hey there, *Parvis*!" the voice came, softly modifying the last syllable of his name, per Parviz's own earlier instructions. ("Think of *Paris,*" he told Germans who had trouble remembering his name, "then add a *V* after the *R* and voilà, you've got me." A slight mispronunciation, he figured, was a small sacrifice for the sake of a good mnemonic.)

He crafted a single sentence to distill the ordeal for the busy journalist. "I was there at the restaurant, at Mykonos, with the four men who died last night."

"I heard. Let's have coffee one of these days to talk it over. Today is insane."

Parviz, stunned by the lukewarm reception, was forming his next sentence when the reporter excused himself and rushed off.

The dismissal caused a wave of panic in Parviz. For years, he had carefully collected journalists the way a connoisseur collects wine. In their company, the raconteur in Parviz found a captive audience. Spinning tales was a skill he had been perfecting since childhood, when he and his friends, who could not afford to go to the movies, pooled their allowances together to buy a single ticket for an emissary to see, then recount the ninety-minute film over the span of hours—so elaborately that the film, if the others ever did see it, invariably fell short of its narration.

Journalists had always been Parviz's most formidable allies. Years ago, after his visa had expired, the same editorial writer he had just spoken to had saved him from deportation by writing a scathing piece on Germany's repressive immigration policy. But now? To whom could he turn now?

As he brooded, the telephone rang. The same voice filled the receiver once more. "I'm sorry, Parvis. It's a crazed morning here. Did you say you, yourself, were at the Mykonos last night?"

"That's what I said."

"Then we must talk instantly."

Café Kranzler was teeming with customers at midmorning, as it had on many mornings in its two hundred years of operation. A waiter in the café's trademark maroon uniform seated Parviz at a table for two. The other chair did not remain empty for long. To his great relief, the old friend who had nearly forsaken him appeared, looking almost as distraught as he felt. The Kurds who had died had been guests of the Social Democratic Party, whose politics the newspaper advocated. That the party had failed to protect its guests was devastating, especially to the editorial writer who was one of its most vocal supporters.

Neither man spoke of what was undeniably on their minds—of fear. Parviz was certain the killers would soon return for him, but said nothing of it. The other sensed it so vividly that the words seemed superfluous. Never had the bold, outspoken Parviz asked not to be named in a piece, or hidden himself from view, as he did on that gray, cloudy morning, behind a pair of sunglasses worn indoors. For the second time, Parviz began recounting the details of the night before, the second of hundreds of times to come. Recollecting the tale did not ease his pain, for he had yet to feel pain, but it shattered the silence he was certain the killers wished to drive him into.

The first few questions established the Doctor's purpose in Berlin, at the conference, then at the dinner with the exiles. Parviz's voice faltered when he talked about the confusion over the time of the meeting, and of Noori's telephone call to him. The answers came easily to him as he walked the listener through the memories, hour by hour, until he was asked, "How did you survive?"

He paused to consider. *Had he?* He did not feel alive in the same way he had the day before. It was as if he had been cast into life's twilight, into an in-between state, where he was at once both alert and disoriented. He spoke again, this time deliberately.

"Around eleven. We'd just finished dinner and were talking. Someone asked Dr. Sharafkandi if the Kurds of Iran wanted to separate and create a country of their own. He objected to that suggestion, saying that his people were not separatists, insisting that the Kurds were even more Iranian than the Persians. It was his way of saying they did not want independence, but autonomy. He said the real issue was how to unify the opposition against the current regime. I was sitting with my back to the entrance, facing the Doctor, and sometime in the middle of all this I felt someone standing beside me. I turned toward him. He looked to be thirty to thirty-five years old and had a mask on. The rest happened at lightning speed. The man had a machine gun but I could not see it. It was under something, maybe a blue handkerchief, or maybe inside something. I don't know. He cursed us, but you must forgive me because I cannot bring myself to repeat his words. And then it happened. Forty bullets, maybe more. I survived by throwing myself under a table."

The next question, the reporter's last, was the one that Parviz had come to answer, the one that had driven him to make the call in the first place. "Who do you think is behind this?"

"Undoubtedly, the regime in Tehran."

Killers often return to the scene of the crime. So do haunted victims. At noon, Parviz found himself on Prager Street. From a distance, he could see a throng at the end of the block. Plainclothes agents and uniformed police officers were milling in front of the restaurant, inside the police barricade. Some spoke into walkie-talkies. Others, with gloved hands, held up and stared into small transparent bags, appearing deep in thought. A few were wielding tape measures, busily sizing things as scientists would. One appeared possessed, tracing and retracing the same steps from the boxes of evergreens to the main entrance, then to the intersection, over and over.

Outside the barricade, dozens of microphones hovered in the air, above the heads of onlookers. Newspapermen shadowed the investigators and shouted questions at them. Stern-faced television anchors paraded before the cameras and spoke feverishly. Phantom drawings of three suspects, barely resembling the killers, were circulating among the crowd. The next day's headlines were in the making.

*"The Berlin Massacre Ordered by Saddam Hussein:
500,000 DM paid for every dead Kurd."*

*"Executed at Dinner: Four Men Die
in a Power Struggle within the Kurdish Party."*

When Parviz was a boy, his mother once asked him to take the wash to the rooftop to hang up on the clothesline. Being only six, he refused. She asked again. He did not budge. She promised him candy, but he was not enticed. She beat him, but all he did was cry. She beat him harder. He only cried harder but did not move. In the end, she threw her hands up and bitterly called her son a "spring" because the harder she pressed him, the more he recoiled, and the more he recoiled, the feistier he became, and the harder he fought back.

Since the night before, Parviz had been pressed hard. Watching lies being fabricated before his eyes was a final blow. He pondered his choices. He could go home . . . *Keep mum, and be afraid of every shadow?*

To walk away from the scene was, for him, to be just as dead as the others. What a disgrace then, to have survived. Or he could . . . *Speak! Speak, now!*

He made his way through the crowd and stood against the police barricade, facing everyone. Fear and fury gripped him once more. The fatigue he had not paused to feel had dulled his senses. Every dark head in the crowd, reminding him of the shooter's head, jolted his nerves. Still, he hushed everyone and started to speak, albeit with a newfound stutter.

"Listen please, all of you! I was here in this restaurant, at the same table with the four people who died. I can tell you exactly what happened."

The chaos came to order. The wayward cameras and microphones lined up before Parviz, the human spring.

By midnight on September 19, 1992, Bruno Jost had examined the scene, which was more gruesome than any he had ever seen. He had talked to colleagues and local and federal police, read witness statements, and looked over the autopsy reports as they came in. He valued these early insights not simply because they advanced his knowledge of the case.

They also became a yardstick by which to measure the quality of future information.

Among his most startling discoveries was something no one, not even the survivors or the relatives of the dead, had considered. A crime of that magnitude could not have happened so cleanly, swiftly, and flawlessly without the help of an insider. Someone at the restaurant had collaborated with the killers. Was he still at large, or among the dead? This would be the first of several questions to gnaw at him in the weeks to come.

He had unearthed more than most investigators could, a credit to two qualities in him that were easily overlooked. Firstly, Jost thought himself a servant to a master named *law*. He did not shy away from the drudgeries of an investigation. He respected, but did not believe in, mediators, which was what he thought of everyone who reported to him. He hardly ever delegated even the lowliest of tasks to assistants. The brilliance of the truth he was to piece together, he believed, was in the luster of every detail that went into it. He feared what might be lost in the journey that a fact made from the lips of a witness to the pen of an overworked agent.

Besides, he could not claim to be a superior to those who had seen what he had not, talked to those he had not, measured the distances he had not walked. To earn the respect of his coworkers, to prevent the possibility of ever being told he was wrong because he had not been present at the scene, he traced in the footsteps of all those who had first been dispatched and repeated every tedious procedure they had performed in his absence.

Secondly, Jost was also a self-effacing man. His unassuming ways—the only item of luxury on him was the wisp of a gold band on his ring finger—deflected attention from him. He so often yielded to colleagues, so easily lent an ear to everyone, that witnesses, experts, or police officers spoke unreservedly in his presence, as if he were merely eavesdropping. A smile readily creased his lips to ease subordinates, as did his lilac gaze. Whatever flaws or shortcomings existed in Jost's character, they did not get in the way of his equanimity. Indeed, nothing caused Jost to lose his stride—not the armed bodyguards shadowing him, the frozen expressions of the corpses he examined, the tantrums of traumatized witnesses, or the cunning of the detainees who spun tale after tale to evade his questions. Nothing upset his peace for long because nothing could surpass in strangeness what he had witnessed as a child.

Until the year he left for college, Bruno Jost lived on the grounds of an insane asylum. His father was an attendant there and had an apartment on the premises. Growing up near the patients had inured Jost to strangeness. Sudden howls, frantic fits, gloomy countenances, bizarre rituals, and violent threats did not intimidate him. He had learned long ago how to stare into havoc and see past it.

That night, the last call Jost received was from an Iraqi Kurdish leader who had also come to Berlin for the annual conference of the Social Democratic Party. Jalal Talebani wished to meet with Jost because he had spent most of the day before with the Doctor. Fear of the killers kept Talebani inside the apartment of a friend, and so he asked Jost to come to him instead.

"I'd warned the Doctor months ago, in Paris, and again at the conference. I'd told him that a plot was in the works for his assassination," Talebani began.

Jost did little to prompt him. He settled into a chair and watched Talebani with eagerness. Talebani had to unburden himself. A few nods from time to time or a gesture was all he, on whom the foreknowledge of the crime now weighed heavily, needed to continue.

"My men in northern Iraq got a tip from an Iranian agent they had arrested. During the interrogation, the agent leaked the news of a plot by Tehran to behead all Kurds by murdering their leadership. But when I told the Doctor, he wasn't impressed. He said, 'You're not telling me anything new. Of course they want to kill me. Saddam wants to kill you, too. Tell me something I don't know!' I thought Vienna would smarten them, get them to up their security, but obviously, it hadn't."

Vienna again. For the second time in thirty-six hours that city's name had come up. Before the interview ended, Jost wrote VIENNA in block letters in his notepad and circled it—a reminder to study that case in the coming days.

On the ride back to his hotel, Jost pondered what he had learned from Talebani. Politicians were a tough lot to trust, especially the aspiring kind who lived in exile. Jost was glad to have the unsolicited account, but it hardly offered him more than hearsay. His main suspect was still the armed Kurdish group, the PKK.

When he arrived at his hotel it was three o'clock in the morning. The next day was scheduled to begin at eight. He slipped between the sheets and sleep spread over him fast like a spell.

Yousef Amin was wide awake aboard a train bound for the town of Rhine in Nordrhein-Westfalen, some four hundred miles from Berlin. He sat alert, gazing at the view that rolled past, as if absolution was something to be granted him through sight. The graffiti-riddled walls of the city tunnels soon gave way to farms, barns, bridges, rivers, and windmills. The landscape changed but his thoughts did not. All he could think of was what had happened in Berlin. His life would have lacked nothing, he reflected, if only he could wipe away September 17, or a few hours, even five minutes, of it. Five minutes seemed like a reasonable wish—small enough to come true.

Going home was a relief, not merely because he had escaped arrest, but because he had escaped the band of men he had once called friends. His troubles with them began four days earlier, when they had all been sitting together at a sidewalk table of a café and the team leader casually said to him, "If I ask you to kill, would you do it for me?"

The team leader, a forbidding figure, was not someone Yousef wished to cross. He hemmed and hawed. "You see, umm, but, brother, ahh, I wish I could but, er, I've got responsibilities now. A family, you know."

"Forget I said anything," the team leader waved his hand in the air. "I was only kidding."

Others in the group berated Yousef, calling him a coward. But he did not budge. Away from his family, Yousef had realized that he was through with living dangerously. He finally had a stake in life. He had youth (he was only twenty-five). He had his girl. And by November, his first wedding anniversary, he was also going to have a son.

Refusing to kill came at an unexpectedly high price. The team no longer trusted Yousef. His giddy manner, which had seemed perfectly innocuous before, now struck them as a liability. They did not take their eyes off him. In the days leading up to September 17, he was allowed out of their sight only for a few minutes, and only to call home. His wife pleaded with him to return but he had said, "I can't. They won't let me."

That they had turned on him became clear when he found himself alone in the apartment on that last morning. After his teammates left on errands, he decided to run to the phone booth at the corner to call his wife. But the door would not open. The lock had been turned and the key missing from its hook.

Being trapped was a familiar experience for Yousef. He was the fifteenth child of a poor family from Lebanon, and believed himself to be the reincarnation of his biblical namesake, Joseph, the son of Jacob. Joseph, too, had left home as a teenager looking to find in strangers what he had not in his kin. Yousef eventually met Abbas Rhayel. Though he was Yousef's junior by three years, Rhayel adopted Yousef like a little brother. When Rhayel decided to move to Beirut, so did Yousef. When Rhayel joined the Hezbollah, Yousef followed. When Rhayel went to receive combat training at a secret camp in Iran, Yousef went along. When Rhayel moved to Europe in 1989, Yousef was beside him. Together they went to Hungary, where smugglers snuck them into Germany. Rhayel was Yousef's guide. He was the one to find Yousef work, albeit of the sinister kind; he was his bridge to other societies, albeit to dangerous ones. He was also the one to enter the restaurant that night and fire the four final shots.

As the train neared Rhine, Yousef's mood brightened. He thought of his wife and her belly full of hope. He would never again allow anything to get in the way of his new life in a land so safe that the worst he ever had to fear was severe weather. The future, at last, held a promise, whose first glimpse, according to the obstetrician, was only six weeks away. He would not let a few minutes of standing guard at the door of a restaurant eclipse his fortune. After all, he had refused to kill.

6

For days, the ghost of Doctor Sharafkandi kept haunting me until I finally had the balls to ask what he wanted. "Hadi *jaan,*" said the ghost cheerily, "being the respectable man that I used to be, I can't rest until I know: Was our dinner tab ever settled?"

—Hadi Khorsandi, exiled Iranian satirist

Friday, September 25, breezy and bright, had all the beguiling signs of a late summer day. But its glory was lost on the hundreds of mourners at Berlin's Socialist cemetery, whose eyes were clouded by tears.

Security was tight. The day before, police had combed the grounds and the neighborhood. Several dozen armed officers monitored the comings and goings of the visitors. The cemetery's memorial hall was filled to capacity. Another throng waited outside. Some paced about aimlessly, others huddled together in threes and fours. Conversation eluded them. Instead, they sucked hard on their cigarettes and exhaled in each other's direction.

When the doors of the memorial hall opened, a stately man, a colleague of Noori's, led the way bearing a basket of red and yellow roses. The pallbearers, wearing sullen expressions, lifted the coffin and began to march. The crowd remained hushed, for as the coffin moved forward the faces they were looking for appeared. Shohreh, dressed in black, followed the coffin stoically. Sara was beside her, chewing gum. In a hot pink jacket, matching headband, and floral-print leggings, she gripped her stuffed rabbit in one hand and her favorite teacher's hand in the other. She looked to suffer from nothing worse than boredom. She seemed ready for a field trip, not the gloomy affair of her father's funeral. There were no tears on her cheeks, not a trembling in her gait as she passed across the vast lawn. Her pace had the irreverence of an ordinary preadolescent girl. Only her gaze flashed with a wrath that far outsized her small frame.

Relatives and close friends walked with the mother and daughter. Parviz hid his inflamed eyes behind sunglasses and carried a large portrait of Noori, cupping one cheek, smiling warmly. Next to Parviz, Mehdi, squeezing his eyelids together to hold back tears, stumbled forward, drunk with grief. Around his neck hung a flimsy string that had been threaded through the edges of a photo of the four dead men.

They came to a set of stone steps, to a display of flowers and photos cascading down the sides. On the landing, Noori's brother positioned himself behind the microphone. An interpreter stood beside him to translate for the Germans in the crowd—reporters, friends, and colleagues of Shohreh and Noori, and a cadre of representatives from the Social Democratic Party.

"On behalf of Noori's family, I thank you all for coming. I've been asked to talk about Noori. Under different circumstances, I could talk about him for hours, for days even. But this shock. I can't yet make a sensible sentence, you see. I can only think of a poem he recited to me when he came back to Iran in 1978. Today it seems that the poem was the story of his own life."

Those who knew Noori had expected his eulogy to include poetry, especially lines from the great modern poet, Ahmad Shamlou. His was the very verse that had ignited the flames of the 1979 revolution in the lives of the young urbanites—middle-aged mourners now—the verse that was ultimately etched on Noori's tombstone:

Not a tale to be told
Not a song to be sung
Not a sound to be heard
Or a thing to be seen
Or a thing to be known

I am shared pain
Shout me . . .

Shohreh sat on the top of the stone stairs. At times, she seemed to be somber but aware; at others, removed, engulfed in a whirlwind of thoughts. One moment she would lean her head, wrapped in black chiffon, against a picture of Noori;

her hand, still adorned with her wedding band, stroked the frame and she looked into the distance, as if she were drifting into a dream. The next moment she had returned, alert, straightening herself and the flowers, dragging her index finger along the glass as if housekeeping could not be postponed and she simply had to dust. Her lips were moving to the words of the poem:

In the quiet, luminous space I have cried with you
For the sake of the living,
And in the dark cemetery I have sung with you
The most beautiful songs
Because this year's dead
Were the most loving of the living . . .

Hundreds had come, mostly exiles who knew Noori personally, or of him through his television and radio interviews, or from his bylines. There were also many who did not know him at all. Nearly a million Iranians were living in exile by 1992, after the greatest exodus in the nation's history. The majority were political refugees—some six thousand of whom had settled in Berlin. That morning, they had come to the cemetery because they shared the same tormented origin and traveled the same tormented trajectory. Noori's history mirrored their own. In the aftermath of the coup in 1953 and the overthrow of the popular prime minister Mossadegh, many university students had headed west, where they founded the Iranian Student Confederation. With offices throughout Europe and the United States, the confederation was the model of the democratic dream the coup had dashed. Scores of young progressives—secular and religious—came together to run the self-fashioned miniature republic in which every season was election season. They elected university representatives, who elected city representatives, who elected country representatives, who elected members of the international executive committee. They raised revenues from membership dues and printed annual budget reports, all according to the egalitarian bylaws they, themselves, had drafted. By the end of its existence in the late 1970s, the confederation had shaped a generation, from whose ranks the new political elite then emerged.

Dozens of graying members of the old confederation, idealists who had rebelled against one bad regime only to pave the way for one still more vicious, were standing at the foot of the stairs, solemnly listening. What pained them the most was not simply that they had become victims, but that they had bred their own executioners. Noori's death was their burden. With the man they had come to bury, they would also bury a piece of their own past, a piece of themselves.

Noori was not all that they had lost. Trust was the other. In the week since the assassination they had pondered the details of that night, leading them to the certainty that their ranks had been infiltrated. One of their own had betrayed them. They were grieving Noori, the Kurds, and the irrevocable errors of their youth. They were also grieving their once undivided community, which was now broken. Fear had chased them out of Iran but had found them again in Berlin. Their safe haven was safe no more.

The procession began to move. Row after row, mourners holding photos, banners, and placards flowed forward until they arrived at the empty plot and circled it. There was a hush. A tall, broad-shouldered woman accompanying Shohreh unfurled an Iranian flag she had carried in a bag. What she did, what everyone did that day, was to follow their intuition, not a script. Quickly, a few arranged themselves behind the green, white, and red flag. Each grabbed a corner and stretched it along the length of the plot. Everyone was overcome by melancholy, but also with pride. For Noori was to be buried in Berlin's Socialist cemetery beside some of Europe's most notable rebels. A horn began to sound from the nearby woods. That its player was not in sight enhanced the majesty of the music. The melody was familiar to most as the beloved melody of their youth. Their lips began to move to the lyrics of the "Internationale."

Arise, ye wretched of the earth, arise, ye prisoners of starvation . . .

When the song ended, six large men in dark suits lowered the mahogany box into the pit. Stepping to the edge, Shohreh looked down. The freshly dug hole was the raw, unsightly truth the eulogies had left out. In it, she saw the shape of her days ahead. Her stoicism vanished. The gypsy within overcame her. She squatted at the edge. In her black skirt suit, her arms wrapped around her shins, she looked like a lone, helpless crow. She began to rock to and fro.

"Oh, Khomeini. Oh, Khomeini . . ." she mumbled, as

if the leader were still alive, as if she had known him well enough to dispense with titles.

"Oh, Khomeini . . . Oh, Khomeini . . ." she repeated, in a tone of concession to a longtime enemy. "Oh, Khomeini . . . Oh, Khomeini . . ." She rocked to and fro, to and fro. She unwrapped her arms and covered her face with her hands, then lifted them to the sky, then clawed the loose earth. The crowd gasped. Their tears burst forth. Several relatives rushed and whisked Sara away. Shohreh repeated her movements and lamented. Face, sky, earth. Face, sky, earth, over and over, in her own mad choreography.

Reporters squeezed to the front. A recent journalism graduate on his very first assignment—Norbert Siegmund—was mesmerized by the widow. All he had ever seen at a funeral were mourners who never lost control or surrendered decorum. But this dazed, slender woman, at war with the earth and sky, moved him immensely. Overcome, he stopped the tape and packed his microphone away to honor the moment.

Hands and knees in the dirt, Shohreh began again. After all, she was the hostess and had to serve her guests, even if all she had to serve was grief. Through a curtain of tears came her monologue. It was a medley of fragments, some mumbled to herself in Persian, others shouted in tortured German for the spectators' sake.

"I know who did this . . . Oh, Khomeini. I know you did this. Oh, Khomeini . . . We'll not always be your prey. We'll avenge ourselves. Oh, Khomeini. I swear on your grave, Noori, we'll take your revenge."

Pointing to the pictures of the four dead, she howled, "Their blood will be a beginning. I know it will."

Then, turning on the crowd, she growled, "Why are you all silent? We can't be silent. You know we can't."

Mehdi's eyes were shut, his face tilted skyward. Parviz had placed the picture frame at his foot and turned his back, his shoulders heaving.

She carried on. "In exile . . . In exile, I'm burying him. In exile, where he never wanted to be. I know who killed them. And they can never pay the price of his blood. His life wasn't for sale. They can never appease their way out of what's coming to them, out of what I, *we,* will do to get them justice. There won't be a deal. I'll be here to remember and to shout the truth until kingdom come: I know who killed them. Khomeini, that's who! Khomeini killed them."

Parviz could not bear to watch her any longer. He feared that strangers hearing her imperfect speech might think less of her or their tragedy. They were grief-stricken not mad, transplanted not rootless. He stepped behind her, slipped his hands under her arms, and lifted her. In his grip, she hung like a marionette, at last hushed.

The mourners walked up to the pit and each dusted the coffin with a fistful of soil. Parviz could not watch them. He turned to Mehdi, grabbed him, and began a loud, unabashed cry. Mehdi, wrapping his arms around Parviz, wept in return. While they embraced, each man wondered if the other was the insider who had betrayed them.

• • •

After the burial, the young journalist lingered. He could not leave. Norbert Siegmund did not know anyone in the crowd, nor did he understand any Persian. But what he had witnessed hardly needed translation. He approached Parviz, whom he recognized from his television interviews, and asked if they could talk. Shohreh's lamentations echoing in his ears, Norbert wanted Parviz to guess at the possible suspects behind the crime.

"Suspects? You want to call them suspects? You can, if you like. But there's nothing plural or mysterious about it. This is the work of Iran's regime. No suspects there. They're the culprits, beyond the shadow of doubt. I'm more sure of that than I am of myself standing here now."

His certainty impressed Norbert. Wishing to prolong the conversation, he played devil's advocate.

"But the federal prosecutor is leaning toward the Kurdish group, the PKK."

"The federal prosecutor can lean whichever way he wants, but it doesn't change the facts. These men who died weren't mafia members or drug dealers. They were visionaries of the highest order, real patriots, after whom other governments name national holidays. What does the federal prosecutor know about what we've paid for in blood and tears for thirteen years?"

Like all exiles, he assumed that everyone's calendars began with 1979.

"You sound adamant," Norbert replied. "Aren't you afraid you might be wrong?"

"I sound adamant because I know my history. This isn't the first time an exile has been killed. There have been many, many deaths like this. Am I afraid? Of course, I am. I'm afraid that those who don't know the history may be fooled. I'm afraid of the truth never seeing the light of day, this charade going on until we're all done away with."

Norbert did not know what Parviz meant by history. But he was not about to detain him in that cemetery for an explanation. He offered his business card to Parviz and suggested that they meet again soon. Parviz tucked the card in his pocket and promised to call him.

After the funeral, the mourners stopped at the cargo section of Berlin's Tegel Airport to send the coffins of the three Kurds off to Paris's Père Lachaise Cemetery where they would have the worthy farewell they could not get at home. When the plane was airborne, the crowd converged, most of them Kurds, on Iran's consulate, an indistinct three-story building on Stavanger Street. The staff inside had been warned of the oncoming protesters. The front gates had been chained and the shutters had been lowered over the windows. Now and then, the lens of a camera was wedged in the blinds. The unruliness outside was clearly on record.

Riot police had already garrisoned the building. Uniformed men brandishing batons, helmets, and shields locked their gaze with empty-handed protesters. As mourners, they had shed what tears they had. Now the fog of grief lifted to reveal their wrath. For them, there was nowhere else to go. This fortress was their destination. Faced with the chain of armed policemen, they stood side by side in a chain of their own and linked arms. Watching their line, the chief of police signaled his men. Visors were lowered, shields were centered at chest level. A tunnel formed—the police on one side, protestors on the other. They stared one another down, waiting for the other to falter.

Then came a shout in Kurdish. The crowd stirred. Each protester placed one foot forward. The police gripped their batons. But what followed was not a charge of angry men. Arms around each other's neck, they simply threw their shoulders up, then thrust them forward. There was a momentary hush. Then another shout came, and they undid the movement, stepping back on the other foot, shoulders releasing, lowering. Heeding the rhythm of an inner beat, they had begun the steps of an old familiar dance. One foot back, another forward, undulating the shoulders over and over, till at last they burst into song, their ancient anthem.

Kass naleh Kurd merduah / Kass naleh Kurd merduah / Kurd zinduah / zinduah ghat na ne vey nala keman.
Let no one say Kurds are dead. Kurds are living. Kurds are living. Their flag will never fall.

They chanted though they had no hope of finding justice for their dead. They had no reason to expect from Germany what the rest of Europe had not given them, no reason to place any faith in German prosecutors, judges, or the justice system. They were certain they would be overruled by the opportunism of politicians. Countries with far less at stake in Iran than Germany had been lenient toward Tehran. Bonn had reason to be even more lenient.

By 1992 trade figures between the two nations had reached 5 billion dollars, making Germany Iran's dominant Western economic partner. Iran's shares in German stocks exceeded 200 million dollars. The two countries had exchanged more than three hundred political, economic, cultural, and legal delegations, half of which included parliamentary members from both sides. In every international summit, Germany rejected, or at least tempered, the tone of American proposals against Iran. Since the end of diplomatic relations between Iran and the United States in 1979, Europe had vied to fill the gap America had left behind. At last, Germany was about to step into the coveted space.

Its close ties with Iran had raised Germany's standing as a global broker between Iran, Israel, and the United States. German officials championing the cause of Iran had initiated a continental effort to recast the image of Iran as an authentic, albeit imperfect, regional democracy. The campaign had been launched that July, only a few weeks before the murders. It was widely trumpeted as the "Critical Dialogue," a diplomatic roundtable with senior Iranian and European officials, with future meetings scheduled for the following December.

With resolute expressions upon their faces, the protesters chanted their slogans. But resoluteness was only a mask. They believed Germany's stakes in Tehran were too high to afford justice for their dead. They were chanting to affirm to each other that they were alive, knew the truth, and were not afraid to be seen or sing their song of perseverance. They knew who was behind the murders but it was immaterial—they were adrift and powerless. They made their demands though they were consumed by a despondence that would prey on their peace, even as they made promising gains.

Two of the leading stars of the Social Democratic Party had agreed to represent the victims' families. The law firms of Otto Schily, who would become interior minister, and Wolfgang Wieland, who would become a member of the Bundestag, Germany's parliament, took on the case pro bono. These names raised the profile of the dead, but that was not all. The second firm also added its most seasoned criminal attorney, Hans Joachim Ehrig, to the team.

Ehrig was the lesser known of the attorneys but an equal in wisdom and passion. He was one of those rare members of the 1960s generation who had adapted admirably to the 1990s. His gaze was still fierce behind the perfectly round lenses of his rimless glasses, his old unruly beard trimmed down to a neat mustache. In him, all the formative bohemian ideals of his youth remained intact without dulling his taste for luxuries like silk ties or sailing. (His sail boat was docked in a lake near his villa in north Germany.) But between ideals or luxuries, the choice came effortlessly to him. He was on his way to spend a long weekend in the countryside at an arts festival when his assistant dropped the Mykonos file on his desk. After scanning it, Ehrig rolled his suitcase into the office closet and was off to a meeting with the victims.

7

> A few days after Ayatollah Khomeini issued a fatwa for my death, a delivery man brought a package to my door. Not recognizing the sender's address, I didn't dare open it. Finally I thought, "Hadi, you can't keep being afraid. You've got to live your life." So I opened it. And do you know what I found inside? Not a bomb, oh no! A pack of opium, and what superb opium it was.
>
> —*Hadi Khorsandi, exiled Iranian satirist*

Yousef Amin was grieving for a loss of his own. By the end of September, his friend Rhayel had come to visit him in Rhine, asking him to leave his family in Germany. The Sportino bag they hoped had been expertly hidden was found under a white Audi at a dealership on Cicero Street. The office of the federal prosecutor had issued a statement announcing the discovery of the murder weapons, the first major breakthrough in the case. It was only a matter of time till they came for Rhayel. In the frantic moments inside the restaurant that night he had forgotten to put on his gloves, leaving his handprint on the gun.

Everyone else on the team had already left the country. The chief shooter had reached Tehran within forty-eight hours after the operation. Their patron, a Berlin grocer named Kazem Darabi who ostensibly employed them but had in fact coordinated and financed the operation, had also flown to Tehran. The driver, on his way to the airport the day before, had delivered some cash to Rhayel and advised him to leave immediately.

Lebanon was beckoning. But for Rhayel, the road back to Beirut passed through Rhine. There was no escape for him without Yousef. Self-restraint was not among Yousef's virtues. The very qualities that made him endearing—his boyish banter and innocent enthusiasm—also made him dangerous in the hands of interrogators. It was for Rhayel to shepherd Yousef out of Germany, as he had shepherded him into it. Convincing Yousef to leave was not easy but Rhayel invoked the fate of his namesake. The biblical Joseph had left the comforts of Egypt to return home, and so must Yousef. Downcast and dejected, Yousef posed at a photographer's studio for the black and white portrait that would be used in a forged passport he was expecting to receive shortly, as was Rhayel. Then they would flee Germany.

Shortly, it turned out, meant several days. By October 4, only one passport had arrived and the second was to be delivered the next day. The two friends spent a melancholy last day together. In the evening, at 17 Heriburg Street, the Amins and their guest turned in early. It was a moonless night in Rhine.

Long before the shades had been drawn on the windows and the lights were turned off in the apartment, the forces of BKA, Germany's federal police, had surrounded the building. Two tips had led them there. The first was a document from the intelligence division at the BfV, the federal office for the protection of the constitution, which had been sent to Bruno Jost. Though only partially disclosed, it detailed the events at the restaurant according to an anonymous but highly reliable source.

The second tip, from British intelligence, revealed the identities and whereabouts of the two suspects who still remained in Germany and their patron, Darabi. Since the fall of the Berlin Wall, the British and Americans had yet to fully surrender the city to their German counterparts and their watch posts were still operating. The British had monitored Darabi for years and knew of his ties to Hezbollah, his frequent visits to Lebanon, and the dubious nature of his various businesses.

Just after midnight, the BKA raided Yousef's residence. Though the federal police were on location hours earlier, they waited for the stroke of midnight to make their arrest, giving themselves the longest possible stretch of the "one day" granted under the law before they had to file formal charges against their detainees.

Rhayel ran to the balcony to escape, but found himself surrounded from every direction. Everyone in the apartment was taken into custody: Rhayel, Yousef, Yousef's brother, and Yousef's pregnant wife. In Tehran, Darabi, confident that all his underlings had escaped, celebrated by buying a women's Rolex watch at a jewelry store on his way to the airport. It would be his last stop before returning to his wife and their handicapped daughter, who depended on the generosity of German health care. By the time his plane landed in Hamburg, his men were already in prison. Hours later Darabi, too, was arrested.

Ordinary Berliners took comfort in the news of the arrests but the exiles felt no safer. There were guilty others still on the loose, some of whom had begun to torment Shohreh. Her telephone rang often, and a strange voice would pour into the receiver, "Can I speak to Noori?"

She usually hung up, but if she did not the caller would say mockingly, "Oops! He isn't there, is he? In that case, can I speak to his pal, the Doctor?"

"Who are you?"

Instead of answering, the voice would break into fiendish laughter just before hanging up. Sometimes she answered the phone and heard a tape recorder playing a passage from the Koran.

Sometimes her daughter would cause a scare. During one episode, Sara ran into her mother's bedroom, screaming, "It's a bomb!"

The bomb was their own egg timer, which had been slipped into a boot on the shoe rack at the entrance to the apartment.

"Talk to her! Ask why she did it. You can't be afraid to talk to your own child," Shohreh's brother had counseled.

But all she had the heart to do was seat Sara at the dining table and ask what she could fix her to eat, reminding her, "We must eat. We must eat so we can be strong. We have to be strong."

Shohreh worried that she was failing Sara. No matter what her daughter did, Shohreh wallowed in guilt. If Sara sulked, Shohreh worried that her child was grieving. If Sara smiled, Shohreh thought it was fake, a smile only for her sake. Her sadness rarely dimmed, and when it did, anxiety flared. The menaces who kept calling had her believe that they were capable of coming after her and Sara, too.

Solace was a rarity, but she found it in bed. She refused to wash the sheets because Noori's scent still lingered in the fabric. She pulled them over her head, breathed the stuffy air, and ran her fingers lightly over his side searching the pillow and mattress for his imprint. She shut her eyes and tried to picture him at his liveliest, trying to wipe away the memory of the corpse that the police had asked her to identify. As her fingertips slid upon the sheets, her mind slipped into reverie. Noori came to life.

"Let your hair fall on my face, little lady. It's better than silk."

He dared to say what most men would not. "Why wear a bra? You mustn't deny others the view of your glorious breasts."

Once he had taken his fill of her glories, he lit a cigarette and dreamed about their future. "Let's get out of here, little naked lady. Let's go to a sunny place, somewhere in Latin America, bask on the beach and never look back."

• • •

Unlike Shohreh, Parviz avoided his bed. He dreaded sleep. If he dozed off, nightmares ravaged his rest and he would awaken drenched in sweat. Every dream ended with him on the brink of death: trapped in a speeding car with failing brakes, standing blindfolded and handcuffed on a chair as a noose was tightened around his neck.

Mornings brought no relief. When he left his apartment, he crossed the threshold certain a sniper was waiting for him to emerge. He turned the corner hesitantly, awaiting a dagger at the bend. If walking became a test of his nerves, he would drive instead. But in his hands, the key felt like a matchstick and his car a heap of kindling ready to ignite. On the road, at each traffic light, the sight of every cyclist who pulled up beside him quickened his blood.

He, like Shohreh, was being shadowed. Fearing his assassins friends rarely visited him. Few had the courage to invite him over. He accepted only one dinner invitation in those early days after the killings. When he had arrived at his host's house and they had sat down to eat, the telephone rang. The caller asked for Parviz, telling the host that it was about an urgent meeting that had to be arranged between Parviz and Mr. Changiz Dastmalchi—Parviz's father who had died years ago. The call was only a reminder that the killers were not finished with him. When the host relayed the message, Parviz rose from the table and said good-bye. He never accepted another invitation, not wishing to expose his friends to the perils of his own life.

Besides, he was no longer sure who was a friend. He no longer trusted his friends, and his friends no longer trusted him. No one knew who had spied on them at the restaurant that September evening. So they treated each other like suspects. Parviz took it upon himself to solve the mystery. He questioned old acquaintances, thinking himself perfectly discreet, but they felt interrogated by him. His inquiries only added to the bitterness of an already bitter community. Some pitied him, others condemned him. He realized it one evening when, walking into a gathering of expatriates, he heard someone murmur, "Oh, look, Lieutenant Columbo is here."

He left immediately. Leaving, retreating further into solitude, came easily to him in those days.

The events of September had robbed Parviz of many friendships, but October brought him a few new ones. Norbert Siegmund, the journalist, was now pursuing the case with an intensity matched only by his own. Norbert's office at the ZDF station was within minutes of Parviz's office at the Red Cross, so they met regularly.

The case was a shared obsession. Parviz recounted the minutiae of that evening often, the clues to the riddle that consumed them. He needed Norbert. Being on the air, having millions listening to his argument, broke the silence he so disdained, giving him a small revenge. Norbert also needed Parviz—the protagonist at the heart of his reporting. Thrust into the midst of the Iranian exile community for the first time, Norbert was finding it a forbidding labyrinth, where Parviz seemed more credible than the rest.

Norbert also needed the focus he drew from the investigation. For years, he had been seeking something elusive—his life's purpose—without luck. At sixteen, he became a social worker to help the jobless. At eighteen, he quit his job, picked up his guitar, and went to India looking for inspiration. When he returned after weeks of wandering, he reconciled his passion for music with the mandates of adulthood by choosing music history as his major in college. But a bad piece of Ukrainian folk music, assigned to him for his thesis by a glum professor, dashed his hope of becoming a music historian. Ukrainian folk was no rock and roll, and the scholarly pursuit of music did not stir him the way playing music had. He switched to journalism so he could become a radio host and spend his days airing his favorite tunes.

His first days on the job coincided with an unusually heavy news cycle. There was the weakening currency, the central bank's fear of inflation—two of the many fallouts of Germany's reunification—and a burgeoning immigration crisis marked by 400,000 new asylum seekers in 1992. The station's experienced reporters were chasing these stories when the assassinations occurred. Therefore, the station manager was forced to send the new disc jockey into the field. There, at the site of Noori's grave on his first assignment, the unexpected requiem he heard had moved Norbert as he had once thought only rock and roll could.

He and Parviz drove through the neighborhoods the assassins had frequented. They downed many shish kebab sandwiches and drank countless cups of tea in the hopes of disguising their anomalous presence in the Shiite haunts of Berlin. There was nothing to be unearthed on an innocuous block, yet just walking the streets the killers had walked prompted conversations they never had inside their offices. They roamed about, looking for proof to back Parviz's claim that the business owner, Darabi, was an intelligence operative working for Tehran.

"He's their thug. Every expatriate in this city knows it. Anyone who's ever demonstrated against the mullahs has felt the blows of his bat."

Parviz talked feverishly, as if convincing Norbert might convince all Germans. The shuttered windows of Darabi's grocery and dry-cleaning stores with TEMPORARILY CLOSED signs hanging from the doorknobs, inflamed him every time.

"Laundry services? Bah! All he laundered was the regime's money. He doesn't make his living selling turnips, I assure you."

During one of these outings an old memory rushed back to him. He recalled that Darabi had manned Iran's booth at the annual Green Week exhibit. Since the late 1920s, Green Week had been Berlin's most festive international affair, a behemoth farmers' market. Nearly half a million visitors came every year to taste the products of fifty countries, Iran among them. Norbert jotted the name down, ideas already brewing in his head, as Parviz strained to recollect. Which year, he could not be sure, but he had no doubt Darabi had been the official representative.

"Some bureaucrat somewhere must have the record of it on file, if you'd look into it. Tie Darabi to Iran's regime and you'll have your proof!"

If Parviz was not with Norbert, he was often off to do what increasingly seemed like an act of penance: visiting Aziz, who was still in the hospital. Aziz was estranged from his wife and had no one to look after him. With Noori gone, Parviz felt a tenderness for Aziz he had never felt before. When Noori had first befriended Aziz, Parviz called them "brothers in alcohol," since the two often drank together. But with time, he saw Aziz's affection for Noori. Each night Noori stepped inside the restaurant, Aziz would open his arms and cheer, "My *mola* has arrived!"

He would link arms with Noori and drag him from table to table, saying, "Meet my *mola,* please! This man, here, is my *mola.*"

Mola, the beloved in the love poems of the poet Rumi.

Instead of shying away from flaws in others, Noori was inspired to correct them. It was a virtue Parviz found at once exasperating and endearing. When Aziz and his wife arrived in Germany a few years earlier, Aziz had told her he did not wish either of them to study German.

"We don't need to learn *their* language. Their Western ways will corrupt and tear us apart," was his answer to her proposal that they take turns watching the baby and attending language classes.

Noori spent hours, alone and alongside their respective families, trying to make a better husband of Aziz. His transformation had not come fast enough to keep his wife from leaving, which, in the end, made him doubt the wisdom of the transformation in the first place.

Reflecting on his marriage of twelve years, he would throw his hands up and exclaim, "Ever since we came to this country, I don't know what my wife wants anymore. Shoes?

I buy her. Clothes? I get her the best. But these two . . ." pointing to Noori and Parviz, "kept coming here, hanging around with their crooked ideas, talking about *emancipating this* and *emancipating that,* until she got to be crooked herself, then upped and left one day."

Aziz sounded jolly but what he said always left Parviz feeling blamed for the couple's breakup. He did not think Aziz's divorce was anyone's doing but his own, but he did blame Noori and himself for the two bullets Aziz had taken. After all, Aziz would never have been in the company of the likes of the Doctor if it were not for them. Their friendship had exposed Aziz to danger and caused his wounds. The least Parviz could do to lessen his own guilt was to visit Aziz at the hospital.

The police, too, came to visit Aziz. Parviz would often arrive as a detective was leaving. The ongoing interrogation evoked even more pity in the visitor, who thought the patient was too frail for questioning. Aziz seemed to have aged years in only a few weeks. Seeing him, Parviz choked back tears and tried his best to appear cheerful. Aziz only moaned.

"What can I do, Aziz *jaan*?" Parviz would say in Persian.

There was always a fresh glass of water to fetch, sheets to untangle, nurses to instruct, inconsiderate visitors to manage or send away. It seemed to Parviz that most visitors came to pry, to satisfy their own curiosity rather than to tend to the patient. One couple had especially exasperated Aziz—grocery store owners who had supplied goods to Mykonos. They came one afternoon. The husband talked without pause, shaking his head, reminiscing, retracing his conversation with Aziz before that terrible night.

"How destiny steers us all, Aziz *jaan*. Your voice is still in my ear, 'Come help me on Thursday night, I've got guests coming.' How you begged me. But Thursdays are my busiest days. Shipments coming in, deliveries to do. There was no way I could help out. How awful I felt turning you down. Or else I'd have been right there with you."

Aziz grumbled that all he had ever spoken of was Friday.

The visitor pressed on, saying, "Believe me, you did. As God is my witness, you did. The Tuesday before, you said, 'Come and help me on Thursday night.' Destiny! How a man can escape anything but destiny."

Aziz shook his head vehemently.

The earnest husband turned to his wife. "Remember, hon? Didn't he ask me to come in on Thursday?"

The tearful wife nodded in assent.

It fell to Parviz to protect his bedridden friend from the needling of visitors. He interrupted and steered the conversation in a different direction.

"Did you know Noori's parents have come from Iran?"

"They are here, those two?" asked the visitor. "Ay! No parent should ever see the day. Oh, cruel destiny!"

Aziz cast a grateful look at Parviz and collapsed into his pillow.

8

> The man who translated the *Satanic Verses* into Arabic was kidnapped. His captors told him that the Ayatollah would spare him only if he'd undo his sin by translating the book back into English. Today, some scholars argue that the retranslated version is a major improvement on Rushdie's original.
>
> —*Hadi Khorsandi, exiled Iranian satirist*

Day after day, Bruno Jost pored over the transcripts from the interrogation of the detainees. Two of the suspects, Rhayel and Darabi, had kept a stoic silence. But Yousef had spoken at length. Jost would lay the pages side by side to piece together the passages he had highlighted throughout, tracing the obvious lies, unconvincing denials, and repeated contradictions, hoping they might lead to the secret the prisoner was clearly keeping.

Some lies were preposterously evident, based on preliminary intelligence he had received.

–Do you belong to a political organization?
–I was with the army for two years. Nothing else.

–Do you have any relations with the Iranian government or its organizations?

–No. I'm only a God-fearing Shiite. If I went to Iran, it was to visit holy sites.

Some lies that were less evident became more so by the denials.

–Mr. Amin, tell us about Abbas Rhayel?

–I don't know anyone by that name.

Abbas Rhayel and Yousef Amin had been an inseparable pair since 1989, when they first entered Germany through the Hungarian border and applied for asylum and other benefits in both Switzerland and Germany.

–You don't know Abbas Rhayel?

–No! Never heard the name.

–The man who was sleeping in your apartment when you were arrested?

–Oh, him! I call him Emad Amash.

Emad Amash was the first in a string of pseudonyms Jost had to master while dealing with the prisoners, who assumed new identities as naturally as they changed wardrobe for a new season.

–How long have you known him?

–Not long at all. We met in Berlin just a little while back.

–Could you please take a look at this passport and tell us why this picture of the man you call Amash is tucked into someone else's passport?

This was the false passport the police had found in the Amin apartment, the one in which Rhayel's photo was to be pasted.

Yousef denied having seen it.

–In that case, can you tell us why your picture and birth certificate were in the folds of Mr. Amash's passport?

–Were they?

–We have information that you took these photos to forge them in a passport.

–Your information is no good. I took these photos for my driver's license and took one extra for a friend in Canada who wants a picture of me for his album.

Lies were nothing new to the seasoned prosecutor. But Yousef's lies were a promising sign—a sign of his reluctance to be detached. If he bothered to lie, it meant that he, unlike his teammates, cared enough to engage them. Jost always preferred a speaking prisoner, even if lying, to a stoically silent one.

–Mr. Amin, where were you on September 17?

–I was in Rhine. I was in Berlin a week earlier for a bit, taking care of some immigration business. When I came to

Rhine it was, I don't remember, either the eleventh or twelfth or thirteenth.

–Who can testify that you were in Rhine on September 17?

–You can ask my wife, her sister, and my brother. They'll tell you I was in Rhine. My brother was in the hospital that day, where I visited him. He was in a bicycle accident two or three days after I came home.

–So you were in Rhine on September 17?

–Then again, the accident could have happened on the seventeenth, and I heard the news of it in Berlin.

–So you were in Berlin on the seventeenth?

–Like I said, I had some immigration business in Berlin, went there, and came back right away. A woman cabdriver drove me home to Heriburg 17. She had a red Volkswagen Passat. I was definitely in Rhine that day.

He was always exact with inconsequential details, hoping they might divert his interrogators' attention.

–But Mr. Amin, your brother told us that you visited him one day after he had been released from the hospital, on September 19, one day after you had arrived in Rhine.

But Yousef's lies ended if they seemed to contradict his wife, brother, and other family members.

–Oh? Then whatever my brother says is correct.

Finally when asked about the considerable cash in his wallet he realized he needed help.

–My wife has been saving it for the family. But I'd really like to speak to a lawyer now.

At the end of one such session, Yousef was shown the full text of his testimony to review. His translator pointed to the dotted line where Yousef was to sign. Talking, it seemed, came more easily to Yousef than did printing his own name beneath the statements. He paused, flipped through the document many times, then asked his translator to write on his behalf:

I am told that it is obvious I am not telling the truth. I must think all this over. I have nothing to add for now.

It was clear to Jost that Yousef was tormented. But it was his partner on the case, a senior federal criminal commissioner named Tony von Trek, who discovered why. Von Trek sat beside Jost during the interrogations and also escorted the prisoner to and from each session. At times, von Trek, playing the part of a tough cop whose main thrill was locking men up, would gather more in the trip between the prisoner's cell and the interrogation room than they would in hours of questioning. (Others would have bragged about such tactful acts but von Trek was beyond boasting, especially with Jost, whom he considered a dear friend.) On the return trip to prison one day, without being prompted, Yousef had begun talking about his impending fatherhood and his wish to witness his son's birth in November. Appearing unimpressed, the commissioner enumerated the obstacles standing in the way of that wish, unless some evidence to clear him were to miraculously surface. Yousef had listened and said nothing. When they reached prison, the commissioner gave his card to Yousef and said that if he ever wanted to tell the truth all he had to do was call. He left Yousef with this parting thought, "The miracle is for you to make happen."

In his cell, Yousef Amin began scribbling on the back pages of the prison manual chained to the wall of his cell, #404 B.

M . . . F?
N?
L?
K F A N Y?
M H?
F A N Y?
N F Y . . .
The meaning of love . . .
Yousef Darayi

He scribbled, and he prayed. But prayer could hardly fill the hours in solitary confinement. The manual had become his journal. He wrote cryptically, in codes and anagrams—a few letters here, a name slightly twisted there, a phrase or sentence—each a glimpse into his foreboding about his slipping resolve. *Rhagheb . . . Darayi . . . Oh, you, Rhagheb. I am Yousef Amin. Speak not! . . . Silence, silence.*

• • •

Yousef was afraid to print the names of his accomplices. Rhayel was an old friend, and Darabi was the patron who had given him a job. Yousef was neither rich nor powerful, but his association with Darabi was his claim to fortune. He boasted of their association using the many photographs he staged alongside Darabi. In one, he directed Rhayel, dressed in a black leather jacket and denim trousers, to stand in profile against shelves full of fruit inside Darabi's grocery. With the plump features of a child, Rhayel shyly fixed his gaze on the crate of onions he was emptying into a trash bag. The bag was held by Darabi, who peered into it with pride. In another photo, the three of them, all bearded, appeared side by side. The burly Yousef, bundled in a sweater and winter jacket, grinned mischievously, his head tilted to the right where the much shorter, balding, and smiling store owner stood, flanked by Rhayel, who towered over them both.

If he wrote too much, he tore out the page fearing what he might have revealed. Only once he gave in to fervor, dragging his pen so ardently that the imprint of his words marked the pages beneath: *Forgive me, I am repentant. My dear wife, forgive me! I am repentant.*

More than a month had passed since the murders when a letter arrived at Parviz's doorstep and lifted his spirits in a way nothing had in weeks.

Dear Mr. Dastmalchi,

The office of the federal police requests your presence at noon on November 12, 1992, in Meckenheim to identify suspects in the assassination of the Iranian opposition on September 17, 1992. For your convenience the following will be provided:

1) *At the Köln-Bonn Airport you will be received by an agent and returned to the airport in the same manner.*
2) *Your presence is very, very crucial. We ask that you accept this request and follow the instructions attached.*
3) *If you have any questions, please contact us for clarification.*

Sincerely,
Garbotz, KHK Criminal High Commissioner

Together with Mehdi, who had received the same letter, Parviz headed to Meckenheim. As they waited for their flight at the airport, Mehdi spotted a member of the Bundestag among the milling travelers. "Isn't that the famous Gregor Gysi over there?"

Parviz dashed toward Gysi, one of Germany's most influential politicians since reunification. Like a traveling salesman, Parviz always carried in his briefcase several packets of information about the case wherever he went. He greeted Gysi, pressed a packet into the parliamentarian's hand and pleaded that he not let corrupt officials sacrifice justice in the name of national interests. Gysi slowed his steps to say that Germany's courts and judges were among the best in the world. As he walked away, Parviz could be heard yelling, "It's not your courts I worry about. It's your politicians who will sell out, before your judges can have their say."

At the federal police headquarters, the witnesses were ushered into separate cubicles. Staring at the seven men on the other side of the glass, Parviz and Mehdi were asked to identify anyone familiar. At first, the suspects were all clad in heavy jackets and gloves, their heads were covered with caps, their faces veiled with bandannas. Parviz focused on their eyes and brows. The attacker he had briefly glimpsed that night had dark penetrating eyes. In the first lineup, he spotted one man that most resembled his recollection. "Number seven," he said to the agent beside him.

In the second round, the suspects took off their jackets and gloves. This time, Parviz examined their arms and torsos for heft, for the attacker had seemed towering and powerful.

Once again, he called out, "Seven."

In the last round, the suspects rolled their sleeves to the elbows, and shed their bandannas and headgear to reveal their faces in full. Again, Parviz chose the same.

The agent asked what role Parviz thought number seven had played that evening. Without a moment's hesitation, he replied, "He was the man standing behind me with the machine gun, the main assassin."

Though he had doubts, he did his best to appear confident. Doubt was virtue to Parviz, because it prompted one to reflect. But this was no time for skepticism. He was at war, and wars were waged with conviction, not rumination.

The agent asked him to confirm his answer.

"Yes," Parviz said again, "I'm perfectly certain I saw number seven shooting in the restaurant on the night of September 17."

Parviz was not alone. Mehdi, too, had chosen the same man from the lineup, though with less certainty.

Number seven was Yousef Amin.

Like the chief gunman, Yousef was tall, broad, and bearded, with thick, dark hair and dark eyes. The thought that others might mistake them for each other had never occurred to Yousef and hearing of it enraged him. To have crossed the chief shooter by refusing to kill, to have suffered the berating by the others afterward, to have been locked up inside the apartment, all for not wanting to be the one to pull the trigger, only to be mistaken for the killer, incensed Yousef. In despair, he called his guard and asked to make a call. Within minutes, the telephone in Tony von Trek's office was ringing.

"I can't sleep. I've no peace. My wife's going to have a baby and I'm afraid of not seeing her or my child for a long time. I want to tell the truth. But if anything I say leaks to the outside, it'll be the death of me and my family."

These were the first words Yousef told the small audience that included the prosecutor and the commissioner. Even in prison, he had received several death threats—promising that if he ever spoke he would never see his son. Yousef pleaded that his confessions not be recorded, or at least be kept confidential. It was a request many prosecutors would have granted in exchange for cherished information. But German laws prohibited bargains, and Bruno Jost could not agree. Still, Yousef spoke. Speaking was his only hope.

His confession gathered like a storm. In the beginning, there came only a few minor details. He tried not to implicate Rhayel or Darabi and denied knowing them at all. Even after seeing that he could not escape the fact of his association with them, he tried to minimize the extent of their friendship. According to Yousef's early accounts, the truly guilty had fled the country and those in custody were only unaware accomplices, like Darabi, who was merely the absentee owner of the apartment the team had used.

But confession begat confession. The more he spoke, the more he had to speak. Over the span of twenty sessions Yousef, both narrator and guide, told his tale. He took his audience on the murderous trail he had traveled in September. From 64 Detmolder Street #B, the graffiti-riddled, moss-colored entrance of Darabi's one-bedroom apartment, to 7 Senftenberger Ring Street, the apartment of Darabi's friend, where the team had spent the days leading up to September 17; to the café where the team leader had asked if Yousef would kill; even to the subway terminal he had crossed through that night. Yousef's description of the BMW led the investigators to the city's central pound where the car, strewn with evidence and fingerprints, had been towed. The confessions alone would have been groundbreaking. The confessions along with the evidence—the recovery of the getaway car, the discovery of the teams' apartments—marked the investigation's greatest triumph yet.

9

> [After the fatwa against my dad] we started to get death threats. The phone would ring. I'd answer, and someone would say, "I'm going to kill you. I'm going to cut your throat!" And I'd be like, "Daaad, I think it's for you."
>
> —*Shappi, daughter of exiled Iranian satirist Hadi Khorsandi*

By mid-November, two months after the assassinations, autumn had reached its maturity. Trees were bare. Gusts of wind unsettled the trash on the asphalt. The brutal cold that drives even the most ardent Berliners indoors was about to begin when Norbert Siegmund set out to follow the footsteps of the killers.

The most critical evidence in the case had been recovered. Three men had been charged with first-degree murder. Two of their accomplices were in custody on lesser charges. The investigators had declared victory. Yet these developments caused no celebration among the exiles. Hope still eluded the likes of

Parviz, Shohreh, and Mehdi. Their victory would mean unveiling the duplicity of the politicians who were keeping the truth from the public. The federal prosecutor was still pointing to the Kurdish armed group, the PKK, as his chief suspect, evoking the fear of a cover-up among the exiles. Caught between two opposing claims—one of victory and the other of hypocrisy—Norbert thought it useless to take sides. Instead, he took to the road.

Darabi's biography guided Norbert's travel. In 1982, Darabi had been arrested and temporarily imprisoned for his part in the death of a German student in a dormitory in Mainz. In 1983, Darabi had established the Iranian Islamic Student Association of Berlin and become the face of the city's main Shiite mosque. In 1987, after six years in university, failing his exams, and being expelled, he had started his businesses.

The road also led Norbert to the headquarters of the Green Week exhibit, an imposing edifice of 115,000 square feet, built to withstand the traffic of thousands of livestock and tourists who fill its grounds every January. But in late November an eerie lull permeated the vast empty space. Norbert found his way to the main office, where a diminutive receptionist greeted him. He asked to see the director but was told no one was around.

"What is it you need?" she asked.

Halfheartedly, he explained that he was looking for information about an Iranian man in custody, someone who may have had a booth at the exhibit, someone guilty who was likely to go free if the truth about him went untold. He offered his card to the receptionist and asked to have her superior contact him when she stopped him.

"Wait here, please!" she said, then disappeared into a room and quickly returned with a file in hand. Addressing Norbert in a whisper, she leaned into him. "This is what you're looking for. The police were already here for it. I kept a copy, just in case."

She handed two pieces of paper to Norbert. The first was an application for a booth at the exhibit; the second, an official letter.

From: The General Consular of the Islamic Republic of Iran

Attention: Ausstellungs-Messe-Kongress-GmbH
AMK Berlin
Post Office 191740
Messedamm 22
1000 Berlin 19

Most respected madams and sirs:

The Consul General of the Islamic Republic of Iran in Berlin hereby confirms that Mr. Kazem Darabi has been empowered by us to clear all the issues or answer any questions that may arise from the Islamic Republic's attendance in Berlin's Green Week from January 22 through February 3, 1991.

Best regards,
M. Amani-Farani
Consul

Norbert read the letter, all the while the receptionist beamed at him. He was stunned, not only to have found the document he had no hope of finding, but also by the courage of the clerk who had jeopardized her job to help him. He took the pages, pressed the woman's hand in his, and left.

Returning to Berlin, he ruminated over the lessons of his journey. He realized his own error. Ever since he began reporting the case, he had looked for a single leading hero. Instead, he had to look to ordinary people—a grieving wife, a traumatized survivor, a minor office worker—to the confluence of unsung figures each of whom had taken a heroic step. He felt exhilarated. He had found his life's purpose and knew exactly what he wanted to be: nothing other than what he already was—an uncompromising reporter determined to unearth the truth.

Norbert contacted Bruno Jost's office for a comment about the letter. Instead of granting him an interview, the press liaison offered a terse response that added nothing new to the federal prosecutor's old statement: *We continue to believe the murders at Mykonos may have been the work of the Kurdish armed group, the PKK.*

With every week that passed the federal prosecutor's silence became more damning. A highly positioned source at BKA, the office of the federal police, had slipped a copy of a new document to Norbert's colleague at the station. The vindication Parviz had been looking for was in Norbert's hand. He called to ask Parviz to come to the station.

"The ballistic tests show that the handgun and the machine gun found in the Sportino bag were manufactured in Spain in the early 1970s," Norbert said as he monitored the expression on Parviz's face.

Parviz, puzzled, wanted to know what Spain could possibly have to do with the case.

"Spain doesn't," the reporter replied, "but Iran does."

The test results revealed that the serial number of the handgun found in the sports bag matched that of a handgun sold by Spain in a 1972 shipment of weaponry to the Iranian Royal Army. The weapons had remained within Iran's national stockpile, which, after the 1979 revolution, had become the property of the new regime. Thus the great likelihood that those in leadership with access to the arsenal had armed the assassins.

Joy transfigured Parviz's face. He pressed his palms together as if in them he had finally captured the nightmares, the fears, and the doubts that had dogged him for weeks. "This is great news," he said over and over. "The best news of all!"

Yet Norbert went on worrying about a cover-up, for the ballistic report had not been officially released. Parviz was less alarmed. Even if the politicians were keeping it a secret, Norbert and his colleagues would not, said the exuberant survivor.

Airing of this particular news, however, was a complicated matter. Norbert believed there were still loose ends to the story. Besides, a program as explosive as the one he had in mind deserved a national, not a local, broadcast. And the next installment of the station's nationwide newsmagazine, *Kontraste,* which aired monthly, was still days away. Parviz would have to do what he loathed: wait.

He caught sight of the whiteboard where the chronology of the assassination and all the following discoveries had been charted in multicolored markers. He scanned the most recent additions.

MACHINEGUN: Made by IMI manufacturers, Uzi model, serial number 075884, 9mm caliber, with a 32-bullet magazine

HANDGUN: Made by Llama manufacturers, Model X-A, 7.65mm caliber, Browning, serial number 517070, 8-bullet magazine. Sold to the Iranian Royal Army on June 15, 1972

He sat quietly for a few moments, his gaze shifting from the board to the reporter. When he spoke again, his voice had lost its sparkle.

"We all chase ghosts. I chase the ghost of a friend. You chase the truth your corrupt officials are about to bury. Wait a few days you say. Bah! It's enough time to ship the bastards back to Iran or Lebanon and call the whole thing off."

Norbert assured him that they were working furiously on the segment they hoped to air on the next broadcast, barring other disasters or breaking events. Parviz shook his head. For him, there was only one disaster, one report that could not be delayed. He looked at the white board once more. In frustration, he copied the descriptions of the guns on a piece of paper and tucked it in his pocket. That piece of information was as much his as it was Norbert's, or the station's. The discovery was theirs, he granted them that. But the suffering that had led them to it was his.

There were other elements still missing from the segment Norbert was planning to produce.

"We say the police have five men in custody but we have nothing to show of them except a few phantom drawings you say are bad anyway. We're TV. Without pictures, people aren't convinced," the reporter argued, hoping to convince his ally.

"Interview me! I can say what I saw that night in the restaurant and then in the lineup. I can describe them."

Norbert persisted, "People have to see what you saw. We need visuals. A photograph."

"Only one?"

"On my honor, Parviz! Even one photo will turn this program into the talk of the country."

What would Noori do? Parviz wondered as he walked home, reminiscing about their days of mischief. For the first time since the killings, he missed Noori instead of grieving for him. If Noori were around, he would know what to do. Noori was a great intellect and an even greater schemer. He had been Parviz's senior by only three years, yet he had taken Parviz under his wing when he had arrived in Berlin in the early 1970s. Noori was the one to get the newcomer into the best dormitory in town, the one to introduce him to other expatriates who helped the bookish eighteen-year-old evolve into a thinker and an activist.

The wind had numbed Parviz's cheeks. But he walked unhurriedly, his attention wholly consumed by the piece of paper in his pocket. The proof was, at long last, in his possession. However indebted he felt to Norbert, his loyalty remained to his old friend. He would do what he could to find the photo Norbert wanted, but he would follow the timeline of his own conscience. He would yield to nothing and no one.

At home, he stationed himself behind his desk and began making calls. The first was to an old acquaintance at the Berlin Office of Foreigners Affairs, who owed him a favor. If there were any photos of Yousef, Rhayel, or Darabi, one had to be on file there. But the police, he was told, had already confiscated the files a few days earlier.

Knowing Yousef had once been an asylum seeker, Parviz turned to a colleague at the Red Cross who worked with Arab speakers. The colleague found a file on Yousef with a photo inside but upon closer examination the documents appeared forged, and the photo was not of Yousef.

Still, Parviz refused to surrender. He turned what he knew of Darabi over in his mind. Darabi had headed the Iranian Islamic Student Association, which had gone through several internal breakups. He called the association and said that he was looking for information about Darabi, who was in prison accused of murder.

"Darabi, the goat boy?" The man who answered struck a note of surprise at the other end.

"Goat boy?" Parviz asked.

"A chin as narrow as his, a nose so hooked . . . what else would you call him? You say *he* coordinated a murder? It can't be," the man said with a chuckle. "He wasn't smart enough. *Coordinate*? He couldn't coordinate his own shoes. Somebody put him up to it."

Parviz suggested Iran and the other burst out, "Without them, he'd not have a pot to piss in. Grocer, my foot."

Then, he added after a few moments, "But you'll never get the Germans to admit it."

Parviz let the gloomy comment pass. Instead, he asked if there was a photo he could see from their early days together.

"Nah," the other answered. "Even if I had one, I'd have ripped it up by now. I told you already, I want nothing to do with him."

It took a few more tries before Parviz finally relented. He admitted his failure to Norbert, then packed his bags and left home that weekend on a short trip to put the matter behind him.

But upon his return on Sunday evening luck, too, returned to him. There were a dozen messages on his answering machine, several of them from the federal police, urging him to get in touch immediately. With every new arrest or discovery, the police called the surviving witnesses to weigh in on their findings. Parviz dialed Mehdi. Whatever the news, Mehdi had to have heard about it.

"They've got a few albums," Mehdi said, "with some hundred or so pictures in them."

Parviz asked if Mehdi had seen anyone familiar.

"Few of Darabi in there, for sure. There's one with him in the middle. The others next to him, I think, are *them*."

Parviz did not call the federal police that evening. He already knew what they wanted of him. They would ask that he go to them, sit in a room, and look through the very images he had tried to find, and which, like so many other pieces of information, they were unlikely to release. He was through being the obedient witness.

Before he closed his eyes that night, he asked himself once more: *What would Noori do*?

Monday dawned with a bright new scheme in Parviz's mind. He dialed the number the caller had left on his machine. When he introduced himself, relief rang in the agent's voice who greeted him.

"What can I do for you?" Parviz asked, trying to sound unaware.

As he had expected, the agent asked that he go to their offices for a Mykonos-related matter.

"I'm afraid I can't," he said without hesitation. "You see, since this whole thing first happened, I've missed too many days of work. If I ask my boss for even another hour off, I risk losing my job."

Then he proposed that they meet at his office instead, so he would not have to be out again.

• • •

The morning was all the time he had to set his plan in motion. He told his secretary not to leave her desk after lunch, because a few "high profile visitors" with little time to spare would be visiting. He instructed her to quickly photocopy a few items—an album or two on his desk open to the exact pages to be duplicated while he and his guests were out of the room.

At two o'clock two agents arrived, bearing an oversized briefcase. Settling in the love seat beside Parviz's desk, they placed the first album in front of him. He began leafing through the pages with great care. In that first volume, he recognized no one. The second album followed. Halfway through, he spotted a familiar face, that of a man with a balding head, hooked nose, and deep-set eyes. Darabi was smiling at him, standing between two other bearded figures who towered over him. The one on the right resembled the man he had picked from the lineup. On the facing page, there were several other images of the same men in various poses.

"That's them," he exclaimed, then pressed a hand against his forehead and shut his eyes.

"It's all difficult, very difficult, to have to look at these pictures and relive that night whenever something like this comes up," Parviz told the visitors.

Seeing the sympathetic expressions on their faces, he asked if they might take a short break. The agents consented. The afternoon being young, the guests welcomed the idea of freshly brewed coffee.

They walked to the common personnel room across the hall. Parviz took his time rinsing the pitcher and setting the coffeemaker. Over the sounds of the dripping and snorting of the machine, the agents talked about the heavy toll investigations always took on victims, casting compassionate glances at Parviz.

As he poured coffee, he asked who they thought was the culprit behind the murders. The agents turned silent, shaking their heads. After a few perfunctory sips Parviz announced that the caffeine had done its magic, rose from his seat, and led the way back to his office for a last round at the albums.

"I've got something you really want, Norbert. Something that will make you quit whatever you're doing to walk over to my office right away," the exuberant Parviz whispered into the receiver, moments after the agents left.

"You found a photo of Darabi?" Norbert asked.

Parviz said that he had done better than that.

"You found a photo of Yousef?"

Pride rang in Parviz's voice as he repeated that he had done even better.

"You found a photo of Rhayel?" Norbert asked, gleeful and impatient.

"I've got a photo of all three!" Parviz burst out.

"This makes me very nervous!" Norbert said, though it was joy, not nervousness, echoing in his voice.

"Let's just pray for the well-being of the unknown secretary in whose key ring hangs a master key, and whose hands run the Xerox at the speed of light."

"Don't move! I'll be right over."

• • •

That night, the first exclusive photo of the men involved in the Mykonos murders aired on the local broadcast *Berliner Abendschau*. The riveting segment was narrated by Norbert over a collage of pictures, beginning with the scene of the crime.

> *Tonight, we focus on the investigation, which, despite all the evidence, has yielded few certainties on the part of the authorities. The federal prosecutor maintains that rival Kurdish groups are likely to have ordered the murders on September 17 at the Mykonos restaurant. But slowly, Iran's regime is emerging as the true culprit. Many feel that the German and international communities are not interested in shedding light on this crime.*

The montage of photos faded into the sight of Parviz and Mehdi seated side-by-side on a leather sofa. Norbert addressed them, and they answered sheepishly, each ending the other's sentence.

"Yes. I went to the federal police headquarters in Meckenheim and looked at the lineup."

"And so did I."

"And I identified the killer who had shot at us that night with a machine gun." Each nodded as the other spoke.

Mehdi added, "I think, though I can't be certain, I recognized the same man in the lineup. I picked him out and was told by an agent afterward that it was a big, important step in the investigation. But no one has since come forward to acknowledge it at all."

Norbert's voice boomed again as highlighted sentences from the consul's letter scrolled across the screen.

But we know Iran is involved because Kazem Darabi represented Iran during the Green Week exhibit.

Then the bespectacled face of another exile appeared.

"I wrote a letter to the German foreign ministry requesting information about the Mykonos investigation. In response, they sent me a letter. Here's what it says: 'We have no conclusive evidence yet. No real signs confirming who is behind this crime one way or another.' "

Anger swept across the interviewee's face as he stared into the camera. After a long pause, he went on to read another passage from the same letter. " 'Despite your . . .' " he poked his chest feverishly, " '. . . *your* claims and accusations of the involvement of the Iranian regime.' "

He lifted his head, stared silently into the camera once more, and added a final ultimatum. "We, the Iranians of Berlin, demand that all documents regarding this case be made public immediately."

The segment caused a sensation, even without the revelations about the ballistic results from the weapons. Ordinary Berliners who, until then, had only seen phantom photos of the accused, were shaken by their real faces. The images renewed the public's fury, but this time the suggestion of a political cover-up spurred an unprecedented outcry.

At dawn, Norbert rang Parviz to warn that the federal police had just contacted the station and their agents were en route to the studio.

"I'm sure they'll want to see you next. Lay low! They're mad as hell!"

That afternoon the director of the criminal division summoned Parviz to his office. Parviz went reluctantly. Without moving from his desk, the director cast a livid look at the visitor and told him to take a seat, pointing to a chair across his desk.

"But put your briefcase by the door first!"

The request sounded odd to Parviz, who asked the reason.

"You know why! You can steal a piece of gum out of someone's mouth and he wouldn't know it," the director grunted. "Just tell me how you stole the photos."

"Photos?" Parviz, startled by the man's fury, tried to stall as he gathered his thoughts. "The ones on the TV program last night?"

The director glared at him in silence, then turned to his secretary and asked, "Won't you return to your desk, please? We need a few moments alone."

As the door shut behind her, the director glared at the visitor once again. Parviz threw his shoulders up, seeming unaffected.

"You have nothing to say?" the director thundered.

Parviz only rose and walked to the door. The director changed his tone and said in a softer voice, "Let me see you to the elevator."

In the hallway, he pressed again. "No one's here, see? I just need to know, for my own sake, how you did it."

"I've done nothing, sir," Parviz said, watching the arrows above the elevator door, avoiding his inquisitor's gaze.

When the doors opened, the director made a last plea. "Why don't we go down on foot?"

They descended the stairs together. At the bottom, the director pointed out that they were on the street, beyond the agency's walls or its surveillance cameras. Sounding defeated, he asked yet again, "Man to man, tell me: how did you do it?"

"Do what?"

"You stole those photos and I must know how."

"I'm not a thief, sir, but since you insist, I'll tell you who did it," Parviz retorted.

"Who?"

"*You* did!"

"*I*? Why would you say such an absurd thing?" the director, furious again, blurted.

"Because I can. Because I'm the victim, and you are the BKA. People will believe what I say over the word of a bureaucrat any day. They themselves will think up why you may have done it—rivalry, corruption, whistle-blowing. There's no limit to the public's imagination."

The director was mum. Parviz wished him a pleasant day, turned on his heel, and walked away. He fought hard to suppress the urge to look back.

10

Despite what many think, there is freedom of speech in Iran. Only, there's no freedom after speech.

—*Hadi Khorsandi, exiled Iranian satirist*

When it came to mastering a case, Bruno Jost had no patience for leisurely introductions. He devoured his subject, now Iran, and not only its politics, but also its art and culture. His guide and Persian-German interpreter, Zamankhan, had drawn up a list of books for him to read, and among other lessons he had taken Jost to a Persian restaurant. The interpreter recommended the kebabs: the grilled meat that readily appealed to the Western palate. But since the urgency of the investigation weighed so heavily on him, Jost ordered what the menu listed as "the most truly Iranian dish of all"—a bowl of Ghormeh Sabzi, an herb stew.

"It goes over the saffron rice," the interpreter instructed. He showed how the dried lime had to be squeezed to let the flavor seep into the mix of leek, parsley, chive, scallion, cilantro, and fenugreek. Then he scooped a spoonful of stew and daintily placed it over a spoonful of rice. He was a highly measured man whose precision extended far beyond syntax (he always introduced himself by pausing over the syllables of his own name, *Za-man-khan*). Jost watched him, then simply emptied the bowl over the mound of rice and dug in; he was a passionate man who readily immersed himself in the unfamiliar.

If the grubby look of the stew made the prosecutor squeamish, his face did not show it. After the first mouthful, he pondered. It was strangely delectable; tart to be sure, but also lush and fragrant—a profusion of flavors that hinted at the distinct origins of each ingredient yet delivered a single exotic taste. Jost did not leave the restaurant till he had a copy of the recipe. His enthusiasm for the dish had as much to do with palate as intellect. He cherished the surprise of seeing herbs he had known only as garnish become a meal and, even more, that it was, per its description, *truly Iranian,* not known among Arabs. The dish—unexpected, and rare—mirrored the surprise of his recent encounter with Iran.

Like most educated Westerners, Bruno Jost held two irreconcilable views of Iran: a rich ancient civilization and a savage theocracy. He discovered the rift in his own perspective, only after beginning to probe into the Mykonos case. One view was of the exotic Persia—its bygone glories and empires, its historic ruins, its poets, and its miniatures and rugs. The other was of the Shiite hub of hostility—the fist-throwing mobs on the evening news, their hateful chants against the West, the fanatical rulers inciting violence. His reverence for Persia had sufficed in the past, but now that he had a murder to solve, it was no longer enough.

To consider Tehran as the mastermind of the Mykonos murders made Jost uneasy because it went against Germany's diplomatic ethos. In 1988, four months after the end of the Iran-Iraq war, Foreign Minister Hans-Dietrich Genscher made history by becoming the first Western European senior official to visit Tehran in many years. He had gone a skeptic and returned an optimist: under the leadership of its new president, Rafsanjani, Iran was ready to embrace Europe once more, or so Genscher believed. The era of radicalism had ended, giving Europe the chance to back the forces of moderation by helping Iran recover from war. German businesses cheered the notion, and so did most Germans.

Mykonos was not the first terrorism case Jost had handled. He had seen his share of corpses in pools of blood. Nor was it his first case dealing with troubled territories beyond his own country: he had investigated several high profile cases involving Turks, Yugoslavs, and Lebanese in the past. But the more he learned about this case, about Iran, the greater grew its allure to the prosecutor. Its intrigue was boundless. To discover, for instance, that the members of the terror team were from Iran and Lebanon and did not all speak the same language had surprised him. They communicated in Arabic, but for the Persian-speaking Iranians on the team, it had been a second language. He no longer dismissed details.

"Why are some turbans black and others white?" he asked Zamankhan, the interpreter. The black turban, he was told, is worn exclusively by those who claimed to be the descendants of the Prophet Muhammad.

A mosque ceased to be simply a place of worship. That, too, he learned when Zamankhan explained that the Imam Jafar Mosque in Berlin, where Darabi was a major benefactor, did not welcome all Muslims. It was a hub for radical Shiites, funded mostly by Tehran.

Though the evidence against Tehran quickly began to outweigh that against the PKK, the prosecutor would not rule the Turkish group out—not publicly. He could not. Bonn was carefully monitoring the case. On September 18, the office of the chief federal prosecutor released Jost's memo naming Tehran a possible suspect. Immediately after its release, the chief federal prosecutor, Alexander von Stahl, was severely reprimanded by the justice ministry. His office was never to release another statement without the justice ministry's approval.

Calls from "concerned colleagues" had come in, advising Jost to let law yield to diplomacy. They counseled that in cases as important as Mykonos, lawyers were best to leave politicians in charge and limit the scope of their investigation, a move that would "surely benefit one's future career."

He courteously listened, then did the only thing he could do—investigate.

Exiled Iranians, too, had besieged his office with messages of their own, demanding that he expand the scope of the investigation beyond the men in custody to implicate their masters. But since he fiercely protected the case from others who wished to influence it, he kept his distance from the exiles. He was wary of political oppositions and of falling prey to a plot by former leaders who might use him to revive their own failed enterprise.

What consumed him was neither the prospects of his future career nor the pressures from invested parties. It was the question of motive. To imagine that Tehran, a government ruling over sixty million citizens, was threatened by a minority of four million seemed implausible to him. Besides, the historians he had consulted unanimously agreed that, compared to the Kurds elsewhere, Iran's Kurds had always led far better lives. Given the ancient history of camaraderie among the Iranians and the Kurds why would Tehran wage war against them?

VIENNA. He thought again of the word he had written in block letters during his first night on the case. From the beginning, the ghost of another Kurdish leader, the Doctor's predecessor, Abdulrahman Ghassemlou, had hovered over the investigation. Ghassemlou and two associates had been shot at an apartment in Vienna in July 1989. The similarities between the two murders—three Kurdish leaders killed in two neighboring countries within three years—were great enough to warrant a collegial visit. So Jost flew to Vienna to consult his counterparts across the border.

In meeting and reviewing the findings of the Austrian investigators, Jost quickly learned some key facts. Ghassemlou was widely popular. There had never been any doubt that his assassins were non-Kurds because in the '80s even his staunchest rivals could not have survived the ravages of the regime and war without his stewardship. Unlike the assassins in Berlin, the ones in Vienna had left a clear trail that had led to Iran's embassy. One assassin had even been caught, but once the ties between him and the embassy were discovered, the Austrian administration had intervened. Within two weeks, the prisoner was escorted onto a plane headed for Tehran. A few outraged parliamentarians launched their own investigations and found that the release had come on the heels of a major weapons deal with Iran.

To the Austrians, the motive was hardly a mystery: Tehran feared Ghassemlou. He had first emerged on the political scene in the early 1970s, and become a national figure by the late 1980s. He was beloved by Kurds and non-Kurds alike. Unlike the Doctor, the globe-trotting Ghassemlou was charismatic—as equally at ease in mountains of Kurdistan as on the sidewalks of Europe, sipping espresso beside his Czech wife. Educated in France, he moved between Paris and Prague as effortlessly as he did between French and the Czech language. After the Ayatollah came to power in 1979, Ghassemlou became the patron saint of all persecuted Iranians who took shelter in Kurdistan. His popularity transcended his own territory. Neither defeated nor driven into exile, he stayed in Iran and became a symbol of both resistance and hope. In 1989, more frail than ever from the bruises of a war whose only conquest had been swaths of ruins and millions dead or maimed, Tehran feared its own demise, and the electrifying Ghassemlou who could bring it about.

What he learned from the Austrians broadened Jost's understanding of the history behind the murders. Tehran had less to fear in the Doctor, who was neither as popular nor as charismatic as his predecessor. But by 1992 there was more to fear in regional developments—in Kuwait, which the Americans had invaded, and in northern Iraq where the Kurds were finally given autonomy. Tehran's motive was a mystery as long as Jost believed the Kurds were a lone, powerless minority. But since the Gulf War, the Kurds were no longer alone. They were a minority backed by America, Iran's archenemy, whose influence threatened to deepen and spread among the neighboring Kurds.

Jost returned home with a radically different assessment of Iran than the one Foreign Minister Genscher had. To the diplomat, the new Tehran had appeared on the brink of moderation. To the prosecutor, all that was new about Tehran was its mask of moderation. Doubts no longer plagued him. He had uncovered the motive, and solved the case. Yet he found no relief in all these discoveries. He had only traded doubt for anxiety. He thought about the near future, a time when he would make his findings public. Could an irate Tehran strike against his family? He considered the dangers he might be exposing his children to. The fallout from the trial ahead would hardly be contained within the courtroom. It was bound to reach into his home, and so he needed Angela's consent to continue on.

"Do the right thing, Bruno. Do what your conscience tells you to do," she said, simply and elegantly, without a moment's hesitation.

Her swift response shook Jost, forcing him to make the very arguments he had expected *her* to make: Their privacy would be lost. They would live under siege for the foreseeable future, with bodyguards following them at every step. They might have to go into hiding. But she did not flinch. She shrugged and said that she knew he would never be content quitting or giving the case less than his all. She knew living with the burden of his cowardice would crush them just as mortally as the dangers his valor might bring upon them.

Angela was the one to prepare their children for the sudden changes that swept through their household. A watch post was built on the sidewalk of their residence, and two guards monitored the house at all hours. Two other guards in plain clothes shadowed Jost outside of home. The reinforcements to the Jost house became the talk of the neighborhood. Rumors began to spread about a surveillance camera lodged in their mailbox, and about the house itself being only a facade hiding the family living in a single room underground. Eight-year-old Alex thrived on the intrigue of his father's new case, but the teenage Barbara dreaded it. Angela, who was not the brooding kind, consoled her daughter by promising not Bruno's safety, but his happiness.

"He'll be a better father if he does what he loves to do."

The inconveniences of life with Bruno were, after all, rooted in the very qualities Angela loved in him—above all his single-minded dedication to the objects of his passion. She drew strength from his clarity of purpose, as if nothing could ever blur his view of the truth. He could be contemplative, but never equivocal. She had learned that about him at seventeen when they first met on a field trip. Two days after they had declared their love to each other, he found out that Angela had yet to break the news of their relationship to the young Frenchman she had been dating. He briefly perused her German-French dictionary and jotted a few words on a piece of paper. Then he went looking for his rival. Finding him, Jost pointed to Angela, and said, "*C'est finis.*"

When the young man seemed puzzled, Jost grabbed Angela's hand and, reverting to German, said, "She's with me now, see? You may be on your way! *Au revoir!*"

Four years later, after she completed her degree in French literature and he had entered law school, they were married.

Despite his newfound certainty about the case, Jost could show no sign of it publicly. The office of the chief federal prosecutor was in Bonn's grip. No interviews were to be granted, no statements to be issued without submitting them to the justice ministry for clearance first. For the moment, Jost did not mind the tyranny; he had an indictment to draft. The flurry of inquiries was certain to sweep him up with the start of the trial. Until then, he reveled in the imposed silence. He had always done his best work in quiet.

To Parviz, however, silence was an insult. Any day that ended without a mention of his murdered friends in the news was another nail in their coffins. The passing of several weeks without a single statement from the federal prosecutor alarmed him. Years of activism had taught Parviz many lessons—above all that justice was a debt to wrest from powerful men who thrived in silence. Clamor was essential, effective, and, most importantly, inexpensive. Such was his state of mind just before he committed one of the great betrayals of his life.

In the early days after the murders, an inexperienced reporter from the *Bild,* a popular tabloid, had approached Parviz. He had cringed upon hearing the name of the publication, but the reporter's eyes, gleaming with enthusiasm, his obvious hunger for a serious story, had disarmed Parviz. The *Bild* was Europe's best-selling paper and had a large circulation worldwide. An article in the *Bild* would thrust the case into the scope of a whole new audience. So had gone the inner reasoning that led him to keep the reporter's contacts.

But reaching a wider audience was hardly what drove Parviz to call the tabloid reporter. It was desperation. The nationwide broadcast Norbert had promised was still days away. The waiting gnawed at him. He worried that it might have to yield to other breaking news. The fresh round of rumors about who had infiltrated the dinner at the Mykonos were now directed at him and Noori, and it added to his restlessness. He had to retaliate, ruthlessly if need be. He believed that the waters of the tragedy he had experienced were deep enough to wash away all his past and the forthcoming sins he had begun contemplating.

From the visit the BKA agents had paid him, Parviz still had nine unpublished photos of the three leading suspects in the case. With nine exclusive photos he could strike a bargain with any reporter, especially a novice toiling at a tabloid with lesser standards of accuracy. He called the young reporter and offered him one of the photos.

It all happened swiftly. The photo ran beside an article and interview with him in the next issue of the *Bild*. The reporter was showered with more praise and congratulatory messages than he had ever received in his career. For him and the paper, the piece was a coup, and it brought some highbrow colleagues to the tabloid reporter's doorstep, probing him about his sources.

"I've Parviz Dastmalchi to thank," he told everyone, including Parviz.

The success of the piece was immediately followed by a second and then a third installment on the Mykonos case, with "never before seen" photos accompanying each. For the fourth article, Parviz offered more than just another exclusive photo.

"I have something else for you, something no one has yet reported," Parviz said, then seductively asked if the reporter, whose confidence in Parviz was at a peak, could guarantee front-page coverage in exchange for the scoop.

The reporter put Parviz on hold, but returned moments later with blessings from his editor. Buoyed by the promise, Parviz unfolded the piece of paper he had been keeping in his shirt pocket, and said, "Here are the results of the ballistic tests on the murder weapons found at the car dealership last September, the ones the police won't disclose."

Parviz gave the full account of the weapons' history and the reporter, at times speaking as if only to himself, fitted the pieces of information together, staggered by the enormity of what he was learning.

"These weapons had been sold to the Iranian Royal Army in 1972. But who supplied the weapons to the hit squad is as important as who sold the weapons to the Iranian Royal Army to begin with, you see," Parviz said, raising the curiosity of his eager listener.

It was for this moment he had chosen the novice. What he subsequently did went against everything he had ever preached to his daughter. Yet he did not waver. "The weapons were sold to Iran by Germany," he added.

To force the hands of the German officials, Parviz calculated, one had to incriminate them. Naming Germany, instead of Spain, as the real supplier would goad the authorities into denying the accusation by coming forth with the truth.

"Germany?" the reporter gasped at the other end. "Good God, Mr. Dastmalchi. What proof do you have for this?"

Parviz quoted a highly positioned but anonymous source at the BKA. Then he wrote down the serial numbers of the weapons, their make and model, and the year they had been manufactured. At the bottom he wrote "sold to Iran by Germany" and faxed the hand-crafted document to the *Bild*.

At dawn the following day, a howl—deep, wrenching, and protracted—shook Norbert's apartment.

"Nooo . . ."

The clock radio had gone off and the half-conscious Norbert heard the weather report interrupted by a breaking story about the murders at Mykonos. He burst out of bed and switched on the television. Every broadcast was running the news of the ballistic tests according to the *Bild*'s most recent issue. Except it was *Germany* not Spain that was being named the original supplier.

"Nooo!" Norbert wailed again as he dialed Parviz's number. His howl was the sound of his broken trust.

Parviz spent the early morning hours of that day in his office, unable to do much. Norbert's angry words kept echoing in his mind. Maybe all his ploys had been paltry and quixotic. Maybe he had achieved nothing. Maybe the sum of all his efforts was a drop in an ocean whose tides ebbed and flowed to the whims of politicians. Maybe, as Norbert insisted through his screams, he was damaging the case by his rash acts. Or maybe, as some fellow exiles had rumored, he was using the assassination to promote himself. Whatever it was that moved him was beyond his control. He could not stop what he had begun. The need to wage war had become another physical urge like eating or keeping warm. He either warred or surrendered to fear, insomnia, and despair. It was how he warded off darkness. War was what he did to affirm, if only to himself, that he was innocent and alive.

11

Hollywood is making a film about Cyrus, so Westerners can learn how it took us 2,500 years to get from a great king to the mullahs of today.

—Hadi Khorsandi, exiled Iranian satirist

It was one of the great ironies in the history of diplomacy: Tehran was overtly boasting about what Europe was trying to hide or amend on its behalf. In November 1992, the supreme leader doubled the reward for the murder of Salman Rushdie. In December, another opposition member was kidnapped and killed in Istanbul. Not long after, at a press conference, the interior minister said that the murdered dissidents in exile were getting their due and had only themselves to blame. Yet these events did not keep the euphoric European businessmen from the 1992 Tehran Trade Fair, nor did they stop conceited officials from holding their scheduled two-day summit of Critical Dialogue with Iran in Edinburgh that December.

The next January, two more dissidents were murdered—one in a car bomb in Ankara, the other gunned down in Iraq. And in March, Bruno Jost circled in red three new spots on the world map—two in Pakistan and a third in Italy, each for a new assassination. In Washington, the secretary of state of the new Clinton administration called Tehran an "international outlaw," yet Europe's fervor would not be diminished. Against that backdrop, Jost was the lone investigator tracking the deadly epidemic his countrymen denied existed. At a time when Europe's exports to Iran had reached a historic peak, the prosecutor's gloomy news was unwelcome.

Denial, like a shadow, had also spread over Moabit's prison cell #404. Yousef Amin, too, had a lot he wished to recant. Rumors about his collaboration with the police were circulating among the inmates, who had begun tormenting him. The few calls he received were either threats or reports of threats his family had received. Yousef had survived several jail terms in Lebanon and nimbly slipped by immigration officials throughout Europe. But for the first time in his life, he found himself under assault with no way out. After twenty interrogation sessions, his inquisitors had simply disappeared. By March 1993 it was Yousef who demanded a meeting with them, promising to make new revelations. These, like the preceding confessions, came in several installments.

"I'm here to tell you that everything I've said so far has been a lie. The truth is something I'm saving for the court and only the court," Yousef said to his audience. They were startled by the dramatic shift in his speech and manners. When Jost asked why he seemed so distressed, Yousef burst into a litany of complaints.

"I want to know why your police sent my family back to Lebanon."

Jost and the commissioner, von Trek, took turns explaining that they had done everything in their power to protect his family. In the end, the family had chosen to return on its own. Yet neither man could get through to Yousef, whose distress grew with their attempts to calm him.

"I begged you to give my family an apartment. Six people cooped up in one room. Your police watching them like dogs. The Kurds and the Iranians weren't enough? My family had to be afraid of your police, too! *You* are why they went back. If you so much as whistled, my family would have had a good life here. They told me they'd write me, and they haven't. I've heard from nobody. Not you, not them. No one. I'd have had more visitors at my grave. I wrote a letter to the Lebanese embassy asking the ambassador to visit me here, and nothing! My lawyer hasn't been around. He says he's too busy reading what you've sent him."

Yousef's predicament was particularly tragic because of his previous credulity. Before the murders, he had believed his friends who reassured him that Iran would quickly negotiate their release if they were captured. After the arrest, he had hoped to strike a bargain with Jost by telling the truth, confident of his own winning wit. Six months in prison had taught him a hard lesson about the absoluteness of Germany's laws, the imperfect ubiquity of his patrons, and the limits of his own charm.

"This is what you've done to me."

He made a gesture, which the stenographer recorded.

Note to file: *The prisoner placed his right fist in the joint of his left elbow and folded his forearm over it. According to the translator, the gesture is a vulgar one but, pertinent to this exchange, it means that the prisoner is in trouble.*

"It's all over. You've done your worst. But I tell you now, everything I said before is wrong. Are you writing this down? Lies! I'm keeping the truth for the judge and the court. Oh, how my head hurts!"

Note to file: *The commissioner accompanied the prisoner to the washroom for a drink of water. When they returned, the prisoner refused to go on, demanding another interpreter. He contends that the current interpreter speaks a different dialect of Arabic.*

As Jost adjourned the meeting, Yousef pointed to the translator and shouted, "He's working for the police. I know it. He's a dirty pig!"

Note to file: *Other insults the prisoner used have been struck from the record.*

After denying his past confessions, Yousef tried to revise what he had previously said about the friends he had betrayed.

"Here's something else. Write it in your papers! Whatever happened, Darabi had nothing to do with it. He knew nothing. Darabi is a good man, nothing to do with anything bad. And also I'm not a member of the Hezbollah."

Jost challenged him. "Mr. Amin, you said yourself that you had joined the Hezbollah in Lebanon."

"I never said I'd anything to do with them. *You* keep squeezing me into Hezbollah."

The commissioner read from the transcripts of several witnesses who had spoken of Yousef's membership in the group and his travels to Iran with his friend Rhayel for combat training.

"So what?" Yousef shot back. "They say what they say. I say what I say. That's all. I got nothing to do with Hezbollah. I've had no training. I've not even gone to school. What do you think I know? Nothing! I'm a nobody. You want me to sign something, okay, I will. You want me to say I'm Khomeini, fine! I'll sign your papers and do what you say. I don't need this. I need peace and quiet, not this. Not you. I'm sick. Can't you see? Look at me! I've asked to go to the infirmary, but no one does anything . . . Iran! Keep saying Iran. I'm Lebanese. Got nothing to do with Iran."

"Why is it then that in your address book you have the phone number of the Iranian consulate in Berlin?"

"Maybe someone gave me the number so someone there could help me. Is there such a number in my book? Is the number any good? Did you try to see if it really is the consulate's number? You should, you know."

Jost paused and, instead of pressing the same point, he asked Yousef if he had been threatened.

"It's the police that has threatened me. I'll say what I want to the judge. I'm a Muslim. I'm not afraid of threats. I'm only afraid of God."

"Mr. Amin, just to be sure, do you clearly understand what we mean here by the word *pressure*, or *threaten*? Perhaps your family in Lebanon has been threatened."

Yousef interrupted angrily. "Don't start talking this way!"

Note to file: *At the time of the dictation of the last two questions, the accused asked that the question about the threat against his family be struck from the transcript. When his request was denied, he jumped out of his chair and broke into tears. He said that it cannot and must not appear in the transcribed protocol. He pleaded with everyone in the visiting room.*

"I'm a human being and you're ruining everything for me. I'll never see my son. I've not seen him since he was born. And I'll not see him if you keep doing this to me."

Yousef refused to speak to the investigators again. He ended his collaboration, just as the investigation ended. By March, Jost submitted the first draft of the indictment to the chief federal prosecutor. More than six months after Alexander von Stahl had assigned Jost to the case, the prosecutor had returned with his findings. The appendices alone, spanning Jost's library of 187 binders, were evidence of an impeccable inquiry conducted on two continents. It included some rare finds: police files dating as far back as 1980, letters from Iran's embassy and consular sections in support of Darabi on several occasions, and statements from refugee affairs agencies throughout Europe, sixty-eight witnesses, and eighteen experts and scholars.

The chief federal prosecutor immediately alerted the ministry of justice. Just as quickly, the order came that he neither sign nor release the indictment until the justice ministry, its liaison at the chancellery, and the foreign ministry had approved it. To yield to the justice minister was reasonable, but to yield to the chancellery and the foreign ministry struck the chief federal prosecutor as a violation of the independence of his office.

If anyone had the power to limit the scope of Bruno Jost's investigation, it was the chief federal prosecutor. Yet contrary to what many, reading through the tea leaves of party affiliation, had forecasted, Alexander von Stahl, a political conservative, proved to be surprisingly original. Though his party had historically been uncritical of Iran in favor of Germany's businesses, von Stahl refused to put any interests above the law. He fiercely protected Jost and his staff. For von Stahl, the nation's security always came first, no matter the political consequences. Under his watch, the streets of his country would not be turned into rogues' gaming grounds, be the victims German or not.

Jost's indictment, fearlessly articulating his findings, began with the words, "I accuse Yousef Amin, Kazem Darabi, and

Abbas Rhayel of collectively conducting, on September 17, 1992, with reprehensible motives, a most heinous act of murder against four human beings in the city of Berlin."

The indictment alone was historic, if only for the single sentence no one on the continent had ever dared pen: "Kazem Darabi, the agent who organized the murders, acted upon the orders of the intelligence ministry of Iran."

Iran, that forbidden name, had at last been spoken.

As illogical, even unlawful, as the justice ministry's instructions were, von Stahl obeyed them and sent copies of the document to all three offices. Naming Iran went against the wishes of some of the most powerful figures in his own party, among them the foreign minister and the deputy justice minister. To accuse Iran's regime of murder was not simply a blow to Tehran, but also to Bonn, Iran's champion in the West.

April arrived without a word from the ministries. The chief federal prosecutor reluctantly waited.

Under the glare of fluorescent lights in the exam room, Parviz stood by, sometimes kissing, sometimes stroking the hand of his daughter, Salomeh. She looked even more frail in the hospital gown. He felt restless on behalf of the aspiring twelve-year-old dancer who had been told to remain still till the doctor returned. Two fainting spells, confounding several internists and pediatricians, had forced the father and daughter to see a cardiologist. Two fainting spells on her part, and a heap of guilt on her father's part.

Ever since the morning after the murders, Parviz had tried to keep her away from the fallout, to shield Salomeh from the news. Before picking her up on Tuesdays, their weekday together, he combed through the apartment to hide all signs of the case from view: photos, letters, phone messages, newspaper clippings. But the more he hid, the more she wanted to know.

"How did it happen, Baba *jaan*? How many were they? Did anyone hit you?"

"They came. They shot. They left. Nothing happened to me. Nothing at all," he would say, wishing to move on.

But her questions continued.

"Did you have blood on you? Did you scream? Did you cry? Did you cry after? Were you scared? Are you scared now?"

The depth of her curiosity astounded him. Once he yelled, "Enough!" and she stopped asking, but he knew she had not stopped thinking the haunting thoughts.

The dream of becoming a dancer had turned her into a reluctant eater, and so he designed intricate plans for her meals. Instead of an elaborate dinner, he lined up an epicure's array of tiny appetizers, which he paraded before his willowy ballerina at intervals. In the small, tidy apartment brimming with music, the father, surrendering to the daughter's whims, had agreed to be a dance student in the tutelage of his diminutive coach. Though tone-deaf and hopelessly uncoordinated, his performances were memorable. What he lacked in talent he compensated for in wit. When he failed to remember his steps, he resorted to buffoonery. He limped cross-eyed across the floor, greeting an imaginary audience not with "guten Tag," German for "good day," but with his own Persian-German concoction, "*gooz-be* Tag," or "fart on your day." Nothing like a bit of vulgarity to bond a part-time father with his preadolescent child.

What he could not fathom was that joy, however abundant, was no substitute for safety, which she no longer felt in his presence. Nor could he imagine her days in school, among the classmates who treated her like a sensation. Only some of the questions she asked him were her own. The rest were ones other children, mocking her father as the "superhero of the nightly news," incessantly posed to her.

When the first fainting spell came over Salomeh, he thought she had starved herself. But when she fainted on a full stomach, he blamed himself and his complicated life for his daughter's malady—the malady no one could, thus far, diagnose. He had tried hard to keep her out of his own gloomy world lest the killers, or the mere idea of them, rob her of a happy childhood. But now it seemed the vacuum he had surrounded her with was robbing her of breath.

Unlike Salomeh, Sara wanted to know nothing. In November, she had asked Shohreh where exactly her father was now and if he was in pain. In December, she had asked if she could buy him Christmas gifts and leave them under the tree until he returned. In February, she had asked if Shohreh intended to marry another man, and if so, was he going to move in with them. By March, she no longer asked. If she heard the name "Mykonos" on the radio, she rushed to turn it off. If she recognized the face of family or friends on television, she walked out of the living room.

To help Sara and her mother cope with Noori's absence, Shohreh's parents briefly moved in with their daughter. Their presence strengthened Shohreh, though she could not tell them that it did. Words failed her. What she had in abundance was tears. Her parents stared at her over breakfast and waited in vain for her to form a sentence as simple as, "How did you sleep?"

Her senses failed her. She rarely felt hunger. She barely tasted the perfunctory bites she took in front of them to reassure them of her appetite. Her parents, a government clerk and a housewife, had led serene and predictable lives. It was the security of their life that had given Shohreh the courage to rebel against them—she could go off to Europe, knowing that no matter what happened, she could always go home, she would always have them. But she wondered: Would Sara not have been better off with a pair of ordinary parents that would have been around for her whole life, rather than a pair of extraordinary ones who would be there only for a short time? All day, she turned these thoughts over in her mind's kiln, blazing with anger.

"To hell with his extraordinariness and every bit of his brilliance," she would mumble.

Noori enraged her now.

Stick with me and you'll be famous like you deserve to be, she remembered him promising the night they first met.

Was his death to be her path to fame? she shouted in her head. Once again, he had abandoned them. All through her pregnancy and delivery she had been alone, while he had been in Kurdistan hiding. Remembering their time apart, she grew even more furious wondering if it had been a warning to her to prepare to raise their child alone. Reason had abandoned her. She no longer thought of Noori's absence as involuntary. He had left them, yet again. The thought came to her when she played their old family movies. She spent one night watching reams of film but found Noori only once, and only for a few seconds: walking with her along the racetrack where Sara had run her first competition. It was as if her husband had sketched their future. Everyone moved, posed, and smiled following Noori's instructions, but he, their director, was invisible. His vision filled the screen, yet he would not be seen. Just like now. His multipocketed sports vest hung on the coat hanger. His Swiss Army knife lay on the mantelpiece. His bonsais withered on the windowsill. The wooden backgammon set he had carved, with the marble pieces he had chiseled, lay on the coffee table he had built. The stack of television guides in the magazine rack bore the highlights of his marker, which determined Sara's weekly viewing allotment. When they finally turned in for the night, the beds they slept in had been built by him. In the morning, the jam they spread on their toast was labeled in his handwriting. He was everywhere, yet nowhere.

• • •

For Shohreh and Parviz, an occasional tea or dinner together was just as painful as it was vital. As they sat down to chat, Sara and Salomeh, old playmates, ran off to play. The girls talked of spells, potions, flying brooms, and their beloved storybook witch Bibi Blocksberg. They would dress up in green, and gather their dark hair in buns and tie it with a red ribbon in the witch's style. They would put on an audio cassette of a Bibi Blocksberg adventure and act out the tale the best they could in the confines of the bedroom. Only Sara went further. If her mother was not watching, she dashed into the street shoeless with a broom in her hand. She dared to live the life she conjured, but Salomeh hesitated. Once, their lives had been similar enough to be interchangeable. But now loss had cast one child starkly distinguishable from the other.

Meanwhile, the parents talked about what consumed them. Who had spied on them that night was still a mystery. They had briefly suspected Mehdi, until the coroner had confirmed Mehdi's devotion. The pattern and location of Noori's wounds showed that at the moment of the shooting, he had been dragged away from the line of fire. Mehdi had done that. He was why Noori was still breathing when the ambulance had arrived. They considered the two others who had joined the dinner unexpectedly that night. But that, too, seemed baseless because they had only come to the table at the urging of Aziz. They even wondered about the dead Kurds, especially the quieter of the Doctor's two deputies. Was the mole among the dead? They would argue and empty one glass of tea after the next, but the mystery remained a mystery.

May was approaching without a word from the ministries. The chief federal prosecutor's patience had reached its limit. When he inquired about the delay, he was told the drafts he had sent were lost. *Lost* flabbergasted him. He sent new copies of the indictment to the ministries and again waited. A few more days passed without a word. It was clear the delay was meant to stall the case long enough for it to fade from the public's attention.

Since the release of the *Bild* article, accusations against the office of the chief federal prosecutor had mounted. The segment that Norbert and his colleague had been preparing aired on the national broadcast *Kontraste*. Its septuagenarian correspondent with his glowing bald head rimmed with a ring of white hair had begun the hour by promising to "break the silence" about the Mykonos case. The target of *Kontraste*'s criticism was the chief federal prosecutor.

The reports enraged von Stahl, whose conduct and integrity had come under attack. Together with Jost, they pondered their predicament. Given how long the perpetrators had been in custody, Jost thought of an ingenious justification for releasing the indictment to Berlin's high criminal court and requesting a trial date: any further delay on the part of the chief federal prosecutor would be a breach of the prisoners' rights. By law, they had to either announce a trial date or set the accused free.

Once more, von Stahl contacted the ministries, this time

with an ultimatum disguised as a legal mandate. Word still did not come. So on May 17, he signed the indictment and submitted it to the Kammergericht, Berlin's highest court. Never had a stroke of his pen spawned so many enemies.

One month later, the court granted the chief federal prosecutor's request for a trial. A date was to be announced shortly after Judge Frithjof Kubsch, the chief of division one overseeing national security cases, was appointed to lead the team of four other judges in the upcoming trial. The court had clearly acknowledged the significance of the case by assigning the highest number of judges to preside over it.

Bruno Jost flew to Berlin to meet with the judges and determine the schedule and protocol for the trial. They agreed the court would convene every Thursday and Friday of every week. There would be two other judges on reserve to cover the absence of any of the main judges and two teams of interpreters to assist the Arab- and Persian-speaking witnesses. The meeting was mostly spent reviewing the indictment, without a mention of its historic significance. It was the first time since World War II that a German court would consider the crimes of a foreign government. Jost came away confident of the judges' regard for the quality of his work. None of them had questioned the validity of his premise. There and then, they established the cordial distance that would define the relationship between the prosecutor and the court, especially Judge Kubsch.

In Karlsruhe, at the headquarters of the chief federal prosecutor, a happy uproar swept through the staff at the prospect of the imminent trial. The triumph owed much to the backbone of Alexander von Stahl. But by releasing the indictment, he had violated too many allegiances. Pressure from every corner was heaped on him. A minor shooting incident in a remote part of Germany was turned into a national scandal that dogged him until July, when the minister of justice asked for his resignation. Only two months after he had signed the indictment, Alexander von Stahl was forced to leave his post, ending his promising career in government.

Years later, in a calmer and more forgiving state, Norbert reflected on the events of spring 1993. From the distance of years, Parviz's betrayal revealed a wisdom he had been too furious to recognize at the time, and the chief federal prosecutor, whom he and others had accused of standing in the way of the truth, proved to have been a captive of even greater powers. He wrote:

> With the arrest of the two Lebanese accomplices in September 1992, and that of the Iranian coordinator of the assassinations, Kazem Darabi, in early October, the investigators should have put to rest all other suspicions about the PKK or rival opposition groups. Still, the federal prosecutor never issued any statements about Tehran having turned into the lead suspect and refused to release any information that so much as alluded to it. In fact, eight months later, when a wealth of other evidence clearly pointed to Iran, the spokesperson for the office of the chief federal prosecutor said in a radio interview, "I can only discuss facts and our findings, not fantasize.

We still believe the PKK or the opposition could have been behind this." Until May 1993, the federal prosecutor had not officially taken a different position. But on May 11, 1993, as a result of a piece of misinformation planted in the journal *Bild* by a member of the Iranian opposition, the chief federal prosecutor finally came forward. That bit of misinformation, purposely designed to force the investigators' hands, worked brilliantly. In a statement released that same day, after many months, the federal prosecutor finally spoke of the true origins of the weapons. A week later, he released the indictment. As it turned out, the federal prosecutor, too, had to break free of others who had been pressuring him all along. But at last, the long reign of silence ended.

12

> When Ayatollah Khomeini was told that Salman Rushdie might undergo plastic surgery to change his appearance, he ordered, "Kill anyone who doesn't look like Rushdie!"
>
> —*Hadi Khorsandi, exiled Iranian satirist*

The federal prosecutor brought his charge against Iran in May 1993. But the magazine *Die Focus* had made the same accusations in its inaugural issue the previous January. The chief federal prosecutor could not be sued, but the magazine was vulnerable. Iran's embassy in Bonn sued *Die Focus* and its reporter Josef Hufelschulte, on charges of slander, for an estimated 500,000 DM. Though the lower court dismissed the case, the embassy appealed the decision. For a second time, the reporter appeared before the judge to defend his piece. Like all good reporters, he refused to reveal his source and agreed to present his evidence to the judge only in a closed session.

The evidence was the final summary of the work of the federal commission on Mykonos. Shortly after the federal prosecutor took over the case, the commission—a body made up of Parliamentarians and representatives from all the agencies involved in the investigation—was appointed to monitor Jost's work and review his findings. It was a watch-dog group that was established early on to minimize the damaging fallout from a politically charged investigation. After several weeks, the Mykonos Commission concluded its work by issuing a summary, which was captured in a single line, "powerful figures within Iran's regime ordered the assassinations at the Mykonos restaurant."

Since the commission's findings, like the indictment, had been kept from the public, one frustrated member had leaked a copy of it to Hufelschulte. That was what the reporter presented to the judge who, after reviewing it, told him to go home. Case dismissed!

The embassy did not relent. It insisted upon its innocence by extending an exclusive invitation to the reporter to spend a few hours with the ambassador and his staff in Bonn. The embassy also offered him a visa to visit Iran for himself, but Hufelschulte traveled only as far as Bonn. He had tea at the embassy, which was rumored to be the hub of Iran's intelligence activities in Western Europe. The reception left him with an even greater distaste for the officials he had so scathingly accused. Prior to the lawsuits and the encounter in Bonn, Hufelschulte was only intrigued by the Mykonos case. Afterward, his interest became a devotion, one that would inevitably lead to Parviz.

Hufelschulte paid Parviz a visit, hoping he might have photos or other material suited for print.

"How much for a photo, assuming it's an exclusive?" the reporter asked after settling onto the love seat in Parviz's office—which seemed shrunken beneath his tall, broad frame.

"I'm not a businessman, you know. It's not money I'm after. I want information," Parviz said in an unusually forward manner.

The reporter paused for a few moments to review all he had to offer, then said, "There was a mole in the restaurant that night. You know that, don't you?"

Parviz nodded, his heart racing at the mention of the word.

"I've got something on that. Is it worth an unpublished photo to you?" the reporter asked casually.

Trying to match the other's coolness, Parviz said that the information, if reliable, was worth a lot more than a photo. Hufelschulte said that his source had served on the federal commission on Mykonos, which impressed Parviz. One of the commission's key findings, he explained, a time line drawn from the confessions of one of the prisoners, pointed to the presence of a spy inside the restaurant.

9 p.m.—the telephone at the team's apartment rings once, followed by another single ring seconds later, signaling the operation's launch.

9:30—the killers arrive but do not strike, certain that their man inside would keep the victims in place for as long as it took—until 10:45.

Hearing Hufelschulte review those events quickened Parviz's blood. His eyes fixed on the reporter's broad face with thick, sharply arched eyebrows—as the moments preceding the killers' entrance passed through his mind. The smell of greasy meat wafting from the table to mix with the cigarette smoke in the air; the smoothness of the glass in one hand, the starched lining of his pants pocket enveloping the other hand; the flickering candles dotting the twilight about them; the sounds of fading conversation; then, seconds later, awakening to another sensory landscape, the sounds of groans and dripping liquid, the coarse carpet pressing against his cheek, the smell of a different smoke rising. These moments that bracketed the deaths—always ready to be summoned—were deathless in his imagination.

The reporter went on.

". . . and when the time finally came, the mole signals the killers to enter."

"No! No one signaled anybody. We were sitting there, talking the whole time. No one moved from the table. You're wrong," Parviz protested.

"One person must have been moving about that night."

"No one! Whatever you've been told, I'm telling you, is wrong. I see it now. I'm sitting there. We're all at the table, the whole time."

"All of you?" the reporter probed. "What about your server, the restaurant owner?"

"What? *Him*?" Parviz exclaimed, pushing his hand into the air in dismissal. "Please! Don't you know he was shot? The wretch has suffered more than all the rest of us."

"But he's the one the police suspects."

Parviz tipped back in his chair, suddenly silent. Hufelschulte, reading the shock on Parviz's face, asked if he needed fresh air. But Parviz did not hear him. He was elsewhere—at the dinner table on that September night. The question echoing in his head, over and over, was the last question he had heard that evening. An image he had since suppressed flooded his mind—of Aziz, not sitting beside them but leaning against the edge of the adjacent table, half standing, pointing to the Doctor, as if to point him out, saying, as if not to ask but to announce him, *Would the Doctor like any more beer?*

Aziz had hardly finished his question when the shooting had begun.

Once Parviz regained his composure, the reporter gave a few more details, including the discrepancies in Aziz's testimony to the police. Aziz claimed to have been inside the restaurant all along, but a witness had seen him pacing the sidewalk minutes before the killers walked in.

"Ah! But who's that witness? An enemy of Aziz's could be making the accusation. You know, we Iranians can be terribly cruel to each other," Parviz said in Aziz's defense as if in defense of his own unraveling confidence.

"No, it's a German, a neighbor, with nothing at stake in this."

That night, Parviz crawled into bed but knew he would not sleep. He would spend another night in the embrace of his most steadfast companion—insomnia. There could be no rest for a man in whom so much had been stirred. Everything he had dismissed as negligible gaffes of a simpleton now needed pondering. Aziz had not looked Shohreh in the eye when she had gone to visit him. He was agitated when his visitors recounted their version of events that afternoon in the hospital. He thought back to his own confusion about the date of the gathering. First had come Aziz's message on the answering machine inviting him to the restaurant on Friday night, then the call from Noori on Thursday evening. If Aziz were the mole, had he tried to change the date of the dinner to keep the scene small and manageable for the killers? Mykonos had never been a bustling restaurant, but it had been quieter than usual that evening. The chef had been ill, and he remembered Aziz shaking his head in regret as he turned customers away. Had the chef really been ill?

Aziz as the mole! The idea withered him through the night. What gnawed at him was not his own betrayal by Aziz, but Noori's. Did Aziz blame his divorce on the liberating influence of Noori? *This is my* mola, Aziz's voice echoed in his ear. The image of him wrapping his arms around Noori kept playing in his mind. Aziz pressed Noori in his embrace with such ardor it was as if Noori was venerable, a totem he prayed to. He seemed so dedicated to Noori that Parviz—who found much intolerable in Aziz (especially the stench of alcohol on his breath)—did not confront Noori about his friendship with the restaurant owner whom they had dubbed "the buffoon."

And why had none of them ever wondered how a penniless refugee could purchase a property as lucrative as a restaurant exactly one year before the murders? Parviz thought and seethed. Had the mole betrayed his *mola*? All through the night the tides of revelation lapped against his memory. *Who was the buffoon now?*

There were fewer bouquets and fewer mourners in Berlin's central cemetery. A year had passed. Shohreh, still in black, made her way to Noori's grave, flanked by Parviz and Mehdi. Sara had been sent to school. It was a quieter occasion, but no less somber. Raw grief had lifted. The solemnity that settled in its place was no less affecting in the eyes of the reporters who congregated in a corner and rolled their tapes.

Standing at the plot, Shohreh suddenly spotted an unsettling presence in the distance. Her heart sank in her chest. She turned to Parviz and whispered, "He's coming this way."

"Who?" Parviz asked, and looked in the direction where Shohreh's eyes had been fixed. Aziz was approaching.

"The traitor! The bastard! Let him come. I'll shred him to pieces with tooth and nail," the inflamed widow hissed.

"You can do no such thing. Keep it together. Let me handle it," Parviz counseled her.

Aziz circled the crowd to take his place next to Shohreh. The murmurs died down. The crowd was as silent as the grass under their feet, as still as the trees around them. No one wanted to miss the sound of the man who had barely spoken in a year.

"Hello," Aziz greeted Shohreh sheepishly.

"Hello," Shohreh replied bitterly and turned away.

"You look well, Aziz," Parviz said, stepping between the two.

"Eh! I'll never be a hundred percent, but what's there to do? I go on breathing," Aziz replied and nodded to a few others.

He was about to move when Parviz grabbed his arm and whispered in his ear, "Aziz, stop by and let's talk before you leave."

"What about?"

"You know what."

"Okay. I'll stay," Aziz assented before disappearing into the crowd.

Shohreh asked what Parviz planned to do next.

"I'll just ask him if he did it. That's all. We should give him a chance to tell his side," Parviz answered.

But when the speeches had been delivered, the poems had been recited, and the melancholic ballads had been sung, Parviz and Shohreh looked up to find Aziz gone.

Two weeks later, in the early hours of dawn, the telephone in Parviz's apartment rang. In a drunken stupor, Aziz had dialed Parviz's number. It took a few moments for Parviz to feel awake enough to say, "In the cemetery, I asked you to stay, but you didn't."

"No, I didn't," Aziz shot back through sobs or drunken hiccups, Parviz could not tell which.

"So, what is this talk you want with me?" Aziz demanded.

"You don't know?"

Only hiccups could be heard at the other end.

"Four people are dead, Aziz, and people say you, *you*, are the reason. They say you work for the regime," Parviz fumed.

"History will prove me innocent," Aziz replied.

"*History*? What history? *This* is history, this conversation between you and me. Have you no shame?"

"I did nothing wrong," Aziz hissed.

"Explain that!"

"I don't need to explain anything."

"Don't you ever call here unless you're ready to answer me, until you can prove you're innocent."

"Suit yourself!" Aziz hiccupped and hung up.

13

Ballot boxes are very good for the human being, provided that the human being is a carpenter and has a large order for making them.

—Hadi Khorsandi, exiled Iranian satirist

On the morning of October 7, 1993, Bruno Jost received a call from Commissioner von Trek. The most major figure in the case, "the main asset," in the investigative vernacular, whom they had long wanted to question, was in Germany. He had quietly flown to Bonn for a confidential two-day visit. Since the visitor was unlikely to cooperate with them, the commissioner had sought permission from his chief to briefly detain him. The permission for the arrest was too politically costly to be granted, Jost and von Trek knew. But the old colleagues, despite their graying hair, had held on to certain relics of youth, especially the love of mischief and adventurism. Even if the "asset" was beyond their reach, the least they could do was to unsettle him, if only momentarily, by the chase.

Jost cleared his schedule for the day and camped at his desk. The two men, who had vowed to remain friends in retirement, would wait till noon for the unlikely approval. Had there been the slightest mistrust between them, daring to make so bold a move would have never occurred to them. But ambition, vernal in nature, thrives on warmth, which they had in abundance between them.

That morning, the reporter Josef Hufelschulte received a fax, whose contents, in journalistic venacular, amounted to a scoop. He reviewed the document, then immediately did what a savvy reporter would—called his sources to weigh in on his find.

"Hey, Parviz! It's Hufelschulte," the reporter greeted, then, quickly dispensing with pleasantries, asked, "What am I to make of Fallahian's visit?"

"Fallahian? As in the intelligence minister?" Parviz asked, clearly startled by the news.

Hufelschulte elaborated: Ali Fallahian, whose ministry had been named in the federal prosecutor's indictment, was in Germany. The visit would have been a secret, if a copy of the minister's itinerary had not been leaked to Hufelschulte. The itinerary, telexed to several agencies—the interior ministry and the border police among others—had been intercepted by an ally of the reporter at one of the agencies.

"He flew into Frankfurt on Iran Air flight seven-twenty-one at eleven-thirty yesterday morning," Hufelschulte recited the highlights, "went downtown, and then later in the day was off to Bonn to the chancellor's mansion for a seven o'clock dinner. This morning, he's visiting his German counterpart, Bernd Schmidbauer, at eleven."

Exile cultivates the archivist in its most wistful subjects. Since the murders, the penchant had become a passion in Parviz. His first concern was to obtain a copy of the itinerary, which Hufelschulte promised to send him.

"But why's he here? Is he meeting with the exiles?" the reporter asked.

"He'd meet us for sure, but only if we rendezvous at the morgue, and only with our corpses. Bah! If he's really here, three weeks before the trial begins, he's here for one reason and one reason alone, and that's to stop the trial."

To have his suspicions confirmed strengthened the reporter's resolve. The next call he made was to the chancellery's office of the intelligence chief, Bernd Schmidbauer. He introduced himself to the aide who took the call and bluntly asked if she could arrange an interview with Minister Fallahian prior to his return to Iran. Caught off guard, the aide denied the minister's presence at the chancellery, which prompted Hufelschulte to recite from the itinerary. The flustered aid placed him on hold, only to return and say that she could not comment on the matter, and hung up.

At eleven in the morning, Bernd Schmidbauer welcomed Minister Fallahian to a small meeting with only a handful of attendees, having dispensed with reception ceremonies lest they compromise the confidentiality of the visit.

Schmidbauer suspected why Fallahian was there. He had foreseen such a day and tried to avert it long ago. He was an advocate of improving relations with Iran, but he was also intelligence chief, and thus privy to the full extent of Tehran's notorious acts. In July 1992, during a private meeting with senior Iranian officials, he had issued this warning.

"You must make me one promise! Iran cannot commit an assassination on Germany's soil. That would place an insurmountable hurdle in the way of our efforts on your country's behalf, especially the Critical Dialogue initiative."

The members of the mission had given their word. But like all things that perish in transit, the promise, too, withered upon touchdown in Tehran.

What passed between Bernd Schmidbauer and Ali Fallahian that morning would remain a mystery for months to come. Only after severe scrutiny, and the costliest scandal of Schmidbauer's career, were the minutes of the meeting released. In it Fallahian, cryptically referred to only as "F," had come to make a bargain with Bonn.

> *. . . F said that Iran has helped Germany a great deal. For instance, Iran pressured the Hamadi clan to release the German hostages held in Lebanon. To return the favor, the consulting minister [Bernd Schmidbauer] should help with an upcoming criminal trial in Berlin in which Iran is wrongly accused. F asked: How do you plan to stop this trial from starting?*

The consulting minister rejected the idea of meddling in the legal proceedings. He said: Berlin's courts are in the hands of the justice ministry and function independently of other government bodies. There is no room or possibility for deal making. We can help you by trying to minimize the political costs of the trial, and our best hope is for Tehran to never conduct such an operation in Germany or Europe.

The Iranian side consistently tried to put the Berlin trial back on the table. Both the consulting minister and his adviser rejected the idea each time. F's request to provide the defendants with diplomatic immunity was also rejected. After repeated references to Iran's past aid to Germany, F presented a list of other offers if only the Mykonos trial could be on the table. The consulting minister once again rejected any deals or exchanges that would have to be based on the trial. He said that he had no such powers and could not represent Germany in the way the minister expected him to.

The words "no such powers" had inflamed the minister, who expected that Germany's highest-ranking intelligence official to be perfectly capable, if he so willed, of putting an end to any trial. Time and again, Ali Fallahian had crossed the boundaries of military life into civilian, from religious life into political—sometimes remaining in both capacities at once. He therefore believed his European equals to be capable of doing the same. Born and raised in Isfahan, a city renowned for cunning peddlers, Ali Fallahian had expected to haggle, but walk away with a deal. With the final rejection, the minister's youthful features—his childlike gap-toothed grin and dark, bushy beard that reached the periphery of his eye sockets—could no longer hide his fury. A man of medium height and a robust and hefty demeanor, the minister rose from his seat and strode out, clearly incensed, his clerical robe flaring in the wind of his rushing feet.

Bruno Jost spent part of that morning reviewing his file on Minister Fallahian. As a judge, Fallahian had presided over summary trials and ordered the executions of hundreds of political prisoners who had fallen under his Sharia rule, earning him the title of "butcher." What implicated him in the September 17 murders—the employment of numerous interlocutors, like Darabi, by his ministry notwithstanding—was the vow he had made in a television interview, nine days before the Berlin murders.

> *We have a special unit to take down the opposition. We've identified their central committees, neutralized and arrested them. At the moment, we have no opposition inside the country. They've all been forced to flee. But overseas, we keep them under surveillance. We've infiltrated their ranks and watch them constantly. We've dealt and continue to deal decisive blows to them within our borders and beyond. For example, we have seriously paralyzed the Democratic Party of Kurdistan and are not yet done with them.*

Some of the most incriminating details had been proudly offered by the minister himself. Passages from Fallahian's own autobiography glorified what others would have agonized to bury. In the effusive prose of an adolescent, he had mapped out his brutal origins. Born in 1949 and raised in a religious family, the minister, referring to himself in the third person, wrote of his first encounter with Islam.

> *The heat of faith began to sizzle in his chest and consume him so early on that he had to seek a remedy, which he found in the heat of love he felt in the company of masters such as Navab Safavi.*

The innocent lovesick impression of the line lifted instantly when Jost learned that Navab Safavi had been the founder of Iran's Fadaiyan Islam, the group responsible for several assassinations in the 1950s.

To call Fallahian a counterpart of Schmidbauer or other European intelligence chiefs was not wrong but it was misleading. In the early years after the 1979 revolution, he had been the Ayatollah's Proteus and had morphed into whatever his master had needed.

His career reached its climax after he left his post as the head of housing and sewage and became special prosecutor. In his appointment letter, the Ayatollah wrote, "Because your honor is familiar with the work of the counterrevolutionaries in every mask and every disguise, it is only fitting to put you in charge so that with the exercise of Islamic law you give evil its due."

And due he gave, on numerous occasions, one of which was an assault against an opposition stronghold, where *he destroyed forty of their homes within twenty-four hours.*

Noon had almost arrived. Jost put on his coat and prepared to leave. In his office Tony von Trek began to do the same. He put on his holster. It was all that appeared forbidding about the lanky and mild-mannered commissioner. In the pocket of his trench coat, he kept a pair of handcuffs. There had been no calls from his superior thus far, and so without objection from above he saw no obstacles to prevent the controversial arrest. But the phone rang. Bonn vehemently objected to his plan. The minister, after all, was a guest of the state.

Ali Fallahian slipped Jost's grasp, but his visit did not remain a secret. Hufelschulte's call upset the peace at the chancellery, where the efforts to contain the news were quickly replaced with ones to control its damage. By that afternoon, Bernd Schmidbauer was forced to hold a news conference. Every reporter posed a variation of the same question—the subject of the discussion with Fallahian. Flashing a politician's insincere smile, Schmidbauer said the meeting had a "purely humanitarian nature."

Asked if he thought Tehran had been the culprit behind the killings as the federal prosecutor alleged, he dismissed the allegation, saying "Those who know the facts would draw vastly different conclusions."

Public opinion quickly turned against Schmidbauer for having accepted the visitors in the first place, though it would be months before the damning evidence would emerge. The press, dubbing him "Minister 008," mocked him for his clumsiness, for being the secret service chief who had failed to keep a simple visit secret. In 1992, the pained countenance of the survivors had compelled journalists to write about the case. By 1993, what compelled them was the look of duplicity on the faces of their own politicians. Schmidbauer had been a champion of the Critical Dialogue with Iran, and the German public, who well knew the burdens of a guilty national conscience, began to question both him and the enterprise. The trial was increasingly becoming a test of the nation's integrity, and the headlines reflected it.

The Mykonos Trial Is a Trial of Germany's Justice System.
Is Our Judiciary Truly Independent?
Are German Laws and Judges for Sale?

The domestic uproar inspired international criticism, including American and British demands for an investigation. Fellow journalists throughout Europe, buoyed by their German colleagues, began to revisit the "unsolved murders" of several other Iranian exiles across the continent. By late October of 1993, even New Yorkers were following the news of the minister's "secret" visit in their daily papers.

Mr. Fallahian and Mr. Schmidbauer may have discussed a deal under which the accused killers now on trial in Berlin would be freed or given lenient treatment. In exchange, the Iranians were said to have offered to free several Germans being held in Iran. Some accounts said Mr. Fallahian had also raised the possibility of releasing Ron Arad, an Israeli Air Force navigator believed to be held by pro-Iranian forces in Lebanon, and lifting the death sentence issued by Ayatollah Ruholla Khomeini and confirmed by the present Iranian Government against the novelist Salman Rushdie . . .

On Hans Joachim Ehrig's desk, the pink stack of "While You Were Away" slips was piled high. The victims' lead attorney was already consumed by the trial although it had not yet begun. Nothing in Ehrig's lawyerly conduct or the nearly industrial appearance of his office betrayed the romantic beneath. Only those who had known him as an idealistic university student in the 1960s could see that with Mykonos, Ehrig had found the kind of case that had lured him into law in the first place.

For the reporters who had inundated him with requests, he struck a cool pose, which made his fierce statements all the more compelling: "This visit is a slap in the face of the investigators. It sullies Germany's reputation in the eyes of the world," he told a reporter at a press conference one day after the news of the secret visit broke. "It appears as if economic interests with Iran overshadow all other concerns against our own ethical values."

"How should Bonn have reacted?"

The few sentences Ehrig offered were not only poignant. They were also visionary. In them, he concisely summarized the past and the potential future mistakes that those involved with the case could be prone to make, and more. He also charted his own expectation for the course of the trial and beyond.

"Arresting Fallahian would have been too much to hope for, but pressuring him was not. Bonn should not have accepted the visit. If this indeed proves to be a government-sanctioned killing, all diplomatic ties must be cut off. I hope everyone working on this case can remain independent and not allow the voice of the *higher masters* to echo in their heads. If this trial moves forward the way it should, it can prevent other such assassinations from taking place."

To the chorus of criticism, the exiles added their voices in the way they knew best. They issued a flyer calling for a demonstration and posted it on the entrance of their businesses in Berlin—cafés, grocery stores, restaurants, and travel agencies. Its tone captured the tenor of a people searching for a voice.

> ***A CALL TO ALL***
> ***Fellow Free-Thinking Iranians!***
> *More than a year since the four opposition members were murdered at the Mykonos restaurant by the elements of the regime, the accused will finally stand trial at 9 a.m. on the morning of Thursday, October 28, 1993. In light of certain recent visits, it is incumbent upon us to condemn the efforts of some German politicians who, directly or indirectly, wish to influence the outcome. There will be a protest march in front of the courthouse where the trial will be held.*

Warning: According to the office of the chief federal prosecutor's instructions, anyone wishing to attend the trial must present a valid ID or passport.

Organized by: The Organization in Defense of Refugees

Place: Northern corner of Turm between Rathenauer and Wilsnaker, reachable by UBahn #9: Turm Street stop

Starting time: 8:00 a.m. on October 28, 1993

That morning, Shohreh's thirteen-month lethargy lifted. She awoke to find herself looking ahead to the breaking day. A strange energy percolated in her veins. Fear, anticipation, and excitement had fused and revived her battered spirit. In the lightless universe where she had been adrift, there was a glimmer at last.

Against all logic, she felt certain that those who had killed her husband were mighty enough to blow up the court and everyone inside it, including her. What she most wanted to prevent would come true: Sara would become an orphan. Yet not even for Sara's sake could she keep away from the court. She could not expect others to brave what she would not brave herself. So the night before, she visited two of Noori's old colleagues and signed Sara's custody over to them, just in case.

The promise of the trial had uplifted her, though she had no hope of victory. She wanted the chance to shame her husband's killers, to show herself standing—unafraid and defiant—before the inevitable secret deal between Iran and Germany would knock her off her stand. Her expectations of the trial were dismal. She had never seen the inside of a courtroom. What she knew of it was what she had seen in the movies—all ceremony and no soul. She expected a corrupt, corpulent, ill-tempered and wigged man to knock a gavel on a bench from time to time. The rumors that Darabi had retained Berlin's best attorneys terrified her. Besides, she could not fathom Fallahian having left Germany without a prize to boast of at home. A deal had already been made, she told Ehrig the day the news of the visit broke.

"Germany is a democracy," he assured her. "No one here, no matter how mighty, is above the law." She had not challenged him, only flashed a deferential smile, but pitied his guileless confidence.

For Sara, all of the mother's cynicism came undone. Shohreh was all enthusiasm when describing the trial to her daughter. A fairy tale was about to unfold: The accused—wretched, tattered, and surely remorseful—could only hope for leniency because their guilt would be a foregone conclusion. The unforgiving judge—Solomon disguised as a middle-aged German—would instantly see through their wickedness. Just as instantly, the attorneys for the accused—acned, avaricious, and stuttering to boot—would be unanimously loathed. Whereas their attorneys, noble and winsome, would triumph within weeks if not days and ride with them in a chariot into the sunset. Sara delighted in her mother's tale, and never questioned the plausibility of a chariot on Berlin's busy streets, or the significance of sunset, which, being too young to know Hollywood endings, signaled only bedtime to her. She set off for school that morning, barely fitting into her own skin.

Shohreh stared into her wardrobe. She did not want to look like a casual observer. The court would be her battlefield and she was dressing for combat. She needed armor, not mere clothes. She took her black skirt and sweater set off the hanger once again. Black, all black, from head to toe, would be her uniform for as long as the trial would last. Black, not simply as a symbol of her grief, but as the essence of the truth, the absoluteness of her need for justice.

She set out for the courthouse. The highest security measures had been put in effect for the opening day of the trial. All traffic within a one-mile radius of the building had been diverted since dawn. All vehicles, even bicycles, were banned from parking nearby. Antiriot vans had been stationed in the neighborhood. Police officers, grenades clipped to their waists, guarded the area. The local shopkeepers—pawnbroker, Turkish restaurateur, legal bookseller—locked their doors and watched the frenzy from inside. There was no view of the main doors, only the backs of the crowd wishing to get inside. The queue snaked around the block. Dozens of reporters were on the steps pointing their microphones in the direction of the attorneys as they passed by. A few were interviewing the expatriates in the queue.

Shohreh arrived flanked by two attorneys so she would not face the mayhem alone.

The eight o'clock march was on. Nearly two hundred exiles were milling about waiting to begin, intently watching the movements of the wiry, quick-footed man who commanded them. There were still placards to hand out, banners to unfurl, order to bring to the disarrayed ranks. Moments before the strike of eight, many were chasing him with their last-minute questions. But Hamid Nowzari, a veteran organizer, simply raised the bullhorn to his mouth and shouted the first slogan:

Schmidbauer, Schmidbauer: Keep your hands off our court!

His left fist revolved in the air several times, and the marchers quickly gathered in a circle in the middle of Turm Street. They marched and chanted, settling into the rhythm of their orderly rebellion. Pausing at the entrance, Shohreh waved to the marchers and exchanged a grateful glance with Hamid. Years ago, she and Hamid had founded a group to see new refugees through their difficult time of transition. Now that group had come to see her through a difficult time of her own.

When the cast of attorneys cleared the front stairs, the reporters turned to the marchers. Their savvy conductor, aware of the attention, quickly changed the slogan. He raised his right hand and half the crowd shouted, *Where are the killers?*

Then he turned to his left—they erupted in an answer, *Hiding in Tehran!*

The reporters' pens rushed across their notepads. The red light of the rolling cameras blinked. Inside the building, the trial was about to begin. Outside on the street, the verdict was already in.

14

> Iran is a nation with 2,500 years of history and an incurable forty-five-minute delay.
>
> —*Hadi Khorsandi, exiled Iranian satirist*

If the venue was any indication, then the Mykonos trial was destined to be one of the continent's greatest trials. It was to be held in the largest courtroom of its kind in Europe, Berlin's High Criminal Court. Under the gilded entrance arch, there is a courtyard of white marble columns rising from a red granite floor and encircling a grand staircase. Daylight streamed in through an oval-shaped window at the midway landing of the stairs, perhaps an architectural metaphor—an all-seeing eye, not of God, but of law.

The interior of the courthouse affected the viewer the way great cathedrals do—invoking reverence. But in Moabit court, reverence and awe were reserved for justice. The ornate, vaulted ceilings, the statues of sword-bearing warriors against the walls, the painted panes of glass at the end of the corridors, and the recurring columns flanking the antechambers that overlooked the courtyard created a beauty, whose vastness dwarfed the viewer. What the kaiser, Wilhelm II, had envisioned as "the Palace of Justice" in the late 1800s was a building that would symbolize the power of his government. A century later, the Iranian expatriates entering it were daunted by its regal quality—by the luster of a tradition whose substance they had yet to know or trust.

The daily drama inside the building matched its appearance. Four million files circulated through the halls. Three hundred judges worked and oversaw hundreds of staff serving them. Much of that work was still being done the way it was in the late nineteenth century. Sacks of mail arrived in the mailroom every morning, where clerks stamped each piece and distributed them through numerous small cubbies. Larger correspondence was placed in bins and rolled to their destinations through the tiled corridors. Deep in the building's underbelly was a warehouse, a legal bazaar of sorts. In its 1,400-square-meter space, knives and guns lay alongside locks of hair and soiled handkerchiefs; a depository of all the evidence presented in the trials over the years: 1906—the trial of a Berlin man who, disguising himself as a policeman, had massacred an entire neighborhood; 1967—the trial of the city police officers accused of shooting Benno Ohnesorg, the German student bystander killed at a demonstration against Iran's Shah Mohammad Reza Pahlavi; 1977—the trials of the members of the terrorist group Red Army Faction; 1992—the trials of the Communist leaders of the former East Germany. To know the history of the Moabit courthouse was to know the history of a nation's struggle for civility.

The building's main entrance was reserved for staff, attorneys, reporters, witnesses, and members of the victims' families. Audience members entered, if they got to enter at all, through an ordinary backdoor that opened onto a labyrinth of dusty, graffiti-riddled stairways, each leading to a different courtroom. Surveillance at the threshold was punishing, to deter casual and undetermined visitors. Security officers gathered the contents of the visitors' pockets into small bins. The wands traced the outline of the incoming bodies, then the hands retraced the same path so thoroughly that it brought color to the subjects' cheeks. Shoes and socks came off next, where some spectators hid a pen and a piece of paper, hoping to circumvent the ban on note taking during the proceedings. Those who intended to remain in the courtroom for the whole day swore off liquids of all kinds since a trip to the lavatory required reentry and a repeat of the grueling process.

The Mykonos trial was assigned to Hall 700, the largest of the courtrooms, the one reserved for the most notable cases. In daytime, the room was drenched in iridescent light that streamed in through the stained-glass wall. Even at night, at its most empty, Hall 700 was not a quiet room, for the sounds of the busy street below seeped in through the glass wall. Two grand chandeliers, each a round beam of eighteen vertically conjoined gold and opaque cups, lit the room, but they lit most brightly the moss-colored tables beneath. Placed side-by-side and dotted with microphones, the tables were for the team of six Arab and Persian translators. Behind them, at either side, two bulletproof glass cages were built for the defendants. The cages were the first alterations that Hall 700 had undergone in many decades.

That Thursday morning of October 28, 1993, the judges stepped through their cloakroom and arrived at the bench. Everyone rose. Chief Judge Kubsch sat in the center, his deputy and his reporter on his either side.

Germany's judiciary was a rigorous enterprise that shunned frills and flair. It disappointed those seeking fame and glory, rewarded only modesty and hard work. The judges were not political appointees, and so less vulnerable to outside influence. They were career professionals who had chosen to become judges upon graduation from law school. They were evaluated by their peers, promoted only for merit according to standards set by those peers. In its anonymity, becoming a judge was like choosing priesthood; in severity, it was like serving in the army.

There was no jury in Judge Kubsch's courtroom. The fate of the trial would not depend on the random assortment of laymen. Nor was there the worry that those deciding the case might not be able to duly understand and assess the facts. Nothing could be confusing to, or misunderstood by, a team of professionals. Therefore, no evidence had to be excluded. The five judges who entered the court that morning would not play referee to two dueling sides. Dueling sides do not exist where the prosecutor is an impartial investigator. These judges had studied the case closely for weeks and come to ask their own questions and make their own judgments. They conducted the proceedings not with the decorous formalities of most other courtrooms, but with the fluidity of a debate. Interruptions and interjections, even by the defendants, regarded as contempt elsewhere, were mostly tolerated in the trial where Judge Kubsch and his team presided.

Once everyone had settled into their seats, the chief judge set the routine he would follow at the start of each session. He leaned into his microphone and announced, "Today we begin hearings on case number 2StE2/93."

Then he looked to his right where Bruno Jost and his deputy sat, dressed in their crimson robes. He acknowledged Jost.

"The prosecution is present."

Then he took stock of the defendants in the glass cages and added, "The defendants are present."

Next, he turned to the team of lawyers for the accused.

"The counsels are here."

And lastly, he nodded to the court translators stationed at the foot of his bench, and reminded them, "The interpreters are also present and abide by their oath to translate accurately and truthfully."

Shohreh sat beside Ehrig. Across from her, clad in black robes, were twelve attorneys representing the accused. The more animated and flamboyant of the accused, Yousef and two other accomplices, were quarantined in one glass cage against the wall she faced. Behind her, Darabi and Rhayel sat in another glass cage. At the far end of the hall, beyond a wooden parapet, several rows of benches were allocated to reporters and spectators. The small balcony above them, once used by the kaiser when he dropped in to observe a trial, had been cordoned off.

On that first day, the audience section was filled to capacity. Seventy viewers, friend and foe—Iranians who knew the dead seated alongside the Lebanese relatives of the accused. For the Iranians, the trial was a bittersweet occasion of both shame and relief. On display before the public's eye was the ordeal that had driven them into exile. There was shame in all that had emerged, but the attention was anodyne. They had not come expecting to win or lose. They had not come expecting anything. Being in that room, their long-standing suffering was receiving its due. Being there, alone, vindicated them, lifted and uplifted them. They had come not knowing what the next day would bring. For all they knew, the first day could be the last. That such a day had come at all was what mattered to them.

The opening day the attorneys for the defense steered the course of the proceedings. They entered a series of motions asking to postpone the trial. They claimed not to have had enough time to fully study the case. They accused the prosecution of not having surrendered all the evidence. They argued that the trial had been founded on faulty charges made in a misguided indictment. Quoting "the most knowledgeable man in the republic," they repeated the words of Bernd Schmidbauer: "Those who know the facts would draw vastly different conclusions."

The trial could not begin, these attorneys argued, until the court had heard from Bernd Schmidbauer. The judges granted the defense's demand by issuing a subpoena for Germany's chief of intelligence. But the trial would not stop for a single witness. The court resumed and then again yielded to new motions. Each time Judge Kubsch called for a recess, the five judges rose, their black chairs swiveling in their wake, and marched to their spartan chamber to consult. What lessened the day's boredom for the audience, on whom the legal details in debate were lost, were the intermittent howls of Yousef complaining of a toothache. Finally, Chief Judge Kubsch adjourned to allow Yousef to go to the infirmary. So ended the lackluster day that had begun with so much promise.

The interruptions continued into the second day. Each time the chief judge called on Jost to recite his indictment, the attorneys for the accused entered yet another motion to delay the opening. Once, even Jost himself refused to begin.

From his corner of the courtroom, the prosecutor had spotted Parviz, one of his key witnesses, in the audience, whose presence prior to testifying would have compromised him as a witness. Jost told the judge that he could not begin with a certain spectator inside the courtroom. Before the judge asked the person's name, Parviz walked out.

By the afternoon, Judge Kubsch's supply of patience had dried up. In his mild yet firm manner, he rejected all other motions. He called on Jost to begin. When the prosecutor finally finished reciting the indictment, the trial had truly begun.

The first witness debuted just as he had last promised. "Everything I've said so far has been a lie, but today I'm going to tell the truth," Yousef Amin bellowed from the witness stand, then, addressing Judge Kubsch he added, "I've been saving it for you, Judge."

He pointed to the bulletproof glass cage where Rhayel and Darabi sat and shouted as the voices of the translators trailed his, "Those are not the real killers. The real killers are a team of Iraqi Kurds still out there, on the loose."

When the judges asked why he had lied before, Yousef blamed the investigators.

"They tried to trick me. You'd think I was an ambassador the way they were treating me at first. They gave me money, put me up in a hotel, and promised me stuff," then, turning dramatically toward his old friends, he continued, "If only I named the good men over there."

That afternoon, the witness told a story far more amusing than deft. He was the hero of his own legend, a victim of cunning interrogators. He had resisted valiantly until they were driven to rage. After losing any hope of his surrender, the mask had fallen from their evil faces and they had begun abusing him. What blame still remained, he placed at the feet of his translators, who did not have proper mastery of either Arabic or the particular dialect he spoke, or they were merely spies.

"Spies, you say, Mr. Amin?" one judge asked.

"Yes! Two hundred percent spies, Judge. With ID cards and everything. I saw their badges with my own eyes," he replied.

On the second day of his testimony, Yousef took the drama to new heights. Returning to the stand, he accused his attorney of both incompetence and spying for several Western intelligence services at once. If the contradiction in his claim was obvious to Yousef, he showed no sign of it. He refused to speak as long as his attorney remained in the room.

Yousef's chief counsel resigned immediately. But unlike several others who would be hired and fired by the defendants throughout the trial, he did not simply quit. He summed up his knowledge of Yousef and his own predicament in a brief statement that he delivered before a group of reporters.

> *I fear the words I am about to speak would further confirm Mr. Amin's distrust in me, yet I am compelled to speak them. I cannot allow criminals to rob me of my humanity by preventing me from doing what's right, no matter the price. Now that I no longer represent Yousef Amin, I can give my true assessment of him and the bind in which he finds himself. Mr. Amin is a pawn in the hands of Iran's fanatical regime which, even in prison and courtroom, keeps its firm grip on him. I know that I am breaking my client's confidence by speaking so, but my greater duty is to the truth.*
>
> *Respectfully,*
> *Luther Bunegart*

A new counsel was quickly assigned to Yousef, but Yousef's conduct did not change. His judges seemed to be sitting not at the bench, but in a bulletproof cage across from his own. The charge he most earnestly repudiated was not murdering four men but collaborating with the investigators.

After five days of testimony, when it became clear that he could not undo his earlier confessions, he gloomily returned to his seat.

Darabi and Rhayel took the stand next, but they refused to answer any questions and were dismissed within minutes.

"Can they get away with this?" Shohreh whispered to Ehrig, who assented with a nod. The less the accused spoke, the more terrified she grew. She felt besieged from every corner. To her left and right were the attorneys she hardly knew. Behind her and before her, men whom she feared and loathed perched in two glass cages. She saw their silence as a sign of their power and became ever more certain that something would soon end the trial, perhaps a deal, perhaps a bomb. She diligently recorded the details of the proceedings, as if her notes were all that were to remain of the trial. Her hand was busy throughout the day, running across the pages of her pad, hardly leaving any margins for the occasional exclamation and question marks—the rare signs of her own reflections. In the moments of quiet, during the recesses, she found time to interject a line or two in parentheses, a commentary summed up in an expletive. She remained faithful to the exchanges, meticulously punctuating her sentences, noting the times of the testimonies down to the minute, peeking over the translators' shoulders to check for the spelling of unfamiliar names. Unlike the judges, she was not keeping these notes for some future deliberation. All she wanted was to know the details of her husband's death. She wanted to bear his history, the way she had once borne his progeny.

In the midst of writing one day, she heard the chief judge call her name. She lifted her head, bewildered. Ehrig leaned into her and said, "It's your turn."

Her moment to testify had come and, though she had long known that it would, the reality startled her just the same.

"Me? But . . . what will I say? I'm not ready," she whispered, anxiety rising in her.

"Just answer the questions. That's all you need to do," he murmured, tugging gently at her arm to lift her along as he stood.

On the stand, she did her best to be a good witness. She kept to the facts, as the lawyers had advised. At times, she shut her eyes to concentrate on the details of the memories she was asked to revisit. She did not cry, even when the questions summoned gasps of sympathy from the audience.

"What did your husband say before leaving that night?"

She had paused to hold back tears and answered without breaking.

"Your honor, he said not to wash the dishes because he was going to do them when he returned."

"Is that all?"

"Then he kissed me and said, 'See you shortly, little lady.' "

She had done well until then but, shifting in her seat, she caught a glance of Darabi on whose lips she detected a smirk. In an instant, the smirk undid her composure. She turned deaf. Her fury was reignited and the room blurred. She saw no one but the man with the hooked nose, balding head, stubbly beard, and deep-set eyes, grinning triumphantly.

She faced Darabi and began addressing him as if they had been in conversation all their lives.

"I'll get you, Mr. Darabi. You may think you're a Muslim, but you're nothing but a disgrace to our religion. I'll show you I'm the better Muslim. I'll fight you and your bosses for as long as I breathe. I—"

Judge Kubsch interrupted her.

"You can't speak this way in this courtroom, Mrs. Dehkordi! No one's guilt or innocence has yet been proven. You may step down!"

Shohreh was shaken, above all, by the judge's austere tone. Who was this caped man who did not bow to her venerable grief, and commanded her so? She pursed her lips lest the thought slip through them. Her attorneys had told her to trust the judge. Kubsch was a veteran who had presided over some of the toughest cases of political crime in recent years. When the former heads of East Germany appeared before him on charges of treason, Judge Kubsch had, after weeks of deliberation, declared the trial altogether unconstitutional. The decision caused a sensation, prompting a nationwide debate. The case was referred to the Constitutional Court, and was upheld—setting a precedence. A victory so great would have inflated most egos. But he had celebrated the landmark event by returning to the bench the next day.

Other survivors took to the stand and felt similarly unsettled. For Mehdi, the feeling set in when Judge Kubsch's deputy asked, "Here, in the transcripts of your statement to the police on the night of September 17th, you say the killers were members of Iran's Revolutionary Guards. Do you have any evidence the court hasn't seen?"

"I say this based on years of observation. I've no doubt the regime is behind this. The Guards or the intelligence ministry or both carried it out."

Judge Kubsch interjected. "Let me remind you that this is a court of law. We're not interested in your political analysis. Please state what facts or evidence you have to back your claim."

Modesty kept Mehdi from saying that he was an accomplished engineer and a beloved athlete. He simply said, "You see, I've no other enemies. There's no one else who wants to kill me."

"And do you have any evidence to prove the Iranian regime wants to kill you? If you don't, please don't speculate."

To ask Mehdi to document so obvious a presence as the inescapable menace that had forced him into exile and haunted him still was to ask that he show the air he breathed. He was offended, but silenced, too. That was the trouble all the exiles would face on the witness stand—how to carve out something tangible from the indurate, misshapen heap of their thirteen years of suffering for those who did not know their experiences.

The scrutiny felt equally harsh to Parviz when his turn came, as if only his errors were the subject of inquiry.

"A few months ago you went to the BKA headquarters in Meckenheim and identified Yousef Amin as the lead shooter at the restaurant that night. How could you say with confidence that Mr. Amin was the man who had shot at your party?"

"Whatever Yousef Amin was doing and wherever he may have been, inside or outside, he was carrying out Tehran's orders," he responded stubbornly.

"This you also say with confidence. Could you tell the court why you are so confident?"

"We in the Iranian opposition have been hounded by the regime for so long that we sense things in a way that's impossible to put into words."

The judge, clearly not convinced, watched Parviz silently for a few moments.

Parviz tried again. "Because many Iranians in the diaspora have been murdered, and whenever a case was properly investigated, Tehran was implicated. Very simple! Take the 1989 murder in Vienna . . ."

The judge raised his hand and stopped him in mid-sentence to put an entirely different question to him. "In your opinion, how did the killers know about the meeting on Thursday?"

"I think they had a mole."

"Do you *think* this, or know this?"

"I think this. I don't have any evidence."

"You said earlier that the killers were near the restaurant at nine-thirty. How do you know that?"

"From the police reports that have been in the papers."

"Have you read all the police's findings?"

"What's been printed, yes. The rest, no, although heaven knows it's not for lack of trying."

Suddenly, Yousef stood up and shouted, "What I want to know is how my pictures have ended up in your hands. That's what I want to know. The police are leaking my pictures. I'm sure of it."

Parviz welcomed the break. He raised his arms, looked up at the ceiling, and said, "You ought to ask Allah how that might have happened."

A long day of grueling testimony was about to end and the judge still had many questions for the witness. He told Parviz to return the next day.

"I'm afraid I can't," Parviz said, surprising the court.

Judge Kubsch frowned and asked why. Parviz reluctantly explained, "Because my daughter needs me, your honor."

The previous morning, he had heard a loud thud from Salomeh's bedroom. She had fainted yet again. Her pulse had dropped. He had rushed her to the clinic, and the cardiologist had finally ordered a pacemaker to be implanted in her.

"She's probably having heart surgery tomorrow. I must be at her side," Parviz continued.

"Don't you have anyone else who could accompany her in your place?" the chief judge pressed without a hint of emotion.

"Sure I do. I've got a dozen people who could be with her. But as her father, I *want* to be with her," Parviz ended, clearly discomfited by having to speak publicly about so private a matter.

The room fell silent. After a pause, Judge Kubsch said, "In that case, please call me tonight after you find out if the surgery is on or not for tomorrow. If it isn't, I'd like you to be here tomorrow."

Parviz called the judge at home that evening. The surgery had been postponed and he could return for another day of testimony. In the absence of microphones and the decorum of the courtroom, Judge Kubsch's voice sounded soft through the receiver.

"How did the visit to the doctor go? Is your daughter better?"

For a few moments, the business of the trial pressed on neither of them, as they talked one man to the other, father to father. Parviz's refusal had been unfathomable to the judge. For years Mrs. Kubsch had been asking her husband to take a few days off for a family vacation, but each time he told her there would be plenty of time for vacations in his retirement. His work was treated as sacred by the household. His son and daughter walked gingerly if they found him at his desk inside his study. Only when they had trouble with their studies of Latin or Greek would their father would attend to them. For all other subjects or troubles he entrusted matters to his wife, who had dedicated herself to the three *K*s: Kinder, Kirche, and Kuche—or children, church, and kitchen. He performed the duty that was also his passion. It was what he expected everyone to do, before Parviz refused him.

The conversation, warm and thoughtful, endeared the judge to Parviz, though he, sworn to skepticism, would not acknowledge his thawing apprehension toward Kubsch to anyone, not even to himself. He was still at war and could not chance dismantling the barricades within.

In the remaining weeks of 1993, Noori's friends who had frequented the restaurant took the stand.

"Do you wish to take the religious or the secular oath?" Judge Kubsch asked the witnesses, who usually chose the secular oath, since their foes, the defendants, had sworn to God.

"I swear to tell the truth and nothing but the truth."

They came expecting to win the court's sympathy, certain that their testimony would deliver a blow to the accused. Instead, they found themselves sternly examined. The judges no longer asked who they thought was behind the killings. They surprised the court by raising a subject the witnesses had hoped to have buried with the corpses of the dead. The two names the expatriates dreaded rang in the chief judge's microphone. "Have you heard the names Nejati and Sedighi?"

Until 1991—twelve years after the rise of Ayatollah Khomeini—the Iranian opposition in Berlin had, despite all the rifts within it, spoken with one voice against the regime in Tehran. But that year, the sudden appearance of two men tore the community apart. Just as Germany's foreign minister had returned from his visit to Tehran vowing to mend the relations between

Europe and Iran, Nejati and Sedighi, using the disarming pseudonyms of "the savior" and "the virtuous" in Persian, had been assigned as envoys of the Iranian president to mend the relations between the expatriates and their homeland. From the Center for Strategic Studies at the president's office, the two senior officials were to deliver President Rafsanjani's message of reconciliation to the diaspora.

Berlin had been their first stop. They had contacted several leading members of the opposition and invited them to a "dialogue." What the subject of that dialogue would be, or how it would come about, was unclear. Yet the proposal had excited most exiles. Noori had called it the historic opening everyone had been waiting for, and gathered friends every Wednesday night at Mykonos to decide the terms of that dialogue. Some had already talked to the envoys on the telephone and believed meeting them privately was harmless, but others believed the meetings had to be held in public.

But a few thought this was the regime's latest scheme to infiltrate the ranks of the opposition and destroy them from within. Whether that was the intention of the envoys or not, their appearance did, indeed, bitterly divide the opposition. Because both men had vanished after September 1992, rumors that they had merely been the first pieces in the premeditated assassination plot had spread. Few remembered feeling optimistic about them, and fewer still would admit to having met them.

Given this history, the testimony of the several exiles who took to the stand was a blur of incoherent statements.

Exile witness 1 said, "Yes, your honor. I've heard of them. I know many people received phone calls from them, and a few met them."

"Who did they call?"

"I know one person they called, because he told me himself that they did."

"Is this man a politician in the opposition against the regime?"

"He's, er, an activist."

They chafed at the word *politician*. They were not politicians in the same way the judges knew politicians to be. They were disenchanted citizens, paid by no one, seeking neither fame nor glory, hoping to rid themselves of their tyrants. Politics, as they knew, was nothing but penance.

"What was the subject of these meetings and phone calls?"

Exile witness 2 said, "They said they wanted to negotiate a solution to bring the educated back to Iran."

"What was the subject of the conversations with the particular friend who you said told you that he had been contacted by them?"

"Well, I suppose Nejati wanted to show he meant well. He knew every last detail of all our backgrounds. He knew that this guy and his wife had fled Iran on foot years ago without their baby girl. He knew the child was still with her grandparents in Iran, and he offered to reunite them."

"Did he reunite them?"

The witness, seeming ashamed, nodded.

"Where is the child now?"

"Nejati made arrangements and, in a few days, the kid flew to Berlin. She's here now."

"What did the father have to do to return the favor?"

"Nothing, your honor, as far as I know."

"Nothing? Do you mean to say the highest officials of the regime you call evil were simply acting charitably?"

"I, I suppose . . . I don't . . . can't say, your honor."

The next witness took the stand and was asked: "Did you meet with them alone or was this an open meeting with others?"

Exile witness 3 said, "Er . . . I met with them alone, in a hotel."

"What did they want from you?"

"They wanted me to return to Iran to help rebuild the country after the war."

"What is your profession?"

"I'm a veterinarian."

"Was the health of your nation's pets and livestock such a pressing priority to force you to meet with your sworn enemy in secret?"

"Er . . . I thought . . . Well, in my analysis . . ."

"Please, no analysis! Just state the facts."

Only the rambunctious Yousef's interruptions gave these witnesses a reprieve.

"Ah! What is this? They all say 'I can't say.' Why don't we just close it all up and be off to Lebanon already?"

The exiles appeared composed. They were dressed in suits, silk scarves tied around their necks, their temples aglow with silvery sideburns. But the trial exposed their inner disarray. It brought them face to face with the errors they had hoped to keep from the court. They had to admit they were accusing the very regime they, themselves, had helped bring to power. At times, the scrutiny felt so harsh it was as if they were being tried for the parts they had played in a revolution some thirteen years earlier. Only on the witness stand, when they failed to convince the judges of the nobility of their reasons in meeting the envoys, did they begin to see their own gullibility in having met them at all. And when they did, they realized they could no longer expect the judges to believe in their wisdom, or hope to convince them of what they knew. Once they had portrayed their rulers in the dark light where those rulers belonged, they had inevitably painted the landscape of their own failings.

By the year's end, the excitement of the opening days had waned. The tedium of the day-to-day proceedings brought boredom and the benches emptied. Inside the courtroom, everyone settled into a routine. Of all the attorneys representing the victims, Ehrig was the only one in court every day. In their own separate cage, Rhayel and Darabi had grown accustomed to their own silence, as had others in the courtroom. They sat through the long hours keeping themselves from dozing off by doodling, or carving letters and shapes with their pens into their wooden benches.

Bruno Jost, however, was listening. No matter how stellar the quality of his investigation or the evidence on his side, he knew the case would be lost if the argument in the courtroom was lost. He watched the proceedings intently.

He had mastered all the documents contained in the 187 binders on the shelves behind him. By 1994 he knew every detail and pronounced all the Persian and Arab names with a native's ease.

Listen fiercely was, for the most part, all he could do once the trial started. Bruno Jost, the federal prosecutor, the impartial investigator, had done his work. His indictment was in. The rest was for the judges to decide. In the courtroom, it was for the judges to ask the questions, for the judges to measure the strength of his argument, the soundness of his logic. He could, and did, rise from time to time to question a witness or make a statement. But they were detours along the road the judges were paving on their own, albeit using the map of his indictment. Jost, the leading man, had yielded the spotlight to the chief judge.

Judge Kubsch's authority was absolute but somehow also gentle. His subtlety had cast him in a paternal light. Everyone sought his approval. Even at the peak of their exasperation with his scrutiny, witnesses never doubted his fairness. When his wife, fearing retribution, suggested that they unlist their address from the phone book he, knowing his own reputation, dismissed the idea.

"If the terrorists are truly looking for me, they won't need the phone book to find me. All we'd get by unlisting ourselves is to lose the friends who are hoping to find us."

The bench brought out the best in the quiet man who was always lost in thought at home behind his desk or tending to the flower beds, speaking only when addressed. His own son, a law student clerking in the same court, often snuck into the audience section at lunch breaks to watch his reclusive father come to life. Kubsch's bottomless patience drove casual viewers and reporters away. His serenity suffused the courtroom, which, for all the hostility inside, might have otherwise been mayhem. He never raised his voice and was sparing with his words. The expressions of his eyes, enlarged by his spectacles, instructed the witnesses more often than his orders. One day, when a witness kept rambling, he waited till the witness had paused to catch his breath, then he simply pressed his hands down into the air and closed his fists, like a conductor ending a symphony, and the witness plopped to his seat. Even the defiant Rhayel and Darabi showed their regard in their own muted fashion by keeping a lamblike demeanor in his presence.

Yet no one revealed Judge Kubsch's mastery better than Yousef, who sought chaos as his only salvation. Using his full repertoire of physical and verbal stunts, Yousef disrupted the proceedings, hoping to win the forgiveness of his former allies. Sometimes he lay his head on the bench, appearing to nap. At other times, he showed up to court in his underwear only to be sent back to dress himself. He broke into song or complained—of prison food or the clamor in his ward. On a few occasions, he feigned insanity and spoke of stray spirits swinging from the courtroom chandeliers, or whispered to the specks of dandruff on his collar. The room burst into laughter at Yousef's antics, but the chief judge, with a nod or the wave of a hand, pacified him each time.

But even under the reign of Judge Kubsch's civility, the old enmities were hard to contain. Darabi lost a grip on himself from time to time. One morning, when the judges were in their chamber, he finally returned the gaze of an old foe in the audience, someone he had faced off against at numerous rallies over the years. From the first day of the trial, the sight of the spectator had rattled him. Once the crowds began to thin, Darabi had expected to be rid of him. But even when endless legal arguments chased the reporters away, and frost brushed the panes of the stained-glass wall in white, that spectator always showed. Coming in from the cold, he and his two friends huddled against the heater, their gaze fixed on Darabi, who was helpless in his glass cage. Being a prisoner on trial had to be punishing. Being a prisoner on trial under the glare of a longtime enemy accented that punishment with torment.

"You're a dead man, Hamid Nowzari," Darabi hissed from his perch.

"Shut up!" was all the shy, amiable community organizer would say in return.

After leading the demonstration outside the courtroom on the opening day of the trial, Hamid had expected to resume his daily routine. Yet the pleasure of watching Darabi in captivity had drawn him in. The novelty soon wore off, and still he found himself returning day after day. There was something irresistible about Hall 700, though even he did not know what it was. He ran through the heady explanations at first. The trial was historic and he was there to affirm the work of the court through his presence. Or the trial was proving him in the right, so he came to revel in his own good judgment. Hamid and his small band of friends thought President Rafsanjani's promise of reform was nothing but a sham. They had been dismissed by other exiles as idealists who were unable to see a political opportunity—a handful of dinosaurs charging headlong toward extinction. Then the murders had occurred. The champions of reform and reconciliation vanished and the dinosaurs, albeit too desolate to gloat, lived on. But, at thirty-six and after ten years in exile, gloating was not as sweet as it had once been.

For a while he thought he was there for friendship's sake. Together with Shohreh, he had founded the refugee organization that, over the years, had become their home away from home. He figured he was there so Shohreh would not be alone. Yet he knew himself well enough to know that loyalty could have carried him only as far as November, with luck, through the early days of December. When 1994 began to loom and he was still returning to the benches, he realized there was no point asking why he was there. He quit his day job and took on a night shift so he would never have to miss a day of court. Going to court was what he had to do; the reason would reveal itself to him some day.

Thus began the monastic life of Hamid Nowzari, who never set foot in a temple except in foreign lands and not without a camera dangling from his shoulder. He was vigorous. Organizing protests, leading demonstrations, stamping his restless feet to the beat of slogans at rallies suited him. But being useful in a courtroom was something he had to learn. It would be years before he would realize that the trial, indeed justice, was what he had been demanding at all the marches throughout his life. A trial never lasted longer than an hour, as so many who had been political prisoners in Iran had described to him. And a judge was a turbaned cleric in the image of Minister Fallahian to whom their guilt was usually a foregone conclusion. In Hall 700, he watched Judge Kubsch and his team, looked at Bruno Jost, listened to Ehrig's every statement, thinking all the while, *This is the shape of a court, the look of a judge, the sound of a real hearing.*

For the time being, he would be the trial's self-appointed ombudsman, there to monitor the proceedings. No one in the room knew Darabi or Iran as well as he did. An expatriate publication gave him permission to be their representative. The court granted him a press pass with which one of his two other companions entered the reporters' booth and took notes. He and a third listened. Sometimes the band of three drafted an ad hoc press release. Hamid's name always appeared at the bottom after the words, "For more information, please contact." In the evening, they brought the scrawled pages home, typed them up, wrote a summary of the day's events, suggested the next day's highlights, and distributed the report to diaspora publications before heading to work. None of them complained of their drudgeries. The ritual was a labor of love, strangely healing.

As the judges were returning to the bench, Darabi glared and shouted at Hamid once again.

"Your wife's a whore."

This expletive particularly amused Hamid, the bachelor. But the fuming Darabi sounded off again.

"Motherfucker! Your mother's a whore, too."

At those words, Hamid shrank. His lifelong orphanhood, beginning at age five with the loss of his mother and father to cancer within months of each other, made him vulnerable against any allusion to his lineage. He said nothing more, only pushed his hand into the air, as if pushing him away. Darabi sneered, undulating his shoulders, dabbing his forehead with the back of his wrist, striking his best homosexual pose then repeating in a high-pitched voice, "Oh, shut up!"

As the lone woman in the courtroom, Shohreh often wondered what it would be like to be left alone in that room without a single compatriot: Who would ever know her experience—not in its docile German translation, but in its feral Persian original? Who would help her if there was no one present but Germans, especially now that Salomeh's condition was keeping Parviz away?

But this never happened because Hamid was always present. In the early days of the trial, Hamid had gone unnoticed. With his slim frame and deep olive complexion, he was easily overlooked amid the many faces. Then one morning, the attorneys for the accused surprised the court by introducing two new witnesses they wished to present the next day. The move upset Ehrig, who asked to postpone the new testimonies so he could study the witnesses. His request was denied. That evening, the spectator became a volunteer researcher. The names of the witnesses had sounded vaguely familiar to him. He spent the night reading through old magazines, and calling other exiles in Berlin to unearth information about them. In the morning, Ehrig's aides had come up empty. Hamid, however, handed a file to Shohreh with the detailed profiles of the new witnesses. The file elated Ehrig, who waved it in the air beaming at the benches.

From that day forward, Hamid's presence seemed as natural, even as essential, as anyone else's in the room. The translators began to greet him. The courtroom guards looked to him as the master of the audience section. If there was a row, they did not move from their posts. They left it to Hamid to restore order to his own domain.

One afternoon Ehrig finally broke the silence between Hamid and himself. In the courthouse's basement canteen, where the attorneys, witnesses, and reporters ate, he spotted Hamid at his usual table. The silent courtroom visitor was perfectly animated in the canteen. The waiters, overjoyed whenever he entered, ushered him to the "Mykonos corner." The canteen staff who had secretly sworn allegiance to him made the witnesses for the accused suffer for service. They huddled around him to hear the latest installment of the trial's drama, which he had learned to tell with enough suspense to last through dessert—always a bowl of Jell-O.

Ehrig picked up his tray, walked to the Mykonos table, and asked if he could join him. Hamid lifted his head from his newspaper, rested his glasses on his forehead, beamed his winsome smile, and said, "With pleasure!"

He had long wished to reach out to Ehrig but feared he might think him another anti-Tehran proselytizer.

Ehrig quickly got to the point. "Who are you?"

Hamid offered a bite-size autobiography. To Ehrig, who had been in college in the late 1960s when German universities were abuzz with Iranian student activists, Hamid's history rang familiar.

"Tell me, how much longer will you keep at this? How long will you keep coming?" Ehrig asked, gently provoking his new acquaintance.

"Not long. Because it won't go on much longer."

Ehrig, surprised by the response, asked why.

"Iran will buy someone powerful enough and that will be the end," Hamid answered confidently.

Ehrig had little patience for cynicism. There were many corrupt officials for sale, he consented—his tone suddenly declarative—but not everyone in Germany was for sale, certainly he, himself, was not for sale.

"You!" Hamid paused and patted the attorney tenderly on the back. Perhaps ingratiating himself was an art he had been born with, or had mastered years ago as a small orphan at the mercy of adults. Whatever its origins, Hamid disarmed everyone with geniality.

"It's not you, Mr. Ehrig. You're as noble as they come," he reassured the attorney. But Hamid felt certain there were greater political motives, trade interests, that would put an end to the trial. Iran would present an offer Germany could not refuse, something that would make sacrificing justice small in exchange.

"I can't convince you of the outcome I don't myself know. But our judiciary is one of the best in the world."

"For your own, yes. But not for foreigners like us. Fallahian has already struck a deal. It's just a matter of time before they call this whole thing off."

"Still, if you bother to come every day, there must be a tiny flicker of hope somewhere inside you . . ." Ehrig said playfully.

"Hope has nothing to do with it. It's about duty. Someone has to bear witness," Hamid said.

"Ah . . . but hope has got everything to do with it, or else you'd be in a museum looking at relics. When you bother to watch the living as ardently as you do, it's hope driving you to it."

Hamid shook his head and smiled. Ehrig, realizing the argument could not be settled, moved on.

"No matter! This is something only time can tell. For now, there's a lot I don't know about this case, and that gets in the way of my job. Will you help fill me in?"

From that day on, Hamid's bowl of Jell-O was always served with an extra spoon—the second for his newfound lunch companion.

15

From: Minister of Islamic Guidance
To: Employees

Since autographing is an ungodly act from the deposed Shah's era, the Committee for the Promotion of Virtue and Prevention of Vice hereby orders revolutionary sisters and brothers to refrain from signing and, instead, use the Islamic method of fingerprinting. Note: Respected sisters must wrap their index finger in the corner of their veils, so that the direct imprint of their fingertip should not arouse the God-fearing brothers. (fingerprinted: Minister of Islamic Guidance)

—*Hadi Khorsandi, exiled Iranian satirist*

"The court calls Mr. Aziz Ghaffari to the witness stand," announced Judge Kubsch on the morning of January 16, 1994.

Aziz entered the courtroom dressed in a knee-length sheepskin coat. The news of his upcoming testimony had been circulating for days, and the expatriates had flocked to the court to hear him. The benches were filled to capacity again and many more had been turned away. Hamid had arrived earlier than usual to shepherd first-time visitors through surveillance at the entrance and ensure that they made a good impression. In court, he told them, the exiles represented the dead: the more civilly they behaved, the more sympathy the dead inspired.

Whatever the case's legal title, on that day it was the case of "Exiles versus the Restaurant Owner." They were mostly old friends of Aziz who had come hoping to see him redeem himself so they could be at peace with the memories of the company they had once kept at Mykonos. Perhaps the rumors of his betrayal were unfounded. That was what they told themselves as they shuffled to their seats. Aziz had been one of their own and they wished to believe in their own collective innocence.

A great gasp came from the audience as Aziz passed them. He had not come alone. There was an attorney at his side—yet another sign of his guilt. Shohreh, pen and paper in hand, glared at him. Aziz kept his eyes on the judges, avoiding everyone else. His gait had been restored and he walked his old carefree walk. The room was unusually quiet, except for the muffled sound of the men's steps on the padded floor. Silence was always Yousef's cue. Spotting Parviz among the audience after many weeks he crowed at the feisty survivor who had come through the shootings unscathed.

"Oh, look! Rambo's here!"

On the stand, when Aziz was asked whether he wished to testify in German or in Persian, he cast a quick glance at the audience and chose Persian. He knew who his real judges were.

The questioning began. No, he had not been able to identify the attackers in the police lineup. No, he could not recall how the attackers were dressed that night. *His chef missing?* He paused, squinting, as if straining to remember, but alas, no, he could not. *Had he asked anyone to help him cook?* No one at all. *But a fellow exile claimed he had asked long in advance to help him serve the party on Thursday evening.* (That fellow exile and his wife, who had visited Aziz in the hospital, were in the audience, fuming.) He, and everyone else for that matter, could say what they liked. He knew what he knew. Noori had told him Friday night from the start.

"You realize you're a suspect here?" Judge Kubsch asked Aziz.

Aziz nodded and said, without flinching, "Yes, I know."

The judge pressed.

"Can you tell us why you might be a suspect?"

"Well, you should ask this from folks who think me a suspect why," was Aziz's cool rejoinder.

The arrogant response drew another gasp from the audience.

"Well, what reasons did the police offer you for their suspicion? You must have been curious to know," Judge Kubsch said with his usual paternal equanimity. "For instance, you had a sizable stash of cash in a plastic bag in your basement, some five thousand marks—"

"Six thousand," Aziz corrected his inquisitor.

"So I must ask this question, though if you're afraid you might somehow be incriminating yourself, you can refuse to answer it. Where did this money come from?"

"I already gave this information to the police when I was in the hospital and they promised to keep it to themselves," he said what seemed to have been rehearsed.

"Did the police tell you they suspected the cash might be your payment for the intelligence you provided the killers?"

"Yes," he said sharply.

"What did you say?"

"It upset me. They could tell that it did."

"One of the defendants here in this courtroom told the police that he heard one of his teammates say a few days before the assassination, 'When it's all over and done with, he'll sell the place.' The assumption is that the 'he' in that sentence was a reference to you. What do you know about this statement?"

"I've heard that Yousef Amin has said this to the police, but it beats me. I'd wanted to sell the place for a long time."

Hearing his own name, Yousef placed his hand on his chest, bowed, and hollered, "You must give the court the facts. Facts, I tell you!"

There were only a few laughs for everyone was too focused on Aziz to pay Yousef much attention. Other questions poured in.

"Have you heard the name Nejati?"

"Yes."

"What do you know about him?"

"Nothing at all," Aziz answered.

"Okay. Let's leave the subject. Take a look at the defendants, please. Does anyone look familiar to you?"

A few sarcastic sounds rose from the audience:

"Get up!" "Take a good look!" "See a friend?"

"Yes, I know the man to the right, Kazem Darabi," Aziz said, after looking to his left and right to examine the two cages a few times.

"Where did you meet him?"

"At his booth during the Green Week. I and a few others took him on, argued with him."

"Do you know what line of work he's in?"

"No. I never knew him, not even his name."

A few in the audience laughed.

"Well, there's someone here who says Mr. Darabi delivered vegetables and groceries to your store."

"People say what they say. I say what I say," Aziz said nonchalantly.

Shohreh wrote and wrote without lifting her head from her notepad. Parviz's face was flushed, and Hamid kept his eyes on his lap all the while Aziz spoke.

"You bought the restaurant in the early weeks of 1991, but then put an ad in the paper that very summer to sell it. Why?"

"Personal problems."

"You had problems in June that disappeared by August, at which point you decided not to sell the place?"

"I'd come into some money that made it possible to keep going."

"How did you come into this money?"

"I can't say. But," Aziz turned to the audience, "you all know very well how I came to this money. It wasn't clean money but it was not blood money, either."

Aziz's attorney asked to confer with his client, and the two left the room for several minutes. The audience felt divided. Most were appalled by Aziz's calculated performance. A few, still doubtful, thought he might have got the cash through the illegal currency exchange that was rampant in the early days after the fall of the Berlin Wall.

The hubbub had yet to die down when Aziz and his attorney returned and asked to talk privately with Judge Kubsch, who disappeared into his chambers with them. When they returned, the judge announced that he had heard a satisfactory explanation about the source of the cash. The subject was closed.

The questions began again.

"After you placed the ad to sell the restaurant, did any buyers come to see it?"

"A group of Lebanese buyers looked at the restaurant very closely. I said that to the police already."

"Lebanese you said, right? Do you have any reason to suspect that these groups had ulterior motives for looking at the property?"

"They kept coming and going, inspecting the place high and low. I didn't think anything of it at the time but, looking back, well, it may not have been so innocent. Who knows, maybe they were checking the place out."

The audience, aghast at the discovery, stirred again.

"You said that throughout the night of September 17th, you went out of the restaurant every once in a while for air."

"If that's what I said to the police, then that's what I did."

"You said the last time you went out for air was about half an hour before the shooting."

"Then that's what I must have done. I don't remember anything now."

"Did you go out for air ten minutes before the shooting?"

"Doesn't seem logical. No, I didn't."

"After the guests arrived, did you ever leave the restaurant?"

"How could I? It was where I lived and worked. Where would I go?"

Tension rose with every exchange now. Parviz, seated in the front row, leaned over the parapet, listening even more intently.

"In other words, you did not stand in front of the restaurant, either?"

"I'd get out for air. That's all."

"You came out to get air half an hour before the shooting, you said before."

"If I went out at all, which I doubt I did."

"There's a witness who saw you outside, looking distressed, minutes before the shooting."

"Distressed? I can't remember having run into a psychiatrist that night."

"She says that from the time she spotted you outside till the time she heard the gunfire, it took only minutes."

Judge Kubsch reminded the witness once again, "You don't have to answer the question. But if you do, you must tell the truth."

Aziz threw his shoulders up and continued in his cool manner. "Whoever this witness is, I'd like to meet her. Anyway, there are people here who were there that night. They know where I was. Why don't you ask them?"

"Are you denying that you went out of the restaurant minutes before the shooting?"

"Yes."

Judge Kubsch stopped the testimony.

"You may step down, Mr. Ghaffari, but your testimony is not over. I'd like you to hear the next witness before we continue."

The judge had never before interrupted one witness to hear from another. He puzzled everyone when he announced, "The court calls Ms. Renata Kakir to the stand."

Through Hall 700's alternate entrance, a young woman entered. She was dressed in a white medical pantsuit, her work uniform, her auburn hair in a tight bun. A chiropractor, the witness had ridden her bicycle from the subway station to the courthouse that morning. On the night of September 17 she had also ridden from the subway station to her home. She lived on Prager Street, in a fourth-floor apartment that overlooked Aziz's restaurant. Though she had never dined at Mykonos, she bought her cigarettes there and made the kind of small talk neighbors make. That night, like most weeknights, she had taken the ten o'clock train, reached her stop at ten-thirty, and some fifteen minutes had passed by the time she, lugging her bicycle, had emerged from the underground and peddled to her block. Aziz was nervously pacing up and down the sidewalk when she reached her door. The two greeted each other. Then she unlocked the door, pressed the call button, rode the elevator to her flat, and parked her bicycle on the balcony, beneath which she had seen shadows scurrying around. When she stepped into her living room, a deafening sound had boomed under her feet. It had been loud enough to make her wonder if the china shelf in the restaurant had buckled and all the dishes had crashed to the floor at once. She rushed to the balcony and peered at the sidewalk but saw nothing. Then the sirens had blared.

The next day, the police had taken her testimony. Together, they had walked the route, bicycle in tow, several times until they set the time of the killing at 10:48.

Judge Kubsch asked, "Your neighbor here denies having seen you that night."

"I don't know why he would. But I'm certain about the truth of what I'm telling you."

"Thank you, Ms. Kakir. You may go."

Aziz returned to the stand but remained resolute. He denied having seen her that night. It took three days of testimony until he was finally dismissed—the court deadlocked over his guilt or innocence.

In the weeks that followed, the witnesses for the accused took the stand like the troupe of a traveling circus. Some stunned the court with their freakish performance, others with the signs of genuine fear in their voices, upon their faces. The former listened to the questions, but answered as if they had heard nothing at all, making their own rehearsed statements instead.

"How do you know Mr. Darabi?"

"Mr. Darabi was always an avid student," one defense witness answered.

"Of what?"

"I don't know for sure, but he's always studying."

"Studying and running several businesses at the same time?"

"Human beings must always learn from birth to death, says the holy Koran."

"Let's focus on one human being here if you could, on Mr. Darabi. He let you live in his house, correct?"

"Never charged me a single coin. He's a nice, nice man. A real Muslim. And he knows German. He helped me because my refugee salary is so small. This man here gives and gives."

"He paid you?"

"Not for any work. He paid me out of the goodness of his heart."

"Did you pay him back?"

The witness shook his head.

"Since you lived with him, did you ever see the other defendants who are here today?"

"I don't know. But I tell you all the Lebanese people of Berlin know and like Mr. Darabi. He's a good man."

"I'm not asking you to judge Mr. Darabi. It's obvious from your answers that you're trying to hide something. Are you under pressure? Do you fear anything?"

"I fear only God."

"Did Mr. Darabi ever speak about Salman Rushdie in the mosque?"

The witness shook his head once more.

"There was a demonstration against Salman Rushdie at the mosque. Was Mr. Darabi not there?"

By this time, the witness spoke less and less and gestured more. He threw his shoulders up.

"Yesterday you said that Mr. Darabi spoke at an anti–Salman Rushdie rally and today you can't remember?"

Darabi interjected from his cage, "We're all against Rushdie. That's no secret."

The court welcomed the comment from Darabi, who had kept silent on the stand.

"Did the defendant talk about the fatwa to kill Salman Rushdie at the mosque? That's the question. But perhaps Mr. Darabi, whose memory is obviously vivid, can answer himself."

In return, Darabi only said, "Later. I'll speak later. In case you haven't noticed, we're gonna be here for a while. Another two more years at least."

Like a pandemic, amnesia seemed to afflict all the witnesses for the accused. When failing memory could not be blamed, the translators were. One week, a witness testified that he had been born and raised in the same Lebanese town as Yousef, had known Yousef all his life, and even traveled with him to Iran to receive combat training. A week later, he squinted at him from the stand as if straining to see, and said that his vision had failed him the week before and Yousef was not the man he thought he knew. When the judges pressed, the hysterical witness begged to be dismissed. "Please, please, don't make me go there again."

"Why? Are you afraid?" Judge Kubsch asked.

The witness only sobbed.

"Have you been threatened?"

He sobbed more intensely and pleaded once more, "If you don't let me go, I may never see my family. I've been instructed to forget everything I know or else I might have a car accident. Believe me, the person who told me about the accident wasn't reading tea leaves either."

The start of the testimonies by the defense witnesses coincided with the appearance of a new face in the reporters' section. The lanky newcomer looked German but sported the quintessential untrimmed beard of a devout Muslim. From the very first day, he took diligent notes. He looked familiar to Hamid, though he could not remember why. Leaving the court one afternoon, he spotted a witness whose testimony was to continue the next day, entering the reporter's car. The view of the two men triggered in Hamid's mind the memory of Darabi alongside the reporter. This was Oscar Brestrich, a convert to Islam, who had appeared on a televised debate defending the fatwa against Rushdie. He had quoted from the New Testament to prove that Christianity, like Islam, condoned the killing of apostates.

At lunch, instead of going to the canteen, Hamid slid into a phone booth to call the station that had broadcast the debate. He asked the operator to connect him to the producer Norbert Siegmund. From their seats in the courtroom, Hamid and Norbert had greeted each other often enough to have formed a friendship. Hamid asked for the transcripts of the debate which, by evening, Ehrig was reviewing.

The next day, another witness took the stand and behaved as cagey as the rest. It was all the provocation Shohreh needed. She had heard about Brestrich's ties to Iran's regime and promised to let Ehrig address the matter in court. Still, seeing Brestrich in his usual spot, busily taking notes, she walked over to the parapet alongside the reporters' section. She pointed to him, her brow knitted, her dark, straight hair slicing the air as she turned furiously back and forth between the judges and the grinning reporter. Her voice, outsizing the dainty expectation her figure inspired, boomed.

"It's him! This man! There can't be a real trial with him here."

Hamid, alarmed, caught her glance and motioned her to *calm down!*

"Mrs. Dehkordi, you're disturbing the court," Judge Kubsch thundered.

But Shohreh pointed and continued, "He's one of theirs. He's their reporter. Ask him! He's the reason why none of them speak. Judge, how can you watch them say nothing at all one after the next? How do you let so many hours be wasted listening to their hogwash?"

"The reporters in this courtroom have proper credentials and the right to be here," Judge Kubsch responded.

But it hardly pacified Shohreh.

"It's been weeks. They keep coming on and saying nothing. *He*'s the reason why. I don't feel safe with him in this courtroom."

"Mrs. Dehkordi, I ask you to take a break to collect yourself."

A guard escorted Shohreh out of the room to a bench in the corridor before getting her a drink of water. Another guard stood watching over her as she wept. A few moments passed and the courtroom doors opened. The chief Arab translator walked out and approached Shohreh. For months, he had watched her despair. This time, he could no longer go on watching. He had to talk to her.

"Hush! You waste your pearls of tears over nothing. What a shame! You worry for no reason, missus. Hush, now!" He handed her the cup of water the guard had fetched.

Shohreh wiped her face and took a sip. The translator, encouraged, went on.

"I've worked in this court for so long. This judge is like no other. You can't see the heart in his chest, but as God is my witness, it beats better than any I know. You'll get what you want."

What she wanted, she remembered, was dead, and no one, not even Judge Kubsch, could give him back to her. Tears overcame her once again. She moaned, "He hates me. He treats me like I'm a lunatic. They've paid him off."

"This judge? Ay, missus! This judge . . ." The translator, searching for a metaphor, knocked on the marble wall behind them and whispered in her ear, "He's a rock. Nothing gets through him but the truth. Come now! You're shedding the light out of your eyes, and won't have them to see the glory of the day that's coming to you. Come, listen to this old Arab! Trust me!"

He put his arms around her, hugged her, and then returned to the courtroom.

By the next day, when Ehrig presented the transcripts to the judges, the police had also spotted witnesses boarding Brestrich's car. Judge Kubsch asked the witness how he had got home after his last court appearance.

"Someone drove me," the witness said.

When the judge asked who, the witness pointed to Oscar Brestrich.

"What did he say to you in his car?" he pressed the witness, who was growing uneasy.

"He turned up the music and told me how to behave on the stand. 'Don't let them provoke you,' he said. I asked him why the music was so loud and he said the police might have bugged his car."

"What else?"

The witness turned silent, refusing to say more.

Brestrich was called to the stand and introduced himself as a reporter for Iran's official news agency, IRNA.

"In what newspaper do your articles run, Mr. Brestrich? Who's your editor?" the judge asked.

"I don't have an editor. I report to Iran's embassy in Bonn."

"Why would a reporter report to an embassy?"

"Why not?" Brestrich answered breezily.

"And you get paid for this job?"

"Handsomely!"

"And the embassy circulates your reports to Iran's intelligence communities?"

"Yes, naturally! They'd be fools not to. It's every government's job to collect intelligence. Why not Iran?"

"You have also been in touch with the witnesses. Why?"

"I help prepare them for your questions."

Judge Kubsch told Brestrich that reporters never reported to embassies, nor did they coach courtroom witnesses. Brestrich dismissed the opinion as puritanical. The witnesses, he argued, were foreigners who did not know the ways of a European court and needed advice from an insider like him: a German who knew the system, but also knew Iran—he had traveled there, met with Ayatollah Khomeini, and taken lessons in Shiism from Kazem Darabi. Without someone like him, the novice witnesses would otherwise be lost in the courtroom.

The judge listened to Brestrich's monologue to the end, then said, "In light of what the court has learned about you, Mr. Brestrich, I revoke your reporting credentials as of today. You can continue to attend the trial, but only as a spectator, not a reporter."

The Arab translator turned to Shohreh, who was seated behind him, and flashed a triumphant smile. With a sigh and a smile, she acknowledged her newfound ally. Then she looked to Hamid and moved her lips to form the words, "Thank you!" Together, they had scored a small victory.

• • •

Other victories followed. Oscar Brestrich never returned to the court. The Austrian chief investigator flew to Berlin to testify about his findings in the 1989 assassination of Abdulrahman Ghassemlou, a case that still remained open. His appearance in court was brief but damning. A four-year probe into the case had led to Tehran. The investigator's final remarks shook the court.

"Iran's leadership has been pursuing a covert policy to annihilate the Kurdish leadership. That much is clear to me. We did our job, investigated the case fully and thoroughly. We traced the killers and found those responsible. The problem wasn't with us, the police, or the investigators. It was with our politicians, who set the guilty free."

The federal intelligence chief Bernd Schmidbauer was once again forced to testify. At first, he tried defending his October 1993 meeting with Minister Fallahian as merely humanitarian. But when a confidential document—the record of the minutes of the meeting—was released to the court, the word "humanitarian" became the punch line to his critics' jokes. The chief spy, dubbed Agent 008, was widely mocked for his ineptitude to even tell a proper lie. The testimony further cast him as a deceitful politician, and launched a series of congressional inquiries that marked the nadir of his career.

Schmidbauer's testimony disillusioned the nation. But Judge Kubsch's handling of him restored both hope and pride to them. Against Schmidbauer's blunders, the judge's subtle virtues glimmered. Reporters took note:

If there has been anything astonishing, anything admirable about the Mykonos trial in Berlin, it is Frithjof Kubsch. He is almost intolerably detailed and knows how to gently leave no room for appeal. It is with these qualities that he is moving the trial forward. This is how he is and how he will prove the motives behind this criminal act that took place on our soil. Until now, this judge, firm yet humble, constructing his quintessentially long sentences, has asked the questions and done the work of the prosecutor and the attorneys at the same time. He has masterfully resisted all the efforts that aimed at disrupting the trial. In the last round of testimonies by Schmidbauer, Kubsch asked Schmidbauer to explain what he meant when he said, "Those who know the details will draw a different conclusion." Kubsch kept at 008 for so long that eventually Schmidbauer was left with no choice but to admit that he had lied.

16

> We don't like going to Iranian restaurants that aren't busy—we prefer the ones where we can ignore a large number of people.
>
> —*Hadi Khorsandi, exiled Iranian satirist*

There it was, inches beneath Salomeh's left collarbone, an unsightly lump, on the brink of bursting. Salomeh had proved far too slender for the pacemaker. The device had so stretched her skin that her doctors, fearing a rupture, thought it best to replant it in the muscle instead. No matter how Parviz pleaded with her, she would not agree to a second operation. She was afraid, and the father who lived in the shadow of death was hardly qualified to advise her about life.

He reasoned that her skin might break at a time when neither he nor her mother were there to help. He could allude to death but could not utter the word itself, not about her. In return, she shocked him by her depth and her forwardness.

"But *babayee,* you give interviews, go on TV, write articles. You could drop dead, too. Shouldn't you have a surgery to sew your mouth up for a while?"

She showed the kind of feistiness he would have admired in anyone but his own thirteen-year-old sick daughter. He tried hard to hide his amusement, his pleasure.

"I swear on the Koran, something bad is gonna happen if you keep this up."

"I thought you were agnostic, *babayee.*"

Her father's vocabulary was not all the precocious child had mastered. His perseverance was another.

"You want me to have surgery so that I live. And I want you to stop being Ambassador Mykonos. There are other survivors who could do the talking for a change."

In the end, he was the one abandoning reason and resorting to bargains.

"If you have the surgery, I'll be by your side every step of the way and do anything, absolutely anything, you say. I'll even shut up, if that's what it takes." Parviz clapped a hand over his mouth, pretending to be mum.

They bickered for days. Salomeh, seeing her father's surrender, began contemplating her wishes. On the day she finally consented to have the surgery, she had won an impressive wish list from her parents. Only the intangibles were left to negotiate.

"Promise to perform for me every day?"

He clicked his heels and saluted her. To show good faith, he staged a coming attraction. Putting his cupped palms together, he raised them to his lips. His cheeks ballooned as he blew hard into the tiny opening between his thumbs. A loud hoot, like a locomotive whistle, filled the air. Once, twice, then a third time.

"All aboard!" Salomeh bellowed jubilantly.

With his fingers at his mouth, he puffed his cheeks out once again. A convincing hissing sound filled the air. A long puff followed a shorter one, the invisible train accelerating, then puff, puff, puff, until the sound tapered. Salomeh waved and blew kisses. Her father's flair for cheap pastimes thrilled her. He made her laugh with nothing more than a twisted nose, a crossed eye, or a lazy tongue. Each time he crossed the threshold between activist and entertainer, Salomeh became hopeful that with enough persistence she could keep him with her at the opposite side of the perilous ground he insisted on treading.

After the surgery, Parviz got on a plane. Since the start of the trial, he had compiled all the documents—articles, photographs, reports—edited them, written his own introductions, and paid to publish them as a two-volume set called *The Mykonos Case*. He referred to them as his *books,* though given their rushed and unfinished presentation—page numbers missing in places, handwritten notes added in the margins of others—they more resembled the private journals of a genius on the verge of madness. He was compelled to produce them in the same way Shohreh was compelled to keep notes and Hamid was to bear witness. The raw look of his white-bound volumes conveyed an urgency other Iranians in the diaspora grasped, and they set Parviz on a tour through their enclaves in Europe and the United States.

It was on the road that he realized his spirit, like the skin on his daughter's chest, was about to break. Fear and mistrust had so swelled in him that he could hardly enjoy the company of those who came to listen to him. He walked away from his readings always on the edge of falling apart. In New York City, a comely woman bearing an armful of his books to be autographed shyly asked if he wished her to take him on a tour of the city. Moved by her beauty, he instantly rejected her offer, certain she was a Mata Hari. In Los Angeles, his hosts, worried for his safety, placed a German shepherd outside his hotel room. But the dog, glowering and baring his teeth each time Parviz neared the door, terrorized him. In Miami, another host took him to the beach. Soon after they had waded in the water, the clouds covered the sun. The host, fearing a storm, swam closer to watch over him, but Parviz, suspicious of him moving in amid the rising tides, kept on swimming away. At last, the anxious host swam back to shore, borrowed the lifeguard's bullhorn, and begged Parviz to get out of the water.

He realized, too, how much he missed Noori's conversation. His good-hearted audiences, with their dull questions and even duller commentary, only reminded him of the erudition of his lost friend. One day, after he had returned to Berlin, he went to the cemetery. Noori's plot was in disarray —dried-up bouquets strewn on the ground, weeds everywhere. Atop his friend's grave, he knelt and wept. In the past, when he suffered a setback, the thought of all the years ahead to make things right uplifted him. But now his loneliness was deeper than ever, and his setback greater than any he had known, and he was nearing fifty. He wept and wept, and when he had no more tears to shed, he stared quietly at the dry soil until nightfall.

"You know what happened in court today?" Shohreh would often ask her reticent daughter as they ate dinner together.

Sara hardly spoke. If she were still grieving, she did so in her mother's absence. To make conversation, Shohreh gave her reports of the trial. They were always smashingly positive: Bruno Jost was brilliant, Hans Joachim Ehrig was an orator of Grecian proportions, and Judge Kubsch, a highly reliable source had leaked to her, was secretly on their side, which explained why he had to treat her harshly in court. Every one of their witnesses performed magnificently, whereas every one of the defendants' witnesses was clownish.

In return, all that could be heard from Sara was the clanking of her utensils against the china plate. If Shohreh pressed, Sara simply asked, "When, then, will it be over?"

The question always dumbfounded the mother for its aptness. There had been several victories throughout the trial, but they had all come at the cost of weeks and months. The trial had entered its third year, as Darabi had promised, and the end was nowhere in sight.

What Sara could not say was that watching her mother go to court terrified her. She feared losing her to the same men who robbed her of a father. More than any verdict or victory, she wanted the ordeal to end. She wanted a quiet, ordinary life without the constant ringing of the telephone, the incessant beeping of their jammed fax machine, the preoccupied face of her mother as she strained to write yet another letter to another congressman, or compose yet another sound bite for another reporter. She wanted peace so that she could sleep with abandon once again. As it was, she was frightened into wakefulness every dawn, sensing a strange presence lurking in her room, though it always vanished when she opened her eyes.

Her mother answered, "Ah! You're missing the point, *moosh mooshak*. We're winning."

But black, in which she was still dressed, was not the shade of victory, not to the twelve-year-old girl. Each time Sara asked when she would shed her mourning clothes, Shohreh denied she was in mourning.

"This is just what I'm doing to remind the others what we've suffered, you see. It's just for a short time."

"It's been two years, *maman*. This is going nowhere."

There was cruelty in Sara's voice but all Shohreh would have the heart to say was that justice, real justice, worked slowly. Yet cruelty was not the worst of what the mother would find in her child.

"What really works is a good gun to shoot those men with. That's the fastest of all!"

Shohreh's blood quickened every time Sara's fury surfaced, but she managed to show a patience that failed her in the courtroom. Shooting was what the savages on trial had done, Shohreh would say. "Savagery was their way. Civility is our way."

Something about the dignity, the certainty with which her mother uttered the words, the way she wove the tangled yarn of the ordeal into *us* and *them, civil* and *savage* was comforting to Sara. It restored to her mind a bit of the order their lives had lost ever since that September night.

Shohreh spoke of civility, but it was sanity that preoccupied her the most. On days she was in court, she felt sane. Around Sara, preparing her meals, she felt sane. When reporters came over and their tapes were rolling, she felt sane. But as soon as she found herself alone, sanity began slipping from her. Stillness terrified her. A dark cloud, a ghoul, haunted her day and night. In solitude, it spread over her and whispered into her ear the very same words that Sara had spoken, *Face it! This is going nowhere.*

Only Noori's mother was able to console her. When they talked on the phone, she detected an anguish in her voice that matched her own. Then, in one conversation, she detected the foreboding traces of a familiar insanity, and dared not talk to her again. In her last telephone call, the old woman, feverish with flu, told Shohreh that she owed her an apology.

"None of this would have happened if I'd not eaten that fish. I let you down, my poor bride, I let you down."

Living in Tehran, Noori's lonesome mother, helpless with age and distance, hardly dared talk about her loss. Her forbidden sorrow, trapped within her, had turned in on itself.

"It was that fish. The minute I swallowed it, something went haywire in my belly. Oh, that fish! It's why he's dead," the old woman said weeping.

"*Maadar jaan,* nothing you ate, nothing you did or didn't do could have prevented what happened," Shohreh said, censoring the word assassination from her lines, certain that their phones were under surveillance.

"People told me to swallow a whole fish alive. They told me if I did it when pregnant, the baby would become smart. I was nineteen and already loved him so. His father was away with the army. I was alone. I reached into the courtyard pool and caught a goldfish by the tail. I dropped it into my mouth. It slid down, flailing all the way into my stomach. There was such twirling and spinning in my belly. When it all stopped, I knew something had changed. I did this to him. If I'd not had that fish, he'd have been a regular boy. He'd have been alive . . ."

Ghouls of a different kind were hounding Bruno Jost. His mere name invoked anger in many. In court, even some judges were growing restless with him. In their chambers one afternoon, one judge lost his patience with the prosecutor's refusal to limit the scope of his accusations. They had gathered to discuss Jost's refusal to drop the charges against Iran's minister of intelligence. The assistant judge thundered at the uncompromising prosecutor:

"What is it you want, Mr. Jost? Will anything ever be enough for you? You've got five men in custody. Lock them up and be done with it! Why can't you?"

His name was on the lips of furious imams at Friday prayers but except for guards, Jost hardly had any protectors. In the holy city of Qom, a wave of angry protestors had left the prayers chanting violent slogans against him. Yet, instead of issuing a statement in support of the prosecutor, Chancellor Kohl sent a conciliatory letter to Tehran expressing his regret for the religious sentiments that the investigation had injured.

Guards never left Jost's side, not even when he was home. So close they kept to him that on Christmas the Josts left gifts for them under the tree, and ate their holiday feast together with the giants who kept feeling for their guns whenever the room fell unusually silent.

Too many forces beyond Jost's reach tugged at the case. The deaths of four men in a Berlin restaurant one September night had spiraled into something far greater than each of their losses. It had become the pawn in many other games. In Germany, it had turned into the centerpiece of partisan politics. Parties used every misstep throughout the case to smear their rivals who, at the time, had been or were still in office. In Berlin, the hearings and investigations into the conduct of responsible local agencies were dragging on, dogging Berlin's secretary of internal affairs, among several figures. Other federal probes into the handling of the case by various agencies and their officials, including Bernd Schmidbauer, had become just as endless as the trial itself.

For all the troubles—scandals, inquiries, humiliations—for the loss of all the diplomatic gains—with Iran and with the rest of Europe and the United States—irate politicians directed their wrath at Jost and exacted their revenge by inventing rumors to smear the prosecutor's reputation.

"That fucking Bruno Jost," a senior foreign ministry official said to the reporter Hufelschulte one night while nursing a glass of whiskey. "He's set up a shadow government in Karlsruhe and is shitting on everything we, in Bonn, worked years for. Goddamn legal debutant picked Mykonos for his goddamn debut and doesn't know when to call it quits and leave it to us. Do you know, by the way, that he's depressed out of his wits? He's on a cocktail of antipsychotic meds. Won't be long before the judges get wind of it."

The rumors reached Jost's boss, who called him to his office.

"Are you in trouble? Is there anything bizarre going on, Mr. Jost, that you wish to tell me about?"

Jost, even-tempered as ever, simply shrugged—nothing at all.

But he did feel exhausted. The trial seemed as endless as the day it had started. Each time Jost thought the last testimony had ended, the team representing the accused produced a new witness. Each time he prepared to deliver his final argument, they presented a new document. There was little he could do against their ploys to prolong the trial. Besides, Judge Kubsch hardly ever rejected the chance to hear from a new witness or consider new discovery. Giving readily in to the unreasonable demands of the accused, Kubsch had been a riddle to many in the courtroom and was becoming one to Jost, too.

But not to the court's chief Persian translator and Jost's trusted guide Zamankhan. He had learned about Judge Kubsch what no one else in the courtroom knew—a detail that in the hands of the trial's enemies could prove fatal. He had stumbled upon it on a quiet February afternoon with the ringing of the doorbell.

A young, willowy blonde woman stood at the door of his residence. The wariness on her face matched his and was reassuring to him. He buzzed her in. She had come for his services. She needed him to translate a file, but asked that he keep it in the strictest confidence. The emphasis seemed odd since the job appeared routine—the usual stack of official documents.

"And you are?" he asked.

The woman, flustered, introduced herself.

"I'm . . . oh, dear me! I'm Ms. Kubsch."

The name shook the translator. For a moment, his gaze froze on her face—distinctly round, just like the judge's, whose features he began to trace upon the young woman's face. Silence overtook them until she broke it.

"My father thinks you're the best at the job and didn't want me to go to anyone else. He said I must see you. He's a bit, how shall I put it, *concerned*. You see, my husband is, like you, Iranian."

He quickly returned his attention to the file once more. Among the pages were old deeds to a home in Tehran, other properties, a birth certificate, and several school diplomas. As he shuffled through them, the gravity of what was in his hands dawned on him. The chief judge's son-in-law had fled Iran, like the victims in the judge's courtroom. Her anxiety was suddenly his. If the news were to leak of Kubsch's ties to an Iranian, especially to one who was on the wrong side of the regime in Tehran, the attorneys for the accused would find what they had been stalling for—a reason to call for a mistrial. The end would be even farther from reach.

That afternoon, the translator became the keeper of Judge Kubsch's secret. The chief judge was no longer the unreadable, unreachable caped figure but a man with a predicament much like his own. Zamankhan had long known and befriended Noori, and yet, at the start of the trial, he severed all ties with Noori's family and other expatriates lest his objectivity be doubted by the court. To become the trial's most meticulous translator was the best he could do for Noori. To help the widow, he would keep his distance from her and those in the community who wished to pry into the court's business through him hoping, in turn, to earn the trust of the police, the investigators, and the prosecutor. It seemed to him that Judge Kubsch had made a similar choice. To protect those dear to him, he would serve the court in an unimpeachable manner to earn the trust of those who were most likely to doubt his objectivity.

The prolonged trial was not without advantages. The attorneys for the accused relied on time to stonewall the prosecution's efforts. But time brought Jost unexpected gifts. The first of those gifts, though not yet the greatest, came in January 1996.

On his way to the canteen during a lunch break, Hamid ran into the prosecutor. The two greeted each other. Jost, without slowing his steps, cheerfully announced, "The Iranians in the audience can expect a bonbon from me this afternoon."

"Really, Mr. Jost? I'm thrilled. Can you say . . ." Hamid called out, hoping to stop Jost long enough to hear more. But he only smiled and rushed past.

At lunch, Ehrig confirmed the news, though he, too, did not know any more. The two devoured their meals and hurried out of the canteen, promising the waitstaff a thorough update at the next meal. Ehrig offered Hamid a pearl of legal wisdom.

"Given the stakes, if the defense can make this last an eternity, they will. But it could backfire. In a case as big as this, surprises are always to be expected. Time may work just as much against them as it does in their favor. They might end up shooting themselves in the foot by dragging it on."

That afternoon, Bruno Jost asked to present a document from the counterterrorism unit of the BfV, the federal office for the protection of the constitution. Soon after he took charge of the case in September 1992, he sent inquiries to all the relevant agencies. At the time, the BfV had forwarded a key document. Portions had been declassified, and the rest was blacked out to protect its source. By December 1995 the safety of the source was no longer a concern. Therefore, the BfV had released the full text to the federal prosecutor's office.

Jost was granted permission to present.

"I wish to enter this document as evidence because it directly substantiates the assertion in the indictment regarding state-sponsored terrorism and Mr. Darabi's role as the coordinator of the operation. If I may read only a few lines.

> *A special unit called the Committee for Special Operations, in tandem with the Ministry of Intelligence, was involved in the murder of the Kurdish leaders in Berlin on September 17, 1992. The unit has long been hounding members of Iran's Democratic Party of Kurdistan and is directly responsible for the 1989 assassination of Abdulrahman Ghassemlou in Vienna.*"

The judges issued a subpoena for the BfV's director, whose appearance on the witness stand inflamed Darabi.

"Nothing! You've got nothing on me," he shouted in German. "All accusations! Nothing but accusations! If you got anything, even one thing, show it right here. But you got nothing!"

"Hush your mouth!" someone in the audience shouted in Persian.

"The motherfuckers are here again. Don't you shits know by now you're no match for me?" he shouted, also in Persian.

No response came. The silence emboldened Darabi, as it always had throughout the trial. Each time they failed to match his belligerence, he grew more vulgar.

"Spineless sons of bitches! I'll get your sissy asses. You wait and see!"

Judge Kubsch called the court to order and the witness began. As Darabi had promised, he offered very little. Citing German national interests, he refused to answer the court's most critical questions. Yet the document, whose authenticity he validated, removed any doubts that had lingered about Minister Fallahian's role in the murders.

The BfV document paved the way for Bruno Jost to do what he had long hoped to—reach beyond the underlings in custody to implicate the masterminds. He charged the minister with murder. In a separate filing in the federal court, he requested an arrest warrant to be issued for Ali Fallahian. Never before had any European prosecutor dared go as far.

Obtaining the BfV document was a triumph. But its blessings were mixed for Shohreh. It proved what she had known the day she buried Noori—that greater powers had ordered the killings. It was the affirmation, the vindication, she had waited four years to have.

But it also revived the rumors about the mole, the infiltrator who had betrayed the meeting at Mykonos. Its revelations credited "a highly reliable source who had been in touch with and present at the restaurant that night." Aziz's testimony, albeit damning, had not proved his guilt and so the mystery had lived on. The old suspicions returned, this time surrounding Noori. They deepened her rift with the community, compounding her solitude. The seven bullets that struck Noori evoked more suspicion than sympathy in some. *The killers must have been determined to silence him, to make sure he'd not walk away alive and talk, or they'd have never wasted so many bullets on him.*

But her ties with the expatriates were coming undone even before this. Her presence was discomfiting to most of them. Always dressed in black, she stood in their way of forgetting their sadness and shame—their collective history and the troubled country they had left behind. No one shunned her, but they seldom included her in their midst. On the rare occasions their paths crossed, they regarded her with pity, or so it appeared to her, in whom grief manifested itself in unattainable expectations of old friends. She felt more at ease with Germans. At work, her superiors were generous with extended leaves, and colleagues, whom she had never imagined depending on, divided the tasks she would leave undone.

And her love for Noori still flourished despite the years, the pain, even her own resolve to move beyond him. His wisdom had proved enduring, his foresight keener than anyone else's. In the aftermath of the Gulf War and the declaration of the no-fly zone over northern Iraq, Noori's predictions had come true. The Kurdish homeland he believed was inevitable had almost formed. His lucidity in articulating the plight of the Kurds in interview after interview—his breadth of knowledge about their predicament, his humility especially—illuminated him more brightly now than ever before. She wondered whether to remind Sara of it—who hardly spoke to her—or let her choose to cope by remembering or forgetting as she wished.

Sara had remained steadfast to her father's memory. Her mother could not see that what ignited her daughter's rage was love. Sara could not break the spell of silence between them, tell her mother what would have allayed her anxieties. She longed to be easy around Shohreh again, but she could not say to her mother what was on her feverish mind. She composed and recomposed the unspoken sentences, which always began, "*Maman,* do you ever see Baba?"

The question was bound to make her mother anxious, but it was how the imaginary conversation always began, though Sara knew her mother would ask what she meant by *see*. She would compel Shohreh to say that her father was dead and no one could see him, which in turn would offend her. The two rarely spoke, and when they did they often circled each other like a pair of tigers, each on the verge of assault—one filled with fury, the other with concern.

Neither mother nor daughter knew of the other's growing devotion to Noori's beloved apparition, something that would have strengthened their bond. The talk Sara would not have with her mother always ended the same way—with the secret she could barely keep in her small chest. *Someone comes into my room in the mornings, not always, but very early whenever it happens. I think it's Baba. I used to be scared, but not any more. But he disappears as soon as I open my eyes. I know it's him because the room always feels wonderful after.*

There was a marked change in the news coverage of the trial. The focus of the press shifted from the defendants in Berlin to their suspected commanders. Article after article trailed the bloody footprints of the killers around the globe until they reached Tehran, where Bruno Jost's shadow had fallen over Minister Fallahian.

On March 14, the federal high court granted the prosecutor's request. An arrest warrant was issued for Iran's intelligence minister. The warrant surpassed the exiles' greatest hopes. The trial's most ambitious victims—Parviz and Shohreh—were satisfied; its most discriminating observers, such as Hamid, were similarly content. Judge Kubsch asked Bruno Jost to submit to his court all the material he had submitted to the federal court, and set an end date for the trial: June 25, 1996. He instructed the prosecutor and the attorneys on both sides to prepare their closing arguments.

No sooner had the judge made his announcement than Bernd Schmidbauer relayed a request to postpone the closing date. A letter from Tehran had reached his office, offering two new witnesses. Bruno Jost, enraged by the move, called it an outright sabotage. Ehrig went even further and called it organized legal vandalism. Yet Judge Kubsch granted the motion and called off the closing till the court had heard from the new witnesses.

The end had slipped away once more. The witnesses were in Tehran. To find, train, and dispatch a team to them was an infinite ordeal. Yet again, Tehran had stonewalled the court and, as the exiles saw it, Judge Kubsch had conceded. In their despair, Ehrig's pearl of wisdom eluded everyone: *In a case as big as this, surprises are always to be expected. Time may work just as in their favor as against them.*

17

Nietzsche's famous *Thus Spoke Zarathustra* finally cleared the censors at the ministry of culture when its title was changed to *Thus Spoke the Ayatollah.*

—Hadi Khorsandi, exiled Iranian satirist

Far away from Berlin, on a March day in 1996, Tehran was as it always is before Nowrouz, the Iranian New Year marking the arrival of spring. The news—good or bad—goes unheeded, and newspapers remain unfolded. The streets teem with passersby bearing bags full of holiday purchases. Joy adds a lilt to the peddlers' calls as they drop portions of steaming boiled beets into paper cones. The police, seasonably mellow, turn a blind eye to undocumented sellers. Sidewalks become temporary bazaars for special holiday goods—the pyramids of unshelled walnuts, mounds of oleaster, trays of wheat sprouts, rows of goldfish in glass bowls. Housewives sniff the simmering pots of wheat germ for the traditional spread called "haft seen," or lift the gills of the whitefish to find the freshest for the dinner of fish and herb rice. Husbands squeeze crates of pansies and bouquets of pussy willow into the overflowing trunks of their cars. Haji Firooz, the Persian Santa, dressed in red, with black-painted face, sings tunes and shakes his tambourine at intersections. The crowds linger until midnight for the half-off sale of unsold goods. By dawn, the ground is strewn with trash in the wake of the shoppers' rampage. In the early morning light, budding leaves dabbed in dew glisten on the bare branches like emerald shards and the snowcapped peaks of the Alborz Mountains in the north shine majestically. The intoxicating scent of spring, what well-traveled Tehranis call "the best air anywhere," lulls the city.

On just such a day, a black Mercedes pulled in front of a two-story home on Koohestan 9 in the city's most affluent district. That brief stop, only a few minutes, changed the fate of the Mykonos trial in a way no one could have fathomed.

Minister Fallahian's deputy emerged from the car. A full-cheeked man with an unruly beard and a receding hairline, he rang the bell of apartment #10 and whispered his name into the intercom: Emami.

The door was buzzed open but the deputy slid his foot in to keep it ajar and rang again.

"Can't come up. Come down a minute!"

Moments later, a shorter, stouter version of him was standing at the threshold. The smile on the shorter man's face quickly vanished for he could see the deputy's look of distress.

"I don't have much time and neither do you. You must pack and get out now," the deputy said.

"Get out? Get out of where? Why?"

"Leave the country! They want to truckicide you. Fallahian's orders! Can't tell you how I know. That alone will kill you. Just go! Find a way to cross the border. Save your questions for later. Don't tell anyone, *anyone,* you're leaving! Border guards have orders to arrest you. How you go, I don't know. But go, or they'll have you gone their way. That's what I came to say."

The deputy grabbed the man's shoulders and their beards brushed against each other in a hurried embrace. Then he disappeared into the backseat of the Mercedes and took off.

Behind the door, he remained frozen at the foot of the stairs. Standing barefoot in a white shirt and a pair of black pants, his eyes fixed to the ground, he was the portrait of a man fallen from grace.

The heirs to the 1979 revolution had come to devour him, one of their brightest children: Abulghassem (Farhad) Messbahi, born on December 17, 1957, the son of a prosperous factory owner, the third of five children in a devout Muslim family. At four, he had learned to read while eavesdropping on his brother's lessons through the open

Truckicide, in the vernacular of Iranian intelligence operatives, is the act or instance of killing the enemy, i.e., an opposition member, singer, writer, or any unpleasant element, by any of various heavy motor vehicles designed for carrying or pulling loads.

windows of the school yard. As a teenager, he gazed into the turquoise dome of the neighborhood mosque every night and prayed, spent summers at seminaries in Qom studying with the foremost clerics. He was among the youngest ever to enter Tehran University and mingle, a mere freshman, with the religious intelligentsia. In 1977 he signed up for the draft but deserted a year later, when the exiled Ayatollah Khomeini ordered all servicemen to abandon their posts. His next stop was inevitable, the only destination for a bright, religious twenty-one-year-old in 1978—the Rafah School, the Ayatollah's Tehran headquarters, where he entered the inner circle.

On February 1, 1979, riding a motorbike, Messbahi shed tears of joy. The Ayatollah had returned from exile and he was one of the guards in his motorcade. By day's end he was kneeling before the leader to kiss his hand, accepting his first official assignment. Messbahi's rise had been swift: chief of Tehran's largest military base, then senior diplomatic attaché to France before the year's end. Under the guise of an attaché, he was to reinvent a new intelligence outpost in Europe. He recruited turncoats from among the opposition and deposited regular installments of cash for them in the hideouts of Hamburg, London, Lisbon, Rome, Geneva, or Brussels. His constant movement across the continent alarmed the French, who deported him and his wife in 1982.

Within days of returning to Tehran, he was promoted to chief of intelligence in Western Europe and flew to Brussels. Deportation brought him and his bride closer to each other.

She, too, joined the ministry to help his cause. Together, they would raise their baby daughter and their brand-new revolution. Adaptable and quick on his feet, he also served as chief negotiator for the release of Western hostages in Iran and in Lebanon, delivering the Ayatollah's message to world leaders.

But each time he returned to Tehran to brief colleagues such as Fallahian, he saw a rift growing between them. He and his friend, Emami, believed they had to defeat the enemy with superior intelligence. They wanted to win in the battle of ideologies. Fallahian and his band argued for bloodshed. They wanted the enemy dead.

In 1987, returning to Tehran to deliver a letter for the Ayatollah from the former U.S. president Jimmy Carter—requesting the release of an American pilot held hostage—Messbahi was quickly flanked by two men on the tarmac of the airport.

"You're going with us," one of them whispered in his ear, then shoved him into a car.

Once they had blindfolded him, the blows came, pounding his face and stomach. Arresting him was absurd, he said to himself, a mistake for which he would receive profuse apologies and perhaps even a promotion. When he was thrown into a solitary cell, he thought someone would soon be on the way to release him. But the person who came only took him to a room where three others sat at a table and they took turns interrogating him, demanding that he admit to being a spy.

"Messbahi! These aren't the days of the Shah," the good interrogator reasoned. "You can't outsmart anyone now. Come clean!"

The bad interrogator, flicking his fingers like he was about to squash a fly, barked, "This is what we do to rebels who won't get in line, who are out of control, whose ways we can't trust, who are too smart for their own good."

His interrogators were reading to him from the manuals he had helped pen, asking him questions he had designed. They whipped him, then ordered him to write a detailed account of his "treasonous activities."

"I'm not a spy," he repeated over and over.

But when their fresh lashes struck the blisters of the old, he began to discover things he did not know about himself. Indeed, he had been a spy, if only they could help him recall for whom, if only they would help him compose the statement of his guilt.

They threw him back into the cell with a pen and a notepad to write a first draft. He was not to make a sound, much less speak, even to ask to be taken to the bathroom. To communicate, he could only tuck a note into the small groove in the wall outside his cell. Each word that escaped his lips cost him twenty lashes, each cough, ten, every sneeze, five.

He turned mute. Because he was not allowed a mirror, he would delay drinking his morning cup of tea until night, just so he could have a surface upon which to trace the contours of his face, lest he forget his own image. After a while, unable to shave, he saw the darkness of his own face disappear into the darkness of the murky tea. He was no longer visible, not even to himself.

Then one morning after nearly four months, they told him to get ready for a visit to the barber. He was about to be granted a furlough. He dared not ask why.

The good interrogator drove him home, but home was not where he knew it to be.

"We thought it best to move your family. It was for your own good."

He rang the bell of a strange door and prepared to behold his wife. But when the door opened, the look in her eyes was empty, loveless.

"Aren't you happy to see me?" he could not help asking her.

"Of course!" she stammered. "Why wouldn't I be? It's just that I didn't expect it."

The good interrogator walked in with him, sat in his living room drinking tea like a guest. That day and every two weeks thereafter, he had to host him, his tormentor, in his own apartment—his harbor.

His friend Emami came to visit, bearing the gloomiest of news: his imprisonment was a declaration of victory by Fallahian and his gang. The ministry was now under their control and they had begun purging their old rivals, starting with him.

"Fine!" he said. "I'll resign and get on."

"Resign?" his friend exclaimed. "You can't resign. School teachers resign. Intelligence operatives strike a bargain. You're still the ministry's employee. You need Fallahian's consent to breathe the air you breathe."

• • •

He went to see Fallahian, but Fallahian would not receive him. He appealed even to President Rafsanjani, and was assured that he would be safe and could go on to other things. Reinventing a life outside of politics intrigued him. It would be a chance to start anew, this time in business. No longer a spook, he fashioned himself into an entrepreneur. He built a factory to produce engine oil and named it Khazar. His old ties to Europe helped him grow fast. But the speed of his success only stirred Fallahian's men. They came to extort shares so large that they exceeded his profits. He had no choice but to close the plant.

Standing frozen behind the door of his apartment building on that March day, he realized that even the president could not save him. He realized that his last and only friend, Emami, had risked everything by coming to him. He realized there was nothing left for him but to flee.

On the eve of the New Year, Messbahi packed his Samsonite briefcase with a comb, a toothbrush, a razor and some shaving cream, a pair of reading glasses, his old tattered volume of the Koran, and $25,000 in cash and headed for the south. His voyage was a gamble. He was betting everything on a seventeen-year-old promise. In his first post before going to Europe he had ordered the release of the chief of one of the largest tribes of the south. On a visit to Tehran, the chief had been arrested for carrying an unregistered gun. Messbahi—then a young and influential official, arguing that the detention could spark a mutiny in the south—had personally walked the chief out of his holding cell. Stunned by the young and powerful savior, the chief, repeating Messbahi's name under his lips, had vowed to return the favor if Messbahi ever happened upon his territory.

Messbahi was going to Zahedan hoping the chief was still alive, hoping he would still remember his vow from long ago, hoping he still commanded enough power to return the favor.

Night had fallen when he reached the chief's compound. The gatekeeper took his name and went into the building. Moments later, a much older and grayer chief emerged and beamed at him. He grabbed him like a lost son who had finally returned.

"*Huzzah!* Come in, dear fellow! Welcome! A thousand welcomes!"

The chief's reception was a boost of life to Messbahi, who was racing against death.

"Heaven knows I want to, but I must leave the country now," Messbahi replied, certain that rejecting the chief's offer would displease him.

"Are you in trouble?" The chief sounded puzzled. He knew Messbahi only as the impervious titan from the capital.

Messbahi nodded.

"*You*?" the chief slapped his thigh and exclaimed. "*You* in trouble with *them*? How could this be? You *are* them."

Messbahi shook his head.

"It can't be. You're humoring an old man."

"I must get out tonight. Will you help me or should I go on my own?"

The chief thundered, "Go on your own? Stop the nonsense, son! You're not going anywhere in the middle of the night. Come in! Eat and rest! We'll take this up tomorrow."

Seeing Messbahi's reluctance, the chief repeated, "Get in, son! You're a guest at my home now, and no guest of mine has ever left without proper welcome. Get in!"

The chief ushered his guest into a room and ordered a servant to prepare a meal. Then, speaking in the local dialect, he addressed his young assistant and the two disappeared into another room, busily talking.

At six o'clock the next morning the chief awakened Messbahi.

"Rise and shine, son!" he said with affection.

They ate breakfast together and afterward the chief handed him a tribal Salwar costume to put on—loose-fitting white pants and a knee-length shirt and vest and said before heading to the street, "Get your things together. We're leaving!"

A dark Buick bearing Iranian plates awaited him at the gates. The chief opened the car door and Messbahi was surprised to find several people already inside—the chief's wife, daughter, son, and two grandchildren. He patted Messbahi on the back, whispering in his ear, "I won't leave you until I put your hand in the hand of a trusted friend at the other side of the border."

The sound of the revving engine faded into the rushing tires on the gravel road. If their destination had a name, no one spoke it. It hailed that morning, a ferocious downpour the likes of which the region had not seen in decades. When the hail let up, the rain came. Through hail and rain, the driver pressed on. At every checkpoint, Messbahi witnessed what he, being a believer, could only call a small miracle. Twice the guards, recognizing the plate numbers of their car, simply bowed and remained doubled over until it passed. At others, the driver stopped, rolled down the window, and exchanged a sentence or two before the bars parted to let them through.

"How come they're not checking us at all?" Messbahi wondered out loud.

"Because they've been taken care of," the chief boasted.

All along the road, he and the chief talked about their families—children, the chief's grandchildren, and loved ones—but never about the reason that had brought them together after so long, never about Messbahi's fall. When they finally arrived at the border bazaar several hours later, the downpour had stopped. Messbahi looked into the horizon and saw a rainbow and, thinking it a sign from God, he got out to pray.

Another car, a Toyota SUV bearing Pakistani plates, was awaiting them. They boarded the Toyota. From that afternoon till the dawn of the next day, they rode over muddy, unpaved roads where they saw only clouds of dust and bright blue skies over dunes as expansive as eternity. For an unforgiving fourteen hours, the driver drove on. His passengers drifted into sleep until at last they were rocked awake by the bouncing tires on bumpy roads. The desert behind them, they were on poorly paved streets now. A new landscape, a run-down town, stretched before Messbahi's eyes. In the narrow alleyways, pedestrians shades darker than he milled about, the men among them dressed in the same costume as he.

The car pulled in front of a modest, two-story home lined with brick walls. The chief stepped out and rang the bell. The door swung open and several children rushed to throw themselves into his embrace. His arms circling their reedy frames, he turned to Messbahi and said, "Welcome to Quetta, son! Come meet my relatives!"

At last, they had arrived in Pakistan, in eternity itself. He prayed again, his lips moving to the words of the scripture, while his wet gaze remained fixed on the chief.

Inside, an elaborate feast had been spread for the guest of honor. Never had a fugitive received so grand a reception. They ate and, when their stomachs were full, they sang folk tunes, and when they had sung long enough they filled their bongs with their purest opium to toast the man of the hour, who, to their great surprise, refused to smoke. By the end, everyone was strewn on the floor in a stupor—everyone but Messbahi, who rose and bid the chief a tearful farewell.

March ended as Messbahi found his bearings in Islamabad and a handful of restaurants where the food did not set his insides on fire. April came and went as he moved from hotel to hotel, never staying in the same one for long. May passed as his asylum request to several European countries was rejected one after another. The record of his deportation from France in 1982 had doomed him. No European Union member would shelter someone who had been turned away from another member country. June delivered yet another blow. All the diplomats he had once known found an excuse to refuse helping him. The shock staggered him into July, which began with a new worry: his stash of cash was fast diminishing.

Without anyone to turn to, Messbahi dialed the last and only number he had not yet dialed and left a message on the answering machine. After he hung up, he fought hard to keep the wave of despair at bay, afraid that the details of his whereabouts on the message would be leaked to Fallahian in return for a handsome reward. The thought of being in custody again drove him to ponder the quickest path to suicide if the minister's men were ever to catch up with him again.

An hour passed. He stretched on the creaky twin bed of his Islamabad hotel room, gazing at the ceiling. The fan whirred. The innkeeper's broom brushed against the floor of the corridor. The faucet in his room dripped from time to time. So many sounds except the one he expected. Anxiety mounted in him. He rose and began to pack to leave for another hotel. As he gathered his few things, the telephone at last rang. The voice he had not heard in years greeted him.

"Mr. Messbahi, this is Banisadr. I hear you're in trouble," former president Abulhassan Banisadr spoke, his calm tenor intact.

The telephone number of the former-president-turned-dissident living in Paris was a secret the Iranian military and government elite tucked in the folds of their passports next to wads of provisional cash reserved for an emergency flight. He was every defector's last resort. He was also their most natural ally, for his history was theirs. Banisadr had been a confidant of the Ayatollah, flown back with him to Iran in 1979, elected the nation's first president in the next year, and soon became the Ayatollah's harshest critic, finally fleeing in 1981. His life had since been dedicated to erasing the blight of his association with the former mentor. He was not a warm man but a genuine nationalist who helped fellow defectors on the condition that they would similarly dedicate themselves to repenting, undoing their past sin for the remainder of their days.

In a few minutes, Messbahi summarized his career and his falling out with Fallahian. When his story came to an end, Banisadr spoke in his usual terse and candid fashion.

"You see, Mr. Messbahi, I'm not yet convinced I ought to help you. I must first find out if you're telling me the truth. But even if you are, I'm not sure what I can do for someone with your kind of past. You're a hard man to pity, having worked for a gang of godless thugs for so long."

Messbahi tried to interject but Banisadr stopped him.

"Let me finish! I'll only help you if you vow to do right by your people now. You must redeem yourself, Mr. Messbahi! Tell me everything you know about that devil Fallahian and the rest of them," the former president demanded, like a priest demanding from a sinner.

"I'll tell you as much as I can. What I don't know, my wife, who's still in Tehran, can help me get," he said with deference.

"Don't talk of your wife. She works for the devil, too. My sources tell me she's been ratting you out to Fallahian for months."

Messbahi gasped. The memory of the disappointment he had detected in her eyes, seeing him after months of detention, rushed back into his mind. He remembered his friend Emami on the day he told him to leave, refusing to say how he knew of the threat against him: *Can't tell you how I know. That alone will kill you.* It had to be his wife's betrayal his friend was sparing him

He held the receiver but said nothing, heard nothing. The former president went on.

"That's what the bastards do. Turn father against son. Wife against husband. They've no morals. They talk of God and act like the devil."

Then he added, "The devil would do well to take a few lessons from them."

Messbahi's attention was drifting farther into the past, reviewing the inexplicable events of the recent years—the way his children seemed to run from him when he went to embrace them; the way he constantly sensed someone had gone through his desk, looking at his files every time he sat down to work.

"You there, Mr. Messbahi?" Banisadr asked when the silence at the other end had lasted too long.

The call brought him back to the conversation. His desperation had strangely lifted to give way to vengeance—against a nemesis who had robbed him of everything, even his wife.

"I'm with you, honorable Mister Banisadr."

Testing his devotion, the former president asked, "What's the regime hiding?" Then, as if tuning an instrument, he asked a second question, striking the perfect pitch.

"Say, what do you know about the 1992 murders at Mykonos?"

That August Berlin was unusually hot. In Hamid's small apartment, the only breeze blew from an old fan. Throughout much of the season, he had spent his days inside, driven to repose on the powder-blue settee of his living room, his eyes languidly scanning the pages of the journals that had piled for several weeks. This was how he filled his daytime hours while the court was in recess. In any ordinary year, he would have gone to a cooler place. But he could not abandon his post while Ehrig was away lest something important elude them in their absence. Yet a new assassination in the suburbs of Paris had put him on alert. Another exile, a former deputy at the ministry of education, had been shot at his home only weeks earlier. Since the killers would not take a vacation, neither would he.

As always, the television was on to ward off the silence in the bachelor flat. As always, it went unwatched. The monastic Hamid, who hardly ate before sunset, bit into an occasional bar of dark chocolate, sipped cold tea, and flipped through the pages of magazines, looking at the lines rather than reading them. The heat had undone his focus. Adult responsibility kept him at the task but a childlike restlessness gnawed at him, clamoring for adventure. In this twilight, his eyes caught a familiar name—Mykonos restaurant. He sat up to read and reread the sentences preceding and succeeding the name carefully.

> *According to a source (a person we'll call C for the purposes of this article), the lead killer who wielded the machine gun at the Mykonos restaurant on the night of September 17, 1992, is a man named Bani-Hashemi . . .*

The line appeared in a diaspora magazine published in France—its author former president Banisadr. Since the murders four years ago, Hamid had mastered every detail about the case and longed to solve its lingering mysteries, among them the identity of the lead killer—the nameless phantom who had tried to lure Yousef to kill; the one who, minutes before the strike of nine that night, had ordered them all, *It's time!* The one who had retrieved the Sportino bag from the trunk of the getaway car and walked with it into the restaurant. The intruder who had announced his presence at the dinner table with an expletive. The machine-gun-wielding assassin who had fired three consecutive rounds. The nameless fugitive finally had a name.

Hamid's drowsiness disappeared. The thrill of discovery set his nerves on fire. At last, at the bottom of a staid afternoon, he had found the adventure he was yearning for.

In thirty years of practice, Ehrig had never returned a business call while on vacation. But when his secretary said Hamid was looking for him, he broke his old vow and dialed the secret co-counsel's number. The news he received was riveting, more invigorating than the fine sand beneath his feet. His excitement showed in the many questions he asked: *Did Hamid know the former president? Was he a trustworthy source or a corrupt politician who would fabricate any lie to inflict damage upon his former allies? Could Hamid find him? Talk to him? Who was his source? Did the source know more about the murders than what was printed in the article? Would the former president be willing to testify in court?*

He asked Hamid to translate the article into German and send a copy to his office. The details of the article itself mattered less to Ehrig. What intrigued him was the prospect of returning to court and surprising the other attorneys, who had delayed the trial with their endless supply of witnesses, with a witness of his own.

Hamid also broke a vow. An uncompromising secularist, he had always kept his distance from the religious opposition. Banisadr, a devout Muslim, had once been at the helm of a government that Hamid had opposed from inception. But on that day he softened. Like any good custodian who would readily place the welfare of his charge above all else, Hamid suspended his own rules. Leafing through the tattered pages of his address book, he found the telephone number of the former president's representative in Germany and requested an audience with him.

Within a few hours, Banisadr had granted Hamid's request with a call. At first, the conversation was dry, their sentences piling like cold logs on a hearth. When they dispensed with introductions to talk about the trial, the case ignited the exchange and they warmed to each other. Since the publication of the article, the source Banisadr had quoted had revealed much more. Once a top operative in the ministry of intelligence, now a defector, he knew a great deal about the assassinations at Mykonos, though getting in touch with him was nearly impossible, given his precarious circumstances in a border country. Banisadr had faxed the defector some questions, and the few answers he had scrawled and faxed back made it clear that he knew too much to walk the streets for long. The former president was doing his all to bring the defector to Europe but the defector's past associations and history made it legally impossible. So Banisadr was looking into alternatives. The former president would not speak of breaking the law, but he was confident that those who did so for the noble end of this case would be absolved by heaven. Most of Banisadr's cryptic lines were lost on Hamid, but not his allusion to a scheme to get the defector out of harm's way.

On the evening of August 21, 1996, the scent of dilled rice with fava beans wafted from the apartment. Hamid rarely cooked but on the few occasions he did, he cooked with the zest of a connoisseur. Throughout the day, pots and pans simmered and sizzled on the stove of his tiny kitchen. He talked to friends and reporters while tasting his concoctions or adding a dash of what needed adding. By sundown, he had prepared a feast for a once unthinkable guest.

At nearly eight o'clock, the police entered Hamid's flat. They peeked into his closets, checked his drawers, searched his cabinets, locked all his windows and entryways. Because he had no curtains, they nailed blankets to the window frames to block the view into the flat. The building was placed under security lockdown for the next several hours. Visitors were turned away as residents looked on warily. An officer stood guard at the main entrance, another on the roof, a third at the apartment's threshold.

Banisadr arrived with two assistants in tow. He beamed his quintessential smile, two bumps forming in the upper cheeks. His dark droopy eyes also smiled behind the large square-framed glasses that had inspired so many cartoonists. Standing across from the former president, Hamid marveled at how similar the man looked compared to the campaign posters he remembered from years earlier: dark hair coiffed back, mustache trimmed, broad forehead smooth, face shaven clean, white shirt buttoned up to the last without a tie. With no trace of trepidation, he cupped two hands around the former president's hand and welcomed him. True to Iranian etiquette, he seated the visitors at the table and rushed to serve dinner.

"Tell us, Hamid *agha,* what should we expect tomorrow?" Banisadr asked, pausing after the first spoonful.

(*Mr. Hamid,* mused the addressee. The president's title for him was a tender blend of formality and affection for his choice of the first name.) Banisadr was to testify at the trial the next day. Those few hours were all they had to prepare him for the witness stand. It was Hamid's only chance to turn a man, by nature a pundit, into a compelling witness—a feat no one thought possible.

The meal proved a catalyst. What a hungry man with a dry mouth and a nagging stomach might have interpreted as criticism simply seemed a friend's wise counsel to a satisfied man, whose senses were filled with the fragrance of herbs, the happy hue of saffron, and the taste of a lamb so succulent that its consumption was, the guests agreed, gastronomic therapy.

"You see, Mr. Banisadr, these Germans have a thing for facts . . ." Hamid began. He had the unusual talent of mangling his own potentially offensive sentences, which always forced the other to articulate them for him and feel charitable in return. He meandered for some time, praising the virtues of brevity as if he were dispensing tips to a convention of grammarians. At last, he began recounting the testimonies of other exiles, who had only befuddled the judges. Pouring a ladle of creamy cucumber and yogurt on the guest's plate, he smoothed over the roughest matters, till it was the president who concluded that the courtroom was not a forum for punditry. By the end, all Hamid had to say explicitly was a warning about the chief defendant, Darabi, who was certain to do what he could to provoke Banisadr and undermine his testimony.

The next morning, the trial was back in the headlines again. Nicknames for Abulhassan Banisadr abounded. Berliners, stunned by the high security surrounding the witness, were eager to hear from the "best protected man in the city," to whom some referred as "Abulhassan Trotsky." The forthcoming testimony of a former president who had turned against his own government made the public curious at first. But curiosity spiraled into sensation when Iran's ambassador to

Germany issued a statement demanding that Germany extradite Banisadr on charges of hijacking. The ambassador was referring to the airplane Banisadr had used to defect. In a television interview, he assailed Bruno Jost's indictment as a list of empty accusations.

"No German government official would ever believe a single one of the prosecutor's statements."

Flashing a confident smile, he went further.

"The judges are sure to vote in Iran's favor. I'm certain of this because I'm certain of our own innocence," the full-cheeked ambassador said, staring into the cameras. Then, dispensing with diplomatic decorum, he assumed the tone of a concerned sheriff.

"I repeat the words of our Majles leader from last week. 'The murders in Berlin are undoubtedly the work of the Americans, and we will not rest until the killers of the Kurdish leaders have been brought to justice.'"

Among serious reporters, the race to the former president for an exclusive interview was on. At times like this, the desire to gain access to a subject overrides all other considerations. Memories fade. Old wounds heal. Past grievances become bygones. At just such a time, Norbert dialed Parviz's number after many months, hoping he could deliver Banisadr to his studio.

"Oh, dear Norbert, don't you worry! Let me work on it and get back to you," Parviz replied in a gay voice, which, to Norbert's ear, was dangerously tinged with mischief. To think that Parviz was going to work on his behalf once again brought him no comfort. Still, it was time to give trust another chance.

On the steps of the courthouse, Parviz caught up with Banisadr. The two had begun to correspond since the murders. Parviz praised Banisadr over and over.

"Your testimony will be smashing. No two ways about it. You must be heard as much as possible as long as you're here in Berlin."

"But the police say I ought not to give any interviews for the sake of my own safety."

"Nonsense! It's the German administration that's trying to keep you under wraps to appease Tehran. Your safety's got nothing to do with it," Parviz answered, adding to the former president's suspicions.

The thought of anyone wishing to silence him angered the former president, who greatly respected the outspoken survivor. He said, "You've lived here long enough to know these Germans. It's unconscionable what you say. I've never put up with duplicity, be it from the mullahs or their Western bedfellows. Let's get on with the interviews then. I'll talk to any journalist you trust."

At these words, Parviz held up his mobile telephone and dialed a number. Norbert answered. Switching from Persian to German, he told Norbert that he was standing beside the one he had been looking for. Norbert asked Parviz to interpret a few questions. When the conversation ended, Norbert, overcome with dread, stopped Parviz.

"Wait! This man next to you, whose answers you translated . . . tell me again, was he *really* who I think it was? Banisadr in the flesh? Right? I mean, you wouldn't—"

"Ah, Norbert! May you someday absolve me! I swear on my Salomeh's life, this was Banisadr himself. Go in peace!"

After many empty weeks, the benches in Hall 700 were once again overflowing with reporters and spectators. Many witnesses had taken the stand thus far, but no one nearly as notable as the former president, once the face of the regime he was about to testify against. The exiles sat taller that day, already boasting that his testimony would vindicate and affirm them.

Judge Kubsch, aware of the tension in the room and anticipating the day's pitfalls, excused all other translators and asked that only Zamankhan interpret. Then he called Banisadr to the stand. The preliminaries had barely begun and already Darabi appeared restless.

"Could you state your profession for the record?" Judge Kubsch addressed the witness.

"I'm the editor in chief of the magazine *Islamic Revolution in Exile*. Prior to this, I was Iran's president, but was removed from office in a coup d'état."

Darabi banged on his bench and roared in German, "Coup? What coup? You lie. You weren't removed. You fled."

"Shhh!" several in the audience sounded in return.

"Shut your mouths! I'm talking to him. He says there was a coup when there was none," Darabi turned in fury to the audience.

"Put a lid on it!" another shot back.

"Motherfuckers, I'm not talking to you. I'm talking to him." He pointed to the witness while he looked at the audience.

Banisadr kept his gaze on the judge, appearing calm.

Sharing the bulletproof cage with Darabi, Rhayel, who had remained stoic throughout the trial, joined the fray. He, too, began grunting the few expletives in Persian he had learned in prison. Four years of trial had done nothing to soften the stony silence of the two defendants before the judges, or diminish their smugness before the audience. They were on their feet, bellowing at the spectators, confident that they would not be outdone as they never had been throughout the trial.

Judge Kubsch silenced the court and returned his attention to the witness, asking him to explain what he meant by a coup.

Darabi, who had barely returned to his seat, shot up again and addressed the chief judge in German.

"He can't explain because there was no coup."

The audience hushed him again. He glared at them, reverting to Persian.

"Shut your shit-holes while I talk!"

That day there were others in the benches who had traveled far to hear the former president, others who were less familiar with the exiles' code of courtroom conduct and less patient with the rowdy pair. One of them got up unexpectedly, pointed to Darabi, and hollered, "The long dick of a donkey up your mother's cunt!"

Darabi, dumbstruck, simply dropped to his seat. To the astonishment of those who had observed him for months, he never spoke another vulgar word for the rest of that day, or the trial.

"Mr. Banisadr, who do you think is responsible for the assassinations at the Mykonos restaurant on September 17, 1992?" The chief judge asked what he had not asked any other witness since the early days of the trial.

The question was what Banisadr had flown from Paris to Berlin to answer. He leaned back in his chair. The trepidation of the opening moments disappeared from his expression as he began to articulate the driving conviction of his life.

"If Ayatollah Khomeini had been alive, I'd say he'd ordered it, because when he was alive, he personally issued and signed such orders. But since his death, there's a small group of elite who call themselves the Committee for Special Operations. They review and order these assassinations inside and outside Iran."

A hush fell over the hall. One of the attorneys rose to his feet but the judge motioned him to wait. The witness, too, aware of the gravity of the moment, paused to ask if he could read from a statement he had prepared. Judge Kubsch nodded an affirmative.

"Here's a summary of everything I know about this case. This information leads me to believe that the assassinations at the Mykonos restaurant were ordered by the highest-ranking members of Iran's leadership. My assertion is based on the word of three separate sources, inside and outside of Iran. I've learned that the point man to oversee this operation was handpicked by the intelligence minister, Ali Fallahian. I've also learned that the lead assassin, named Bani-Hashemi, who shot the victims with a machine gun and fled Germany on a plane that same night, came to Berlin via Poland in early September and executed the plan with the help of Mr. Darabi. He is a tall and hefty fellow, in his mid- to late thirties, with light brown eyes. He is soft-spoken but wears a grim expression on his face."

Yousef interjected, "Judge, just so I know, please tell me is 'grim expression' a fact or an analysis?"

The courtroom, intently focused on Banisadr, disregarded him.

When the statement ended, the judges and the attorneys began.

"How do you know these things, Mr. Banisadr?"

"From the three sources I mentioned."

"Who and where are these sources?"

"I can't divulge their names. One is in Iran and the other two are out of the country. My third source used to be one of the highest-ranking intelligence officers in the ministry but he has recently defected."

"So, for the sake of clarity in this courtroom, may we give them a name just so we can follow your argument?"

Banisadr looked at Judge Kubsch and, seeing him nod, he assented. The three sources were thus anointed: the one inside the country would be called A, the second, B, and the third, the defector, C.

A new question followed.

"Tell us what you know about the involvement of Iran's leadership in this operation."

"According to source C, Ayatollah Khomeini ordered the assassinations of some five hundred Iranians, mostly opposition members, but also artists, comedians . . . you name it! A few of these folks were killed while he was living. After his death, the Committee for Special Operations took over to finish off the rest. The killers are always highly rewarded. I've got thirteen names of individuals who have committed crimes in Europe or elsewhere, returned to Iran, and are now in government as ministers and legislators. Such is the nature of the men the world community wants to do diplomacy with."

The attorneys for the accused did not challenge Banisadr, who had proved affecting and knowledgeable—not wishing to prolong his presence in court. Instead, they hoped to undo his testimony by challenging his sources. At the end of the second day of testimony, they requested that the sources themselves be subpoenaed so the court could hear directly from them. Judge Kubsch turned to the witness. Banisadr contemplated the matter for a few moments, then said that if the judge would guarantee anonymity, his best source would testify in a closed court. The judge assured the former president by citing all the previous cases where his court had made such provisions for special witnesses.

At recess, Banisadr handed a tightly folded piece of paper to Judge Kubsch, who passed it to Bruno Jost. Jost unfolded it to find a single name, the password to the mystery called C.

• • •

It was not difficult to establish the bona fides of a defector as high ranking as Messbahi. German intelligence agencies had monitored him for years. What preyed on the mind of the prosecutor, who had shepherded the case for four years, was whether he could rely on Messbahi as a witness. Dealing with defectors was a dubious affair. Jost could not be certain that the sudden escape of such a senior operative was not another ploy designed by Minister Fallahian to infiltrate the trial. He knew enough key witnesses who had undone years of judicial work by changing their testimony on the stand. Truth was not what Jost feared. He feared only deception—falling prey to a scheme and discovering only too late that the witness had been a pawn. Jost would not gamble his reputation or the case over the fairy tale of a witness who could lead him to an even greater victory. His ambitions had never surpassed his reason.

But also for the sake of the case, he could not help hoping Messbahi was true. He wished for some evidence to show Messbahi would be a reliable witness, for a sign, however small, to prove he was no longer loyal to the same bosses.

18

"Hadi Khorsandi walks because of me. He breathes because of me. I'm the reason he's alive," Messbahi told the former president—his voice tinged with a passion that survived the poor long-distance transmission between Islamabad and Paris. The revelation came in response to the former president's toughest and most frank question.

"What's to prove that you, Mr. Messbahi, aren't another killer just like all the rest of them at the ministry?"

The story Messbahi told was the best defense of his innocence. In summer 1984, when he was the intelligence chief posted in Western Europe, a visitor from Tehran came to see him. The man had come to personally deliver a missive engraved with the imprint of the Ayatollah's ring. It read:

In the name of Allah the Beneficent the Merciful

Because of insulting the prophet of Islam, blessed be he and all his kin, Hadi Khorsandi must hereby be executed.

Stamped: Ruhollah Khomeini

The letter stunned Messbahi. He did not lift his eyes from the page, lest they betray his disgust to its messenger. He was a fan of Khorsandi's, Iran's foremost humorist. A mostly apolitical satirist under the Shah, Khorsandi had been radicalized by the rise of the Ayatollah to power, sparing neither the mullahs nor their opposition, or the servile press that aired their propaganda. He had lived in exile since 1981 and had dedicated himself to deriding the clergy, whose talk of God, piety, good and evil, and the inner workings of heaven and hell had become a boundless reservoir of material to him. Islam was his new muse, and the Prophet Muhammad the subject of his creative obsession. From his London apartment, he channeled his bitterness into scathing parodies on Shiism—into poems, essays, cartoons, and short stories—that he wrote, edited, and printed in his own weekly, *Asghar Agha*. A close associate of the Ayatollah's spotted one particular joke mocking the Prophet Muhammad and brought it to the Ayatollah's attention. Thus had come the fatwa. There had been other assassinations in Europe, but Messbahi had never been asked to oversee them. This particular fatwa was an exception. Perhaps it was a test.

Messbahi, however devious or flawed, was not a killer.

No matter how high he rose in the ranks of spookery, he was, and would always remain, his father's son. Years ago, when the old man learned of his son's profession, he issued an ultimatum to him.

"I'd have much rather you'd chosen a different line of work. But if this is what you must do, I tell you now: you can wash away every stain but blood. If your hands are ever stained with the blood of another, I won't call you *son* again."

To the envoy who had delivered the letter, Messbahi showed no signs of trepidation. Did Messbahi need men, money, weapons, or whatever else the operation might require? the envoy inquired. Messbahi only thanked him and said that he had all he needed. *All,* he had repeated emphatically, as he thought of the one thing he did not have, the one thing the envoy could never supply him—the will to kill.

Since Messbahi could not openly disobey his orders, he devised a scheme to execute and botch the operation at the same time. First, he assembled a hit squad made up of several Algerian Islamists, for whom he translated the fatwa from its original Persian into French. Then he invented a code name to use instead of the satirist's real name, in conversation and correspondence (the code was Harandi, the name of Iran's chess champion, whom Khorsandi greatly admired). In the days that followed, they monitored the satirist and took photos of him, his neighborhood, and his residence. They studied him long enough to learn his daily routines, including the time of day he left his apartment to take a solitary stroll every morning.

One day before the operation, Messbahi sent a message to the envoy in Tehran.

"The celebration is set for tomorrow."

The response came. "Celebrate away! Have a good time!"

The same day, he traveled to Vienna to distance himself from what was to come. There, hours before the attack, he walked into an indistinct phone booth and made an anonymous call to British intelligence.

"Tomorrow, around six o'clock in the morning, two heavyset Algerians will walk along the avenue where the Iranian exile Khorsandi lives. They plan to kill him when he leaves his home for a stroll at eight."

The British acted on the tip and ordered the Khorsandis to vacate their residence. Shortly thereafter, the men who fit Messbahi's description began to prowl the block. By eight o'clock they had been arrested.

Jost, who had already heard the British account of that attempt was pleased to find that it corroborated the defector's story to the former president. Indeed, an anonymous call had led to the arrest of seven men and their cache of weapons. Jost told Banisadr of his wish to speak with the defector. He would do everything in his power to ensure his safety if he were to testify in court. He would appear as a secret witness in a closed session, or could enter into a witness protection program if he testified openly. Getting him to Berlin, he regretted to admit, was beyond his legal reach.

• • •

One September morning, many weeks and two dozen hotels later, Messbahi checked out of his room in Islamabad for the last time. He was headed for Karachi. After several grueling inquisitions, former president Banisadr had finally judged Messbahi genuine and resolved to help him. At last, he was leaving with the essentials he did not have when he had first entered Pakistan: a passport and a visa to Europe—two things the former president arranged in exchange for his testimony at the trial in Berlin.

For the moment, he was a Swede, the proof of which he patted in his shirt pocket every few minutes. His photo had been forged in a Swedish passport above another's name. Through years of living undercover, Messbahi had come to think of names as seasons and he was always prepared for their inevitable change. He relished each new title and treasured his cache of identification cards. Still, his new passport was an oddity. Above the strange name, his own recent photo seemed even stranger. He marveled at it as if it belonged to someone else. For most of his adult life, his face had been eclipsed by a full black beard, giving him a coarse and unfeeling appearance. What the beard had not covered, his oversized black-framed glasses had. But in Pakistan, he dispensed with the glasses and shaved his face clean. His once massive portrait shrank into an almost diminutive one, exposing a beauty mark he had nearly forgotten on his left cheek. Suddenly, the former senior intelligence agent looked almost sweet, like a freshly picked fruit en route to the airport to be shipped to more agreeable climates.

• • •

The customs officer at the Karachi airport flipped through the pages of the dubious passport. Then, looking Messbahi up and down several times, he asked with a bureaucratic grimace, "When did you come to Pakistan?"

"In late March."

"So where's your entry stamp?"

"Gracious! Is it not there?"

The officer cast a knowing glance at him and shook his head. He leafed through the pages again and asked a second question.

"So where's the rest of you?"

"What do you mean?" Messbahi asked with a smile.

"It says in here you're 176 centimeters tall," the officer said, looking down at him. He knitted his brows and asked, his voice full of sarcasm, "Pray tell, are you 176 centimeters?"

Messbahi, who stood at only 164 centimeters, reached into his pocket and, keeping his breezy tone, apologized.

"What was I thinking? Of course, it's here. Right here!"

He pulled out two one-thousand-rupee bills and slipped them into the officer's hand. The officer dropped his gaze at the notes. Then, seeming unmoved, he ordered, "Arrest him!"

An underling walked up to Messbahi. Dressed in an ill-fitting uniform, he pointed to a chair. Messbahi plopped into it. For the next few minutes, the elder kept examining the passport while the younger stood guard over the implausible Swede. Messbahi, growing anxious, reached into his pocket once again. This time he pulled out a much heftier wad in a silver clip. He extended it, a sum of $2,550, to the younger officer, who passed it to his superior. He scanned the wad and resumed.

"Is this all you've got?"

"Search me all you want. This is everything."

"Five thousand is what will get you past this border."

Messbahi raised his hand, asking permission to get out of his chair. He leaned into him and whispered in a tone of resignation.

"You see, brother, this is what I've got. Either you want it or you don't. You can demand a million, but I don't have a single coin left on me. Take this, or take me into custody."

The officer disappeared into a room. His underling watched over Messbahi, who had begun muttering a prayer under his breath. The boarding call for his flight was blaring through the terminal when the superior reappeared. He waved the detainee to approach him and asked in a murmur, "If this is all you've got, how are you going to make it out of the airport when you get there?"

"I always put my trust in Imam Ali. He'll see me through," replied Messbahi and went on praying, more audibly than before.

"You, Shiia?" The officer smiled a genuine smile for the first time.

Messbahi nodded without interrupting his prayer. The officer pulled a fifty-dollar bill from the bundle and tucked it into the fold of the passport, which now bore an exit stamp. Pressing it into Messbahi's hand, he whispered in his ear, "Godspeed, brother!"

• • •

By early fall, Witness C was no longer the intangible object of the court's curiosity. Before stunned spectators, Agent Messbahi, the most senior intelligence operative ever to defect from Iran's ministry of intelligence, took the stand in several sessions from October till the following February. Known to foreign and secret service officials alike, he was the kind of witness that prosecutors dream of. He was so credible that even Iran's embassy in Bonn could only turn over a few minor embezzlement charges against him. Though his testimony came on the heels of dozens of other witnesses, he mesmerized the court with his knowledge. Each of his measured and unsentimental responses, full of byzantine details about the characters and their circumstances, gave his statements an arresting authenticity. What so many exiles had pleaded before the judges to no avail, what President Banisadr had tried to convince the court of through the force of his celebrity, Messbahi methodically reasoned like a mathematician, yet without abstraction. So intensely focused was the exacting witness on the stand that he frequently needed to take a break. His head pounded with the pressure he put himself under to remember, and to do so with precision.

Even the defendants, especially Darabi, in whose address book Messbahi's phone number had been found, hung their heads in disbelief and kept mum. As for Hamid, Shohreh, and Parviz, they, too, were silent, though a mischievous glance or two betrayed the happy clamor within them. The testimony of the defector lifted them. With tangible facts, the witness filled in the outlines of what they had long intuited. He gave them the unforgettable image of the truth, in one exchange above all.

"Mr. Messbahi, you say that the Committee for Special Operations orders and oversees assassinations. Could you say who they are?" Judge Kubsch asked.

"It's a small group made up of the Supreme Leader, the president, the foreign minister, the minister of intelligence, and the chief of the Revolutionary Guards."

"Are these ad hoc meetings or do they take place regularly?"

"They are quite a ritual, convening relatively regularly and always in the same place."

"Where?"

"In one of the former Shah's residences, called the Turquoise Palace."

Tehran was reeling from the groundbreaking testimony. At a Friday prayer, President Rafsanjani threatened to expose what he claimed to be a "secret dossier" on Germany.

"We'll file a complaint against companies like Siemens for not completing work on our nuclear plant. And that will just be the beginning."

The head of Iran's judiciary issued a statement accusing Germany of violating the international rules of neutrality. Iran's foreign minister, in one of several press appearances, assailed their ally.

"We stand ready to sign a contract worth twenty-five billion with the Germans, if only they could stop letting themselves be manipulated by the Israelis and the Americans. What more could the Germans want? We've given them a foothold in the Gulf, Central Asia, and the Middle

East against the Americans and in return, they put on this Mykonos mockery."

Germany's ambassador to Tehran was summoned to the foreign ministry and warned that his administration would be held accountable for the accusations the federal prosecutor had mounted against Iran's leadership. Angry pro-Tehran protesters swarmed the gates of the German embassy demanding an apology, threatening to bring on what other irate protesters had at the American embassy twenty years earlier. The residence of the German cultural attaché was raided by members of the Revolutionary Guards at a dinner in honor of several prominent Iranian writers and intellectuals. The Guards charged in, took films of the alcoholic beverages on the tables, rounded up the guests, and hauled them away to prison on charges of "illegal contacts with foreign elements."

Other arrests and detentions followed as the trial's final days loomed. Tehran had abandoned secret attempts at subverting the trial. In desperation, the regime had resorted to blatant brutality against German citizens working in Iran or secular writers and intellectuals. A German businessman was charged with rape and put on death row. The editor in chief of a popular literary monthly, en route to Germany, was snatched on the tarmac by Fallahian's men, while for weeks Tehran accused Bonn of his kidnapping. Still, the court's work continued.

On February 14, 1997, the trial's closing procedures began. The charges against Aziz were dropped, as his guilt had not been proven to the court beyond the shadow of doubt. The attorneys for the accused once again asked to postpone the closing until they had received a draft of the federal prosecutor's final statement. This time, Jost did not wait for Judge Kubsch. He announced with uncharacteristic firmness that he would not turn a single page over to anyone at any cost, and returned, with a resolute countenance, to his seat, surprising the court, even himself, with the outburst, which had been four years in the making.

For the next three days, the prosecution presented its closing statement. Citing the testimony of Messbahi, the prosecutor implicated Iran's leadership. When Jost rested, one of the attorneys for the accused attempted a rebuttal by offering to present yet several new witnesses, but Darabi interrupted. He rose to his feet and spoke, this time with a somber tone.

"No! I don't want anyone to make any statements for me. I'll make my own statement. Let's face it, I'm the one who's been used."

Requesting the help of the best translator in court Darabi, with Zamankhan at his side, drafted a twenty-seven-page letter in his own defense. For the first time, defeat tinged the defendant's voice. For the first time, he alluded to his own bad fortune, to having been used as a pawn. To those who had waited years to hear from him, *used* was itself a confession. He painted himself as an unknowing party to a crime others had committed.

"I didn't know what I was getting into when I first got involved with these men here. I knew nothing of what they had planned. Imagine a friend asking for the key to your car, saying he wants to go to the post office to pick up a big heavy parcel. Then you hear on the evening news that this friend has used your car to rob a bank. Are you to blame for the robbery if all you had done was to lend your car for what you thought was a good deed? This is my problem! First, the prosecutor built a case against me based on the lies of Yousef Amin. Then the members of the opposition in this audience poisoned this court against me. That fellow," he pointed at Hamid, "over there, and all sorts of others, with their television friends and CNN crews and former presidents in tow, used this opportunity to trash me just because I'm ideologically opposed to them. But my being ideologically different from them doesn't make me a murderer."

Ehrig erupted the moment Darabi rested.

"At last, you speak, Mr. Darabi. And it's your right to speak. But it's not your right to choose only the portions you wish from a four-year trial. You, sir, *drove* the people who robbed the imaginary bank."

The lawyers defending Rhayel no longer denied their client's role in the murders. They only argued that the trial had proven that Rhayel, a devoted Shiite, had carried out the orders of his spiritual leader, who according to the prosecutor's own statement resided in Tehran. Therefore, the defendant had not acted on his own, but had executed the command of a higher authority. It was that authority, the Supreme Leader, who had to be held accountable, not his mere follower. No sooner had they completed their plea on Rhayel's behalf than he countered them—denying their argument. He had followed no one's orders but his own. There was no one responsible for the crime but him. Then he returned, as stoically as ever, to his seat.

With the end of the four-year act looming, Yousef also decided to address the court.

"I want to thank Judge Kubsch for being such a good judge, and Judge Zastrow, who's not with us any more, may he rest in peace. And Judge Alban, who is also a very good judge, and Judge Noeldeke over there, who was here always and worked very hard, and Judge Klemt, who is very very nice, and the court doctor way over in the back, who came rain or shine. I also want to thank all the translators . . ." He went on to name each one by one, ". . . and the security guards by the door, who guarded this place so well, and the attorneys . . ." Another list of names followed.

His gratitude might have been sincere, but the endless catalog of names he had carefully rehearsed caused the usual uproar of laughter, striking everyone as Yousef's last gag.

When there was no one left to thank, Yousef did what he knew best: he reversed his own previous testimony yet again.

"I also want to thank the prosecutor, Mr. Bruno Jost, and the police who first interrogated me. I am sorry I ever said that they paid or threatened me. The truth is that they didn't. All I want is for this trial to finish, so that I can go home to my wife and child. That's all. If you have no pity for me, please pity my little son."

• • •

At last the time came for Ehrig to make his closing statement. To the attorney who had never missed a day of court, a summary of the four-year ordeal was the best last statement of all.

"Ladies and gentlemen! This crime had been ordered. How do we know this? We know this because since the fall of the Soviet Union and the establishment of the no-fly zone by the U.S. forces over northern Iraq, Iran has quashed the demands of its own Kurds for independence more vehemently than ever. There are also ideological reasons at work here. As one of our experts quoted, Ayatollah Khomeini had demanded that 'the Kurds choose between being Muslims following the orders of Allah and their Kurdish nationalism.' Further evidence? The assassination of Abdulrahman Ghassemlou in 1989 in Vienna. Or the statement by Minister Ali Fallahian on Iranian television days prior to the assassinations, in which he sets targeting the Democratic Party of Kurdistan as one of the ministry's top priorities and reminds the viewers of the past blows the party had been dealt and the future ones that are yet to come. Or the meeting between Mr. Schmidbauer and Minister Ali Fallahian prior to the start of this trial; and Iran's foreign minister's repeated request for the better treatment of the prisoners. Not just for Kazem Darabi, the only Iranian citizen in custody, but also for the other four accused who are not Iranians. Iran has extended citizenship to the Lebanese men here, in the same way that Stalin declared the Soviet Union the paternal home of all the downtrodden. Or in his testimony, Yousef Amin quotes Abbas Rhayel as having said, 'If you are ever arrested, don't worry! Iran is behind us.' Or the statement of Mr. Jalal Talebani, the Iraqi Kurdish leader, about the intelligence his men had gathered on a plan to assassinate the main victim in this case, Dr. Sharafkandi. Or the source of the weapons used in the assassination, which the ballistic studies proved to have been Iranian in origin. Or the source of the silencers, also Iran. Or the fact that two Iranians were involved in this operation. And that the main gunman shouts an expletive at the victims, not to mention the myriad evidence provided by the German intelligence, and then the damning testimony of Witness C, former president Banisadr, and others who have shown the court how the regime in Tehran has deemed this operation a victory."

Attorney Otto Schily, whose firm had accepted the Doctor's case from the start, followed Ehrig. The presence of Schily—a political celebrity—was a boost to Shohreh and the exiles in the courtroom who had feared their own anonymity all along.

"These men did not know their victims, nor did they harbor any personal enmity toward them. There is but one possibility for their motive: they killed because their masters in Tehran ordered them to do so. The assassination of Dr. Sharafkandi and his colleagues did not once move Iran to inquire why the lives of its citizens were not better protected when they were in Germany for an international conference, nor have there been any words of regret or sympathy sounded by Iran in response to this crime. The regime never once took any steps to investigate. Nor has Iran shown any desire to cooperate with the investigation. To the contrary, Iran's regime only moved into action when the accused were arrested, and tried its best to prevent them from standing trial. The mask fell off Tehran's face when it tried to intervene on behalf of the accused. That alone is an admission of culpability.

"We cannot allow the hubbub in Tehran to disturb our peace, because only in peace can the judges arrive at their decision. The question is not only who committed these crimes. Names must be named, even those of the people who have evaded arrest and are not standing trial here. This will surely have political consequences for German-Iranian relations. That's for the politicians to worry about. The court must tell the truth in all its clarity and disregard all other concerns. The terrorism Iran conducts is one of the most hateful forms of organized crime. Any concession would be a sign of weakness on our part, and great disrespect to our lawful way of life, and could only serve to embolden Tehran. The people of Germany want to have friendly relations with the people of Iran. We regard their culture and civilization highly. But the universality of human rights, our right to live according to our own lawful order, demand that we take the strongest stance against acts of terror.

"For much too long, European governments have watched Iran's violent behavior. A regime that touts terror and even commands it must not be the recipient of our loans or red carpet receptions. After all Iran has done to stonewall this trial, in these last days we hear vulgar calls and unfounded accusations coming from them again. Our federal prosecutors have been threatened with death. I fear such threats will only get louder in the days before the judgment. Which is why I must emphasize once more: we are indebted to the federal prosecutor. This gratitude is most heartfelt especially by the victims' families. If there are those in Tehran who think it is possible to make threats against our prosecutors without impunity, they must know that doing so is a declaration of war against all of Germany. Soon the judges will issue their final judgment in the name of the people of Germany. I am confident their judgment will be a fair one. This is my greatest hope because we all have a shared duty. All of us—citizens, men and women, and even those who are our guests—must live in safety and without fear."

19

At dawn on April 10, all the streets leading to the Moabit court were blocked from a mile away. Snipers had been stationed on the rooftops overlooking the entrance. Police and military personnel paced the vicinity in pairs. Iranian expatriates from all over Europe had converged on Berlin. For all they had suffered, this day would be a reckoning. Hundreds were circulating at the four corners of the intersection surrounding the court, preparing for a demonstration. The trial that had lasted nearly four years, placed 176 witnesses on the stand in 246 sessions, and cost three million dollars was about to end.

That morning, Shohreh, still in black, wore her brightest smile. For the first time, Sara accompanied her. The presence of her daughter at her side heartened her. She was no longer the vulnerable little girl but a blossoming fourteen-year-old young woman. The night before, Sara had returned home, cutting her school trip short. The thought of her inexhaustible mother alone on the last day of court had moved her to leave. Away from Shohreh, she had been able to see her mother in a new light. The steady flow of her mother's presence had lightened the burden of her grief. She was joyous that morning.

"What will today bring?" Shohreh kept saying under her breath. But Sara hardly cared. She had not come for the judgment. She had come to watch the end of the trial that put her mother's life on hold. She had come to see the future begin. She had come to say farewell to her mother in black. She tried not to think about the next hour, when she would be in the same room as the killers, breathing the same air. She tried not to think of their eyes meeting, her stomach churning. April 10 was not a day for the unpleasant. She had come to collect her share of peace.

Parviz waved to the women from the sidewalk. He had arrived too late and the audience section was already full to capacity. He paced the pavement as nervously as he had once paced the waiting room of the hospital where his daughter was delivered. The accused were about to get their sentence, and he was about to be relieved of his. Waging war had come at a great cost to him. He had done many things he was not proud of. Restless in bed again the night before, he had counted the days since that night at the restaurant: one thousand six hundred and sixty-five days. He had not bothered with weeks or months because time's other denominations diminished the immensity of his experience. A question had kept him awake and fueled his anxious steps on the sidewalk. What would this day bring? He clung to hope and paced.

Hall 700 had been mobbed in the past, yet never had the crowd included the ranks of Germany's deputy foreign minister or the U.S. ambassador. Among the reporters, even members of Iran's official radio and television were present. For the first time in decades, the balcony, which was once reserved only for nobility, had been opened to accommodate the overflow. The spectators were excited and bolder than ever before, offering their unsolicited views to the reporters.

"We've come to see if the engine of your justice works as well as the ones in your cars!"

They, too, had come to pass a judgment. They wanted to know if the busts lining the halls and the portraits hanging on the walls would prove to be more than mere decor.

Bruno Jost sat next to his deputy, both in the same crimson robes. The night before, the two had celebrated their final evening on the case at a Yugoslav restaurant. The ordeal of his life, the case that had kept him in hotel rooms away from home for half of every week for nearly five years, was about to end. That he was there to see it, alive despite all the threats, was what many might have called a miracle. Jost, being a rationalist, only called it extraordinary. Sitting exactly where he had for so many days, he had not a single regret. He felt content. He had done all he could in the precise way a conscientious prosecutor should have.

He would change nothing, take nothing back. All that remained for him to do was to hope and delight in the thought of returning home and resuming his life's old rhythms. He would sleep for the first few days, hibernate like a bear. Throughout the trial nothing, not the threats to his safety or the indignant treatment of colleagues or the endless hours of work, weighed on him as much as the gaze of the exiles in the courtroom did. Those voiceless men and women kept their punishing stare on him every day. It had been arduous being besieged by their presence, but in the end, their unspoken expectation had driven him out of the comfort of what he knew, into the folds of unknown but consequential things. He was content, indeed, and also grateful for the journey, already wistful, but relieved, too, to see it end.

The five judges appeared at the threshold of the gallery's entry and the room came to order. The whispers died out. Excitement had never betrayed the expressions of the judges until that day. They walked to their seats led by Judge Kubsch, whose steps seemed rushed. Perfect silence blanketed the room. An expatriate shifted in his seat and others glared at him. Any sound that did not emanate from Judge Kubsch tested the nerves. Silence, usually the sign of calm, was only a levee that morning against the swelling waves of anticipation lapping behind it.

He spoke in a voice that quivered for the first time. Looking in the direction of the audience, he addressed them first.

"Before I announce the judgment, I must ask a few things of you. This is a courtroom. Please do not interrupt. We have copies of your passport pages and know your identities. The guards have been instructed to escort out those who upset the proceedings immediately. Hold your applause and protests. As you well know, there are many in line downstairs wishing to get in. So, if there are any interruptions, though there have hardly been any throughout this trial, you'll be removed from the court to let the others get in."

Then he turned to Shohreh and added, "I also ask the family members of the victims and the accused not to get emotional. The translators will be given a copy of the judgment, which they will translate for them, if need be."

No one stirred. All eyes were still upon him. It was nine-thirty in the morning when Judge Kubsch rose to his feet. Everyone followed his lead. He forgot to begin, as he always had, with the words "in the name of the people." Instead, he began with the sentences:

"For their role in killing four people, Kazem Darabi and Abbas Rhayel are sentenced to life in prison. Their two accomplices, Yousef Amin and Muhammad Atris, are sentenced to eleven and five years, respectively. Attaollah Ayad is free, however, the court will not compensate him for any fees or losses. Now you may be seated."

Everyone settled into a seat. Yousef Amin was smiling. Rhayel and Darabi slumped, their eyes cast down, perfectly defeated. Judge Kubsch continued.

"It was clear from the beginning that this would be a long trial. And so it was. The defendants exercised their right not to speak and so they added to the court's burden to work even harder on their behalf. There were many other unforeseen complications, too, that prolonged the trial. The proceedings had to be translated into at least two other languages at all times. Some witnesses were presented much too late and, furthermore, they were only available in other parts of the world—Iran, Canada, Lebanon. It took a long time to find, train, and send judges and reporters to hear their testimonies.

"The media says that it is Iran that is on trial in this courtroom. This is not true. We do not try anyone in absentia. When a defendant had a toothache, we canceled the trial because our court could never convene in the absence of a defendant. We do not try anyone who cannot be present. So 'governmental terrorism' has never been on trial in this courtroom."

The statement sent a jolt of anxiety through Hamid, who, fearing what Judge Kubsch might say next, shut his eyes. He had spent the night before preparing for the two possibilities of this day. Were the judges to rule in the exiles' favor, he would unfurl the banners that read:

CUT ALL TIES WITH IRAN!
RECALL AMBASSADORS FROM TEHRAN!
MINISTER KINKEL: YOUR COLLEAGUE IS A TERRORIST

And if they were to rule otherwise, he would display different ones:

A DARK AND SHAMEFUL DAY
FOR THE GERMAN JUSTICE SYSTEM
JUDGES COWED BY POLITICAL PRESSURE

The room was silent for a few moments until Judge Kubsch resumed.

"But!" he emphasized the word on which his reasoning turned. "We can talk about acts that have taken place against the backdrop of governmental terrorism, even if that government is not present to defend itself. According to the law, we must explore crime in its proper context. Our goal here was never to explore the context, but it became necessary as we tried to understand the motives behind these crimes. Within the framework of this investigation, finding the culpability of others, including individuals and institutions, also became necessary. The accused here are not the true culprits of this crime . . ."

Hamid opened his eyes. He sat up and inhaled deeply, at once suffused with ease. Ehrig pressed Shohreh's arm and she leaned against him. For the next several minutes, Judge Kubsch traced the history of the Kurds' persecution, since the rise of the Ayatollah, to the killings at the Mykonos restaurant. By then, tension had fallen away from him and he was speaking in the same measured and deliberate voice everyone knew. Speaking the lines the exiles had never thought he would, never believed any foreigner capable of understanding their tale well enough to compose, Judge Kubsch uttered what to their exhausted ears was a lullaby, one of vindication.

"The orders for the crime that took place on September 17, 1992, in Berlin came from Iran's Supreme Leader."

Hearing the judge list the names, Hamid shot up. Other exiles followed suit. They could not act against the judge's wishes and burst into cheers, so they remained silent but standing. Joyous, Hamid began to tap on the back of the bench before him. Others, who had looked to him for a sign, did the same. The happy drumming of the spectators filled the air. Shohreh burst into tears. She wrapped her arms around her daughter and the sound of their weeping mingled with the tapping knuckles. Her kisses—fast and numerous—trickled on her daughter's head and cheeks. For so many years, the expatriates in the courtroom, refugees in an unknown territory, had knocked on Berlin's doors, breathed Berlin's air, walked upon Berlin's pavements, slept in Berlin's nights. But belonging, ever mercurial, had never taken hold of them, for without justice, belonging never does. They were knocking because with that judgment, they had finally been affirmed and met by dignity. They were knocking no longer to get in, but to announce that they had, at last, arrived.

Bruno Jost darted out of the room to call his office in Karlsruhe with the news. So did several journalists who rushed out to file their stories: "History made in a German Court" the next day's headlines would read. "Unprecedented in the History of the World." For the first time, a court had implicated in crime leaders who were still in power.

Outside, the mobile phone in Parviz's hand rang and the voice at the other end said, "They named names, Parviz. They named everyone."

"Who's everyone?"

"All of them."

"Darabi, Rhayel, Amin, you mean?"

"No, the bosses."

"No, no! Wait! You're excited and are getting ahead of yourself."

"Parviz, listen to me! We won!"

"You're mistaken. Don't interpret what the judge said. Tell me verbatim what you heard!"

"Kubsch named—"

But before Parviz could hear the words, the crowd outside erupted. Screams of joy filled the air. Parviz wept. Several journalists ran to him, microphones and cameras in hand, and asked, "Mr. Dastmalchi, what do you think about today's judgment?"

"I . . . I . . ." But the ever articulate survivor could not complete his sentence. He tried to regain his composure once more and began again: "I . . . I . . ." But four and half years of tears kept welling up in his eyes. He only wept. That morning, tears made up his entire lexicon. They were all the statement he could offer for an answer.

The droves that had come to protest no longer wished to shout their tired slogans. They threw aside their placards, set down their bullhorns, and rolled up their banners. Now was not the time to protest. From the several large speakers that had been hauled to the corners of the intersection earlier that day, a familiar music began to blare. Man and woman, young and old, teamed in twos, extended their arms into the air, knees bent, hips slowly gyrating to the lyrics of "Baba Karam," the most decadent Persian dance tune. They circled each other in slow steps, arching their necks, throwing an eyebrow up to strike their most flirtatious looks, then laughed. They kicked the air and laughed. Those with hats tipped their hats to cover their foreheads and undulated their shoulders as they rounded their partners, all the while laughing.

Outside Hall 700, Hamid, who had smuggled two stacks of flyers inside, threw them over the banisters of the mezzanine by the fistful. The pages shimmered like confetti against the gilded air of the court's interior. He rolled out a banner and hung it over the banister.

CUT ALL TIES WITH IRAN

The guards rushed to stop him. Tearful and delirious, he barely resisted as they handcuffed him. Ehrig, seeing Hamid, hurried forth. He threw his arms around Hamid and pressed him in his embrace, their shoulders bobbing as they cried. It was only when Hamid began to slip from his hold that Ehrig became aware of the guards and entreated them to release him.

Those streaming out of Hall 700 lingered at the entrance. Shohreh wrapped her arms around whoever came to shake her hand. She had nothing to say. The last time joy had so intoxicated her she was in white, dancing with Noori at their wedding, feeling nothing but a blur of light and weightlessness, hearing only the music of her own beating heart.

A journalist walked up to Sara and asked how she felt. Sara, who had never answered a question from a reporter, beamed and spoke her first public statement.

"I'm so glad it's all over!"

Standing in her living room, far away from Berlin, Angela Jost stared at the television set, tears rolling down her cheeks. Her son had been excused from class by a teacher who broke the news to him in the middle of a lesson. He held his mother's hand, high on pride.

That afternoon, following the recommendation of German intelligence officials, the five judges who had presided over the trial were moved to an undisclosed location under heavy security. They were each given a room at a small inn far away from Berlin. After a few hours in their rooms, one of the younger judges ventured into town with two bodyguards to look for a restaurant where they could celebrate the final day of the most grueling trial of their careers. Some time passed before the adventurous judge returned to the inn to report to his colleagues.

"I've found the most charming spot. A cozy café nearby, where we could certainly eat and have a few drinks. But I doubt anyone would dare go there."

When another judge asked why, he said, "Because it's called Mykonos."

In April 1997, in a long overdue act of protest against the Iranian government's terror campaign throughout Europe, Germany requested the removal of the Iranian ambassador and fourteen of his employees who worked in the intelligence section of the embassy. Subsequently, all EU member countries recalled their ambassadors and shut down their embassies in Tehran. European diplomatic ties with Tehran were severed for less than six months, but the result of this brief break was astounding. It brought Iran's assassinations against the exiles to a halt in Western Europe. The Ayatollah's list of five hundred never was completed. Not a bomb had been dropped on Tehran, and no blood had been shed. The historic triumph came on the heels of justice. A unified and resolute West finally stood against Tehran. The judgment from Mykonos, and Europe's rally behind it, remains the most crippling blow ever delivered to the sinister men who snuffed out the lives of the best and the brightest of their nation.

Epilogue

In the final year of the Mykonos proceedings, Judge Kubsch was diagnosed with leukemia. But because he did not wish to delay or compromise the trial, he refused to begin treatment until after the court had issued its judgment. During the long days of treatment his assistant, Judge Alban, dutifully delivered twenty-page installments of the judgment to the hospital for the ailing colleague to review and revise. The final text, over one hundred thousand words in length, was released to the attorneys in December 1998.

A copy of the judgment made its way to Hamid's desk. He reprinted the document as a book with a prologue by Ehrig. A few days after its publication, Judge Alban called

Hamid. From prison, Darabi had called the judge to ask for his own copy. But the legal edition, being an unwieldy format, was not suitable for non-scholarly readers. The judge had told the prisoner that his "enemies" had published the same document as a regular book and offered to send him that version instead.

Before Judge Alban had completed his conversation with Hamid, Judge Kubsch came on the line and asked, "How did you ever get a copy of the judgment? It's not for the public, you know, only for our own internal use."

Hamid laughed and said, "It came in the mail, your honor."

"In which mail?"

"The same mail of good fortune that delivered you to us refugees here in Berlin, your honor."

"My dear sir, as a judge I'm obligated to tell you that what you've done is illegal. And now that I have, could you kindly forward a copy to my office? I'll put my deputy on to make the arrangements."

Judge Alban returned again to give Hamid a forwarding address, and asked for a clean copy, one without any markings or notes in the margins. Then he added, "Please, remember to give us a bank account to deposit the fee for the book."

Hamid rushed to say, "But judge, you must not even mention money! This is a token of our gratitude, a small gift from us to you."

Judge Alban laughed and said, "You hopeless oriental! I'm a judge. If I don't pay you, I'd be in hot water!"

The defendants appealed the judgment and the case was referred to the Federal High Court. Hoping to influence the appeals process, Tehran arrested a German businessman on charges of rape and issued a death sentence for him. Bonn did not balk. In 1998, after a year's consideration, the federal court upheld Kubsch's judgment. True to his reputation, he proved "unappealable" once more.

Bonn, too, arrested an Iranian on charges of espionage. The arrest became the occasion for a happy reunion. Bruno Jost was assigned to the case, and Judge Kubsch presided over the trial, and Hamid and company went on to permanently keep their night shifts in order to attend the trial in daytime. The room, too, was the same Hall 700. Throughout this trial, Judge Kubsch appeared wan and exhausted, yet he carried on. In late December 1999, Hamid ran into him on his way to the men's room and wished the judge a "happy and healthy new year." Kubsch smiled in return and said that "happy" could prove true but he doubted "healthy" was ahead for him. He died the following October. His death came weeks before the retirement he had long promised his wife would be spent vacationing and taking the trips he had postponed for decades.

In 2004, a group of Iranian exiles, spearheaded by Hamid, filed a request with the Berlin city hall to install a memorial plaque at the site of the restaurant. Yet another long battle between Berlin and the Iranian embassy ensued. At the end, the permission for the plaque was granted. Erected on four stubby legs on the sidewalk of 2a Prager Street, the plaque, inscribed in red, reads:

Here, at the site of the former Mykonos Restaurant, on Septembr 17, 1992, the prominent representatives of the Democratic Party of Kurdistan, Dr. Sadegh Sharafkandi, Fattah Abdoli, Homayoun Ardalan, and the Berliner politician, Noori Dehkordi, were murdered by powers in Tehran. They died in the battle for freedom and human rights.

The restaurant has since undergone several incarnations. Despite all the resurfacing, remodeling, and change of supervision, the food and the ambience remain reminiscent of its Mykonos years—remarkably mediocre. It last was a Vietnamese place called Miss Saigon, which shut down in 2010.

Fourteen years since the trial ended, the case remains open. The lead assassin was never apprehended. Bani-Hashemi, who flew out of Germany that same night, remains at large.

Of the five men in custody, Atris, was released after serving three years but was rearrested soon thereafter on new charges, and eventually fled Germany. After completing his sentence of ten years, Yousef Amin was deported to Lebanon.

Kazem Darabi was regularly visited by his devoted wife in prison, where he managed to father another child. In 2007, after having served fifteen years, his appeal was granted and he was returned to Iran in December. He received a hero's welcome at Tehran's airport, where he vowed to the flock of reporters to write the full account of his innocence in a forthcoming book. Darabi's codefendant Abbas Rhayel was also granted appeal and deported to Lebanon at the same time.

Iran's ambassador to Germany during the Mykonos years, Moussavian, who had insisted that the allegations against Tehran "were a joke" and that Iran would never violate human rights or participate in an extra-judicial killing, had his own falling out with the regime. In 2007, he published a book about Iranian-German relations based on his years as the ambassador. Within a week after its release, he, charged with espionage, was jailed. The book was banned and was confiscated from bookstores throughout the country. Yet a copy of it lingers on the shelves of a little-known Iranian-American writer, somewhere deep in the Connecticut woods.

The minister Ali Fallahian resigned from his post as the chief of intelligence in 1997. An arrest warrant was issued by the Interpol for his involvement in the 1994 bombings of the Jewish Center in Buenos Aires, Argentina. Today, he is a member of the Assembly of Experts of Leadership, which oversees the selection of the Supreme Leader. Those named in the judgment are still in power. Former foreign minister Velayati is the special foreign affairs envoy to the office of Supreme Leader, in effect performing the role of a shadow foreign minister. Former president Rafsanjani is both the head of the Expediency Council—which wields legislative powers—and the head of Assembly of Experts of Leadership. The Revolutionary Guards chief remains the most powerful figure in the country.

Two years after calling on Messbahi in Tehran to warn him of a plot for his murder and urge him to leave the country, the deputy minister of intelligence Saeed Emami was arrested on charges of espionage. He died in custody in 1999 under mysterious circumstances.

Messbahi entered the German witness protection program after testifying in court in 1996. He lives somewhere in relative safety on planet Earth. He still follows the events of Iran very closely and runs his own underground think tank from his nameless bunker. In January 2007, the aforementioned writer sat with him for three consecutive days and lent an ear to his ordeal.

Senior Criminal Commissioner, Tony von Trek, died suddenly of an aggressive tumor in the early 2000s. His loss was grieved by many of his colleagues, but most of all by Jost. The reporter Norbert Siegmund went on to receive a doctorate in political science. His thesis was entitled "The Mykonos Process." He continues to work as a journalist. Josef Hufelschulte still reports for *Die Focus*.

The news of the judgment traveled the world. Inside Iran, several angry clerics made threats against Bruno Jost. As a result, the European Union issued a statement, calling "any threat against the federal prosecutor, the court, or Germany, a threat against all of Europe."

In January 1998, one of Germany's most popular magazines, *Die Zeit,* named Bruno Jost one of the Ten Most Important People of Germany, though neither the title nor his historic performance and valor throughout the trial earned him any more than personal satisfaction. He routinely subjected his new assistants to a tasting of Iranian cuisine, namely to Ghormeh Sabzi, at the local Persian restaurant, where he, alongside his family, mother, son-in-law to be, and their two bodyguards, had celebrated the judgment of the case. He retired from his post as a senior federal prosecutor in spring 2009 and is contemplating taking up beekeeping.

The satirist Hadi Khorsandi has survived his fatwa. He has added standup to his repertoire, which he calls "Khorsandup." For a blossoming actor in his early seventies, he does remarkably well onstage.

The restaurant owner Aziz Ghaffari moved to Iran, remarried, and refashioned himself yet again, this time as a pharmacy owner. He is the only survivor of that assassination to have ever returned to the country. The German daily *Der Tagesspiegel,* in a 1996 article, accused Aziz of having been a spy for Iran's ministry of intelligence. He never disputed the paper's charges, much less filed suit for defamation. Mystery still surrounds him, as do the endless speculations about who the mole might have been if not Aziz.

With the trial behind them, Sara and Shohreh Dehkordi moved into a new apartment where their living room windows open onto a quiet and wooded street. Shohreh went on to become a therapist, specializing in grief. Her dream is to someday meet the women who were widowed in 9/11 and create a support network for victims of terrorism. For the first time in years, she and Sara went to the site of the old Mykonos restaurant for the ribbon-cutting ceremony of the memorial plaque.

Sara is pursuing a doctoral degree in political science. She has followed in her father's footsteps and become an activist, though she does not know why being among Iranians always brings on feelings of melancholy in her. From time to time, she cheers herself by playing the old Bibi Blocksberg cassettes and listening to the tales of the beloved witch. She no longer believes that she ought to fight terrorists with guns, but is determined to fight them all the same. She lives on her own, in a studio apartment where an enormous poster of a smiling Nelson Mandela is tacked to the main door.

Today, more than two million Iranians live outside of Iran, one hundred and fifty thousand of them in Germany, of whom nearly ten thousand reside in Berlin. The latter are the refugees whom Hamid Nowzari continues to serve through his small refugee organization. As a token of remembrance of the historic experience, Hamid has kept his odd work hours of night shifts and weekends, ever ready to witness another trial. He and two colleagues went on to write two critical books on the subject of the Mykonos trials. He is also the main custodian at the Iranian Archives of Documents and Research, where this author spent many wintery days reading and feeding spadefuls to one of the few remaining coal-fired room heaters in all of Western Europe.

Parviz Dastmalchi went on to edit and publish collected essays and documents about the case, some of which he has dedicated to Bruno Jost and Frithjof Kubsch. When he finally called Bruno Jost to thank him for his work, Jost simply said, "I didn't do what I did to please the Iranian opposition. I was only doing my job."

In the interim years, he produced a dozen more books, bringing his total of edited, translated, and originally penned volumes to an impressive twenty-five. His translation of Karl

Popper's writings was published in Iran in 2004 and was reprinted several times. Always looking for a new adventure, he openly traveled to Israel in November 2008, placing himself among the very few non-Jewish Iranians to ever dare make the trip.

Time Line

1946 • Democratic Party of Kurdistan of Iran (DPKI) is established.

1964 • Shah Mohammad Reza Pahlavi sends Ayatollah Khomeini into exile.

1979 • On January 21, due to nationwide protests against the monarchy, the Shah of Iran leaves and installs Shapur Bakhtiar as prime minister to quell the unrest.

• On February 1, Ayatollah Khomeini returns to Iran from exile in Paris.

• On February 11, the victory of the revolution is announced. Soon thereafter, summary execution of army leaders on the rooftop of Ayatollah Khomeini's residence follow.

- In August, Ayatollah Khomeini declares jihad against the Kurds.
- On November 4, the U.S. embassy in Tehran is seized.
- In December, the Shah's nephew Shahriar Shafigh is assassinated in France.

1980
- In July, former press counselor to the Iranian Embassy, Tabatabai, is assassinated at his residence in Washington, D.C.
- In September, Iraq invades Iran.
- In February Abulhassan Banisadr becomes president.

1981
- Ronald Reagan becomes the fortieth president of the United States. The American hostages return to the United States as he is taking his oath of office.
- In June, President Banisadr and his government fall. He flees to France.
- In December, the DPKI declares the overthrow of the Iranian regime as one of its goals.

1982
- Iran establishes Hezbollah in Lebanon to expand its influence within the region.
- An assassination attempt is made on the former Iranian prime minister Shapur Bakhtiar in France.

1983
- Hezbollah attacks the U.S. Marine Corp barracks in the Lebanon killing 241 American servicemen.

1988
- The Iran-Iraq war ends.
- Ayatollah Khomeini issues a fatwa against Salman Rushdie, calling for his death.

1989
- In June, Ayatollah Khomeini dies.
- In July, the leader of the DPKI, Ghassemlou, and two of his colleagues are assassinated in Vienna.
- The Berlin Wall falls.

1990
- In April, a member of the Iranian opposition, Kazem Rajavi, is assassinated in Switzerland. The French return several terrorists to Iran citing national interest.

1991
- The politician and entrepreneur Abdulrahman Boroumand is assassinated in France.
- Former Prime Minister Shapur Bakhtiar and his assistant are assassinated at his residence in Paris.
- The fall of the Soviet empire.
- The two Germanys are united.

1992
- In August, the popular singer Fereydoun Farrokhzad is stabbed to death at his residence near Bonn, Germany.
- In September, the Mykonos terror team enters Germany.
- The annual conference of the Social Democratic Party of Germany begins to which the DPKI sends its top three officials.
- On September 17, Jalal Talebani, then a Kurdish dissident, meets Sadegh Sharafkandi at the conference and warns him of an assassination plot against him. That night, at about 10:45 p.m., the three Iranian Kurdish leaders, along with their long-standing friend Noori Dehkordi, are shot to death at the Mykonos restaurant in Berlin.

- On September 18, Germany's chief federal prosecutor, Alexander von Stahl, announces in a press release that the murders at Mykonos involve the nation's national security and thus assigns a prosecutor, from his office, Bruno Jost, to take on the case.
- In December, at their Edinburgh meeting, EU members pass a resolution to begin a "critical dialogue" with Iran, aimed at creating closer Iran-European relations.

1993
- In May, Chief Federal Prosecutor Alexander von Stahl submits the indictment to the Berlin Court.
- In August, von Stahl is forced to resign from his post.
- Trade between Iran and Germany reaches an historic high: 7 billion DM, making Germany Iran's premier trading partner.
- The opposition leader Muhammad Hussein Naghdi is assassinated in Rome, Italy.
- In early October, Iran's minister of information Ali Fallahian makes a secret visit to Germany.
- On October 29 the Mykonos trial begins.

1996
- The German Supreme Court issues an arrest warrant for Iran's minister of intelligence, Fallahian.
- In May, Iran's former deputy minister of education, Reza Mazlouman, is assassinated in France.
- In July, six leading writers and intellectuals, members of the PEN chapter in Iran, are invited to the home of the German ambassador's cultural

attaché in Tehran. The dinner is raided by the Revolutionary Guards.

- In November, the prominent Iranian writer and editor Faraj Sarkohi disappears on his way to visit his family in Hamburg, Germany.

1997
- On April 10, the judgment of Berlin's high criminal court is announced.
- In their show of support for the judgment, all EU member nations shut their embassies in Tehran.
- In May, the reformist presidential candidate Khatami wins election by a landslide.

Glossary

Agha. Mister (Persian)
Baba or Babayee. Father (Persian)
Iman Ali. The cousin and son-in-law of Prophet Muhammad and the first iman of the Shiite Muslims.
Jaan. Dear (Persian)
Kaak. Brother (Kurdish)
Maadar. Mother (Persian)
Majles. Parliament (Persian)
Maman. Mother. Originally French, the term is popularly used by Iranians
Mola. Beloved mentor (Persian)
Moosh mooshak. Little mouse (Persian)
Peshmarga. Freedom fighter (Kurdish)

Characters

The Victims

Noori Dehkordi—Murder victim and organizer of the meeting at the Mykonos restaurant; an opponent of Iran's regime and supporter of the Kurds

Sadegh Sharafkandi—Mykonos murder victim, nicknamed "The Doctor"; chairman of Iran's Democratic Party of Kurdistan (DPKI), 1989–1992

Fattah Abdoli—Mykonos murder victim, DPKI deputy

Homayoun Ardalan—Mykonos murder victim, DPKI deputy

Parviz Dastmalchi—Survivor; author and close friend of Noori, and the most outspoken survivor of the Mykonos assassinations

Mehdi Ebrahimzadeh—Survivor; leading political activist
Aziz Ghaffari—Survivor; owner of the Mykonos restaurant
Shohreh Badii Dehkordi—Widow of Noori Dehkordi; political activist
Sara Dehkordi—Daughter of Noori and Shohreh Dehkordi
Salomeh Dastmalchi—Daughter of Parviz Dastmalchi

The Perpetrators
Abdulrahman Bani-Hashemi—Leader of the terror team, still at large
Abbas Rhayel—Terror team's second assassin, friend to Yousef
Yousef Amin—Terror team's watchman
Kazem Darabi—Coordinator and financier of the operation; member of Iran's Ministry of Intelligence
Attaullah Ayad—Member of the terror team

The Key German Players
Alexander von Stahl—Germany's Chief Federal Prosecutor, 1990–1993
Bruno Jost—Federal Prosecutor for the Mykonos case, 1992–1997
Hans Joachim Ehrig—Lead Attorney for the victims, 1992–1997
Otto Schily—Attorney and Former Interior Minister
Klaus Kinkel—Foreign Minister 1992–1998
Helmut Kohl—Chancellor 1982–1998
Frithjof Kubsch—Chief Judge presiding over the Mykonos trial from 1992–1997

Judge Jurgen Zastrow—One of the Mykonos trial's five judges
Judge Alban—Chief Judge Kubsch's deputy
Gregor Gysi—Attorney and member of the Bundestag
Wolfgang Wieland—Attorney for the victims 1992–1997
Bernd Schmidbauer—Federal Intelligence Chief 1991–1998
Klaus Grunewald—Middle East Director, Federal Office for the Protection of the Constitution

The Iranian Regime
Shah Mohammad Reza Pahlavi—King of Iran's last monarchy 1941–1979
Ali Akbar Hashemi Rafsanjani—President 1989–1997
Hussein Moussavian—Ambassador to Bonn 1990–1997
Ali Akbar Velayati—Foreign Minister 1981–1997
Ayatollah Ali Khamanei—Supreme Leader 1989–present
Abulhassan Banisadr—President 1980–1982

Miscellaneous Characters
Abulghassem Farhad Messbahi or **Witness C**
Renata Kakir—Resident of Prager Street and trial witness
Abdulrahman Ghassemlou—Popular leader of the Democratic Party of Kurdistan, assassinated in Vienna in 1989
Hadi Khorsandi—Exiled Iranian satirist against whom Ayatollah Khomeini issued a fatwa in 1980
Hamid Nowzari—Political activist
Abulghassem Zamankhan—The trial's chief Persian interpreter
Norbert Siegmund—Young journalist who worked with Parviz to uncover the truth of Mykonos
Josef Hufelschulte—Journalist for FOCUS

Note on Sources

In 2005, when I first began to look into the story of the Mykonos assassinations, I quickly learned that sifting through the urban legend and the truth would be a monumental task. Therefore, establishing a timeline of events and the arc of the narrative alone became my first goal. To that end, I conducted hundreds of hours of interviews with the following individuals, among others:

Jalil Azadikhah, Shohreh Badi'i-Dehkordi, Bob Baer, Abolhassan Banisadr, Mehran Barati, Minu Barati, Nasrin Bassiri, Roya Boroumand, Fred Burton, Chief-in-charge of Hall 700 at Berlin's Moabit Court, Parviz Dastmalchi, Salomeh Dastmalchi, Sara Dehkordi, Wilhelm Dietl, Rudolf Dolzer, Mehdi

Ebrahimzadeh, Hans Joachim Ehrig, Ali Ferdowsi, Owen Fiss, Dieter Grimm, Ashraf Golpaygani, Alexander Jost, Angela Jost, Barbara Jost, Bruno Jost, Hadi Khorsandi, Werner Kolhoff, Martin Kubsch, John Langbein, Abolghassem Messbahi, Hamid Nowzari, Owner of Ms. Saigon (formerly known as the Mykonos Restaurant), Mehran Payandeh, Ahmad Rafat, Habib Rahiab, Ewald Riethmüller, Kambiz Rousta, Hamid Sadr, Sahraoui, Ali Sajjadi, Bahman Sarayi-Moghadam, Mohsen Sazegara, Norbert Siegmund, Rudolf Steinberg, David Unger, Sandra Volck, Alexander von Stahl, R. James Woolsey, Abolghassem Zamankhan.

The reporting of the following journalists proved to be invaluable to my work:

Wilhelm Dietl and Josef Hufelschulte in *Die Focus*; Sigrid Avaresh and Werner Kolhoff in *Berliner Zeitung*; Rudiger Scheidges in *Der Taagespiegel*; Norbert Siegmund and Susanne Opalka in *SFB* and *ZDF* for local and national television broadcasts; and Dorothea Jung in *Deutschland Radio*. The publications *Suddeutsche Zeitung, Der Spiegel, Der Bild,* and *Die Welt* also helped fill in certain gaps in my knowledge of the story.

It came to me as a great surprise to find that because of the distinct nature of the German legal system, no trial transcripts existed for this case. However, as journalists and members of the victims' families were allowed to take notes during the proceedings, I was able to glean aspects of the experience through the private journals of Shohreh Dehkordi. The daily filings of Hamid Nowzari and his collaborators and a few other Iranian journalists in the following Persian publications were similarly illuminating:

Abolhassan Banisadr, Ed. *Enghelab Eslami; Biweekly* (Paris); *Mujahed,* the Publication of Iran's People's Mujahedin; Parviz Ghelichkhani, Ed. *Arash Quarterly* (Paris); *Kurdistan,* the Democratic Party of Iranian Kurdistan's Monthly; *Kar,* Publication of Sazman-e Etehad-e Fadayian; *Iran, Terror, Sarkoob,* the Publication of the Committee Against Terror (Berlin, Paris).

Researching a case as lengthy and complex as this should have taken years. But because I had access to the Archives for Iranian Research and Documents and the Archives of the Iranian Political Refugee Association in Berlin, where nearly everything ever written on the case is meticulously gathered and organized, the work took only months. I owe much to the archives and the many volumes that Parviz Dastmalchi diligently printed between 1992–1998. The following is a listing of those and several of my other key primary soures:

The Attorney General of the Federal Court. Anklageschrift [Indictment]. 17 May 1993.

Dastmalchi, Parviz. *The Mykonos Documents: September 1992–April 1997.* Berlin: Azad Press, 1997.

Dastmalchi, Parviz. *The Fall: Mykonos IV.* Berlin: Azad Press, 1994.

Dastmalchi, Parviz. *Governmental Terrorism in the Islamic Republic of Iran*. Berlin: Azad Press, 1995.

Dastmalchi, Parviz. *Democracy and Law*. Berlin: Azad Press, 1996.

Dastmalchi, Parviz. *The Text of the Mykonos Judgment*. Berlin: Azad Press, 2000.

Khodagholi, Abbas, Hamid Nowzari, and Mehran Paydande, Eds. *The Criminal System: The Mykonos Documents*. Berlin: Nima Books, 2000.

Khodagholi, Abbas, Hamid Nowzari, and Mehran Paydande. *There's Still a Judge in Berlin: Mykonos Murder and Process*. Berlin: Nima Books, 2000.

Kubsch, F. *The Mykonos-Judgment*. Edited by Hans-Joachim Ehrig. Berlin: Archive for Research and Documentation Iran-Berlin and Association of Iranian Refugees (Berlin), 1999.

Siegmund, Norbert. *The Mykonos Process*. Berlin: LIT Verlag Münster, 2001.

Selected Articles and Bibliography

"Historic Figures: Ayatollah Khomeini (1900–1989)." BBC. http://www.bbc.co.uk/history/historic_figures/khomeini_ayatollah.shtml

"The Mystic Who Lit the Fires of Hatred." *Time*. 7 January 1980.

"The Connection: An Exclusive Look at How Iran Hunts Down Its Opponents Abroad." *Time*. 21 March 1994.

Afshari, Reza. *Human Rights in Iran: The Abuse of Cultural Relativism*. Philadelphia: University of Pennsylvania Press, 2001.

Bunegart, Luther. Memorandum to Press: On Being Dismissed by Yousef Amin as Counsel. 25 November 1993.

Clawson, Patrick. "Europe's 'Critical Dialog' with Iran: Pressure for Change." *PolicyWatch* 242. 9 April 1997.

Farhand, Mansour. "Iran Wants to Assassinate Me. Why?" *New York Times*. 8 December 1993.

Federal Criminal Police Office of Germany. Summary of Facts. 13 November 1992.

Federal Criminal Police Office of Germany. Final Report. 22 August 1993.

Frase, S. J. and T. Weigend. "German Criminal Justice as a Guide to American Law Reform: Similar Problems, Better Solutions?" *Boston College International and Comparative Law Review* 18:2, 1995.

Grünewald, Federal Office for the Protection of the Constitution. Memorandum to Chief Federal Prosecutor's Office of the Federal High Court. 22 April 1993.

Haass, R. and M. L. O'Sullivan, Eds. *Honey and Vinegar: Incentives, Sanctions, and Foreign Policy.* Washington D.C.: Brookings Institution Press, 2000.

Hufelschulte, Josef. "Mullahs Want to Take Revenge on Bonn." *Focus Magazine.* 18 January 1993.

Jost, Bruno, Senior Public Prosecutor. Federal Criminal Police Office of Germany. *Preliminary Investigation of Ali Fallahian for Murder Among Other Things.* 4 December 1995.

Khorsandi, Hadi. *The Ayatollah and I*. London: Readers International, 1987.

Khorsandi, Shappi. *A Beginner's Guide to Acting English*. London: Ebury Press, 2009.

Kinzer, Stephen. "Trial Begins in Berlin for Iranian Charged in Dissident's Death." *New York Times*. 29 October 1993.

Koohi-Kamali, Fereshteh. "Nationalism in Iranian Kurdistan." *The Kurds: A Contemporary Overview*. Ed. Philip G. Kreyenbroek and Stefan Sperl. London: Routledge, 1992. 171–192.

Langbein, John. *Comparative Criminal Procedure: Germany*. Eagan, MN: West Group, 1977.

Lazariev, M.S., S.K. Mahvi, M.A. Hasratian, and U.E. Zhigalina. *Kurdistan's History*. Moscow: Forough, 1999.

Markham, James M. "Bonn May Balk at Extraditing Terror Suspect." *New York Times*. 17 January 1987.

Matin-Asgari, Afshin. *Iranian Student Opposition to the Shah*. Costa Mesa, CA: Mazda Publishers, 2001.

McDowall, David. *The Kurds: A Nation Denied*. Austin, TX: Minority Rights Publications, 1992.

Menashri, David. "Khomeini's Policy toward Ethnic and Religious Minorities." *Ethnicity, Pluralism, and the State in the Middle East*. Ed. Milton J. Esman and Itamar Rabinovich. Ithaca, NY: Cornell, 1988. 216–17.

Mussavian, S. H. *Challenges of the Iran-West Relations: Analysis of Iran-Germany Relations*. Tehran: Center for Strategic Studies, 2006.

Norton, Augustus Richard. *Hezbollah: A Short History*. Princeton, NJ: Princeton University Press, 2007.

Pilz, Peter. *Eskorte nach Teheran: Der Österreichische Rechtsstaat und die Kurdenmorde*. Vienna: Ibera & Molden, 1997.

Sancton, Thomas. "Iran's State of Terror." *Time*. 11 November 1996.

Schmitt, Michael N. "State-Sponsored Assassination in International and Domestic Law." *Yale Journal of International Law* 17 (1992).

Shahrooz, Kaveh. "With Revolutionary Rage and Rancor: A Preliminary Report on the 1988 Massacre of Iran's Political Prisoners." *Harvard Human Rights Journal* 20 (2007).

Shamlou, Ahmad. *Fresh Air: Book of Poems*. Tehran: Morvarid Publishers, 1958.

Tyler, Patrick E. "Iranian Seen as Victim of Assassination Plan." *The Washington Post*. 9 September 1989.

U.N. Commission on Human Rights. *Report of the Special Rapporteur for Extrajudicial, Summary, or Arbitrary Executions, Transparency and the Imposition of the Death Penalty*. New York. March 2006.

Walsh, James. "Iran's Smoking Gun." *Time*. 21 April 1997.

Wolst, Federal High Court Judge. Haftbefehl, Der Minister für Nachrichtendienste und Sicherheitsangelegenheiten der Islamischen Republik Iran Ali Fallahian [Arrest Warrant, for Ali Fallahian, the Minister of Intelligence and Security of the Islamic Republic of Iran, Ali Fallahian]. 14 March 1996. Die Agenten schlafen nur. *Der Spiegel*. 25 March 1996.

Radio, Television, Films, Audiovisual, Memos, and Electronic Material

Abdolrahman Boroumand Foundation. www.iranrights.org.

Allamehzadeh, Reza, Director. *Holy Crime*. 1994

Asghar Agha: Persian Satirical Monthly. Ed. Hadi Khorsandi. www.AsgharAgha.com

BBC Television. *The Terror Network*. 19 May 1997.

The Dehkordi family home videos.

Democratic Party of Iranian Kurdistan. www.pdki.org.

The personal Web site of Ali Fallahian. www.fallahian.ir.

Radio Farda Archives. "The Mykonos Assassinations Special." September 2007.

Iran Human Rights Documentation Center. www.iranhrdc.org.

Iranian.com (Online community for Iranian diaspora). Published by Jahanshah Javid. www.iranian.com

Khorsandi, H. *Khorsandup Comedy* (DVD). 2005